THE
REFERENCE
SHELF

THE INFORMATION

REVOLUTION

Edited by DONALD ALTSCHILLER

THE REFERENCE SHELF

Volume 67 Number 5

H. W. WILSON

New York   Dublin   1995

THE REFERENCE SHELF

The books in this series contain reprints of articles, excerpts from books, and addresses on current issues and social trends in the United States and other countries. There are six separately bound numbers in each volume, all of which are generally published in the same calendar year. One number is a collection of recent speeches; each of the others is devoted to a single subject and gives background information and discussion from various points of view, concluding with a comprehensive bibliography that contains books and pamphlets and abstracts of additional articles on the subject. Books in the series may be purchased individually or on subscription.

Library of Congress Cataloging-in-Publication Data

The information revolution / edited by Donald Altschiller.
    p.   cm. — (The Reference shelf ; v. 67, no. 5)
  Includes bibliographical references.
  ISBN 0-8242-0872-2
  1. Information superhighway—United States.   I. Altschiller, Donald.   II. Series.
HE7572.U6154   1995
384.3—dc20

                                                    95-23641
                                                    CIP

Cover: An operator enters data into a mainframe computer.

Photo: AP/Wide World Photos

Printed in the United States of America

CONTENTS

PREFACE

> We are in great haste to construct a magnetic telegraph from Maine to Texas, but Maine and Texas, it may be, have nothing important to communicate
>
> —Henry David Thoreau (1849)

The Information Revolution has arrived. Cable television, CD-ROM's, interactive videos, laser discs, electronic mail delivery—concepts unknown a decade ago—are not staple items of daily life. Unlike conventional media, modern technology allows for the conversion of messages into electronic "bytes" of information—the language of computers. This breakthrough has been compared to another technological revolution of more than 500 years ago: the invention of movable type.

Although Vice President Gore is often credited with coining the term "information highway," the phrase was first used by author Ralph Lee Smith. In his 1972 book, *The Wired Nation,* he described the federal subsidies for interstate highways and suggested a "similar national commitment for an electronic highway system to facilitate the exchange of information and ideas."

The result of such a commitment was the much-heralded Internet. Its predecessor was initiated in August 1968 when the U.S. Department of Defense required a network to connect its widely dispersed computers. A quarter of a century later the Internet has become a web of more than 40,000 networks linking an estimated 30 million users in more than 100 countries.

While the highway metaphor illuminates the strengths of an interconnected society, it also suggests possible problems. Writing in the computer journal *Communications of the ACM* Peter G. Neumann notes some of them: traffic jams, road kill, drunken drivers, and car jackers, as well as drag races, joy riders, toll bridges and crashes. Furthermore, a 1995 *Newsweek* poll showed that 23% of the respondents believed that computers would help stratify society into those who could afford developing technologies and those of lesser means.

Nonetheless, most Americans feel that computers serve important functions in their lives. In the same poll, 73% of workers believed computers improve their working conditions, and 45% of those surveyed used a computer almost every day.

Yet, Thoreau's observation about the telegraph made almost 150 years ago still resonates. Technology has provided an ever-increasingly efficient medium of communication, but do we really have something to say?

This compilation examines the philosophical, cultural, political, and economic consequences of the Information Revolution. The first section surveys the history and future of the information superhighway. The second section describes its economic impact on the American and world economy. This new technology has spawned legal and legislative debate, discussed in the third and fourth sections of the book. Finally, the last section examines the cultural and social issues arising from the new communications technology.

The editor wishes to thank The H. W. Wilson General Publications staff for its assistance and the authors and publishers who have granted permission to reprint their material in this compilation.

DONALD ALTSCHILLER

June 1995

I. OVERVIEW OF THE INFORMATION REVOLUTION

EDITOR'S INTRODUCTION

In 1993, a commission established by Vice President Al Gore issued a blueprint for the much-touted information superhighway. The first article, "The National Information Infrastructure: Agenda for Action," contains excerpts from the report of the commission. The next article, reprinted from *Computerworld,* features interviews with the inventors of Arpanet, the forerunner of the Internet. In the section's last article, "A Magna Carta for the Knowledge Age," published in *New Perspectives Quarterly,* social critics offer philosophical and historical observations about the information revolution.

THE NATIONAL INFORMATION INFRASTRUCTURE: AGENDA FOR ACTION[1]

Executive Summary

All Americans have a stake in the construction of an advanced National Information Infrastructure (NII), a seamless web of communications networks, computers, databases, and consumer electronics that will put vast amounts of information at users' fingertips. Development of the NII can help unleash an information revolution that will change forever the way people live, work, and interact with each other:

• People could live almost anywhere they wanted, without foregoing opportunities for useful and fulfilling employment, by "telecommuting" to their offices through an electronic highway.

[1]Report published by the Executive Office of the President, Washington D.C., 1993.

• The best schools, teachers, and courses would be available to all students, without regard to geography, distance, resources, or disability.

• Services that improve America's health care system and respond to other important social needs could be available on-line, without waiting in line, when and where you needed them.

Private sector firms are already developing and deploying that infrastructure today. Nevertheless, there remain essential roles for government in this process. Carefully crafted government action will complement and enhance the efforts of the private sector and assure the growth of an information infrastructure available to all Americans at reasonable cost. In developing our policy initiatives in this area, the Administration will work in close partnership with business, labor, academia, the public, Congress, and state and local government. Our efforts will be guided by the following principles and objectives:

• Promote private sector investment, through appropriate tax and regulatory policies.

• Extend the "universal service" concept to ensure that information resources are available to all at affordable prices. Because information means empowerment—and employment—the government has a duty to ensure that all Americans have access to the resources and job creation potential of the Information Age.

• Act as catalyst to promote technological innovation and new applications. Commit important government research programs and grants to help the private sector develop and demonstrate technologies needed for the NII, and develop the applications and services that will maximize its value to users.

• Promote seamless, interactive, user-driven operation of the NII. As the NII evolves into a "network of networks," government will ensure that users can transfer information across networks easily and efficiently. To increase the likelihood that the NII will be both interactive and, to a large extent, user-driven, government must reform regulations and policies that may inadvertently hamper the development of interactive applications.

• Ensure information security and network reliability. The NII must be trustworthy and secure, protecting the privacy of its users. Government action will also ensure that the overall system remains reliable, quickly repairable in the event of a failure and, perhaps most importantly, easy to use.

• Improve management of the radio frequency spectrum, an increasingly critical resource.

• Protect intellectual property rights. The Administration will investigate how to strengthen domestic copyright laws and international intellectual property treaties to prevent piracy and to protect the integrity of intellectual property.

• Coordinate with other levels of government and with other nations. Because information crosses state, regional, and national boundaries, coordination is critical to avoid needless obstacles and prevent unfair policies that handicap U.S. industry.

• Provide access to government information and improve government procurement. The Administration will seek to ensure that Federal agencies, in concert with state and local governments, use the NII to expand the information available to the public, ensuring that the immense reservoir of government information is available to the public easily and equitably. Additionally, Federal procurement policies for telecommunications and information services and equipment will be designed to promote important technical developments for the NII and to provide attractive incentives for the private sector to contribute to NII development.

The time for action is now. Every day brings news of change: new technologies, like hand-held computerized assistants; new ventures and mergers combining businesses that not long ago seemed discrete and insular; new legal decisions that challenge the separation of computer, cable, and telephone industries. These changes promise substantial benefits for the American people, but only if government understands fully their implications and begins working with the private sector and other interested parties to shape the evolution of the communications infrastructure.

The benefits of the NII for the nation are immense. An advanced information infrastructure will enable U.S. firms to compete and win in the global economy, generating good jobs for the American people and economic growth for the nation. As importantly, the NII can transform the lives of the American people—ameliorating the constraints of geography, disability, and economic status—giving all Americans a fair opportunity to go as far as their talents and ambitions will take them.

I. The Promise of the NII

Imagine you had a device that combined a telephone, a TV, a camcorder, and a personal computer. No matter where you went or what time it was, your child could see you and talk to you, you could watch a replay of your team's last game, you could browse the latest additions to the library, or you could find the best prices in town on groceries, furniture, clothes—whatever you needed. Imagine further the dramatic changes in your life if:

• The best schools, teachers, and courses were available to all students, without regard to geography, distance, resources, or disability.

• The vast resources of art, literature, and science were available everywhere, not just in large institutions or big-city libraries and museums.

• Services that improve America's health-care system and respond to other important social needs were available on-line, without waiting in line, when and where you needed them.

• You could live in many places without foregoing opportunities for useful and fulfilling employment, by "telecommuting" to your office through an electronic highway instead of by automobile, bus or train.

• Small manufacturers could get orders from all over the world electronically—with detailed specifications—in a form that the machines could use to produce the necessary items.

• You could see the latest movies, play your favorite video games, or bank and shop from the comfort of your home whenever you chose.

• You could obtain government information directly or through local organizations like libraries, apply for and receive government benefits electronically, and get in touch with government officials easily.

• Individual government agencies, businesses and other entities all could exchange information electronically—reducing paperwork and improving service.

Information is one of the nation's most critical economic resources, for service industries as well as manufacturing, for economic as well as national security. By one estimate, two-thirds of U.S. workers are in information-related jobs, and the rest are in industries that rely heavily on information. In an era of global markets and global competition, the technologies to create, manipulate, manage and use information are of strategic importance for the United States. Those technologies will help U.S. businesses remain competitive and create challenging, high-paying jobs. They also will fuel economic growth which, in turn, will generate a steadily-increasing standard of living for all Americans.

That is why the Administration has launched the National Information Infrastructure initiative. We are committed to working with business, labor, academia, public interest groups, Congress, and state and local government to ensure the development of a National Information Infrastructure (NII) that enables all Americans to access information and communicate with each other using voice, data, images or video at anytime, anywhere. By encouraging private sector investment in the NII's development, and through government programs to improve access to essential services, we will promote U.S. competitiveness, job creation and solutions to pressing social problems.

II. What Is the NII?

The phrase "information infrastructure" has an expansive meaning. The NII includes more than just the physical facilities used to transmit, store, process, and display voice, data, and images. It encompasses:

• A wide range and ever-expanding range of equipment including cameras, scanners, keyboards, telephones, fax machines, computers, switches, compact disks, video and audio tape, cable, wire, satellites, optical fiber transmission lines, microwave nets, switches, televisions, monitors, printers, and much more.

The NII will integrate and interconnect these physical components in a technologically neutral manner so that no one industry will be favored over any other. Most importantly, the NII requires building foundations for living in the Information Age and for making these technological advances useful to the public, business, libraries, and other nongovernmental entities. That is why, beyond the physical components of the infrastructure, the value of the National Information Infrastructure to users and the nation will depend in large part on the quality of its other elements:

• The information itself, which may be in the form of video programming, scientific or business databases, images, sound recordings, library archives, and other media. Vast quantities of that information exist today in government agencies and even more valuable information is produced every day in our laboratories, studios, publishing houses, and elsewhere.

• Applications and software that allow users to access, manipulate, organize, and digest the proliferating mass of information that the NII's facilities will put at their fingertips.

• The network standards and transmission codes that facilitate interconnection and interoperation between networks, and ensure the privacy of persons and the security of the information carried, as well as the security and reliability of the networks.

• The people—largely in the private sector—who create the information, develop applications and services, construct the facilities, and train others to tap its potential. Many of these people will be vendors, operators, and service providers working for private industry.

Every component of the information infrastructure must be developed and integrated if America is to capture the promise of the Information Age.

The Administration's NII initiative will promote and support full development of each component. Regulatory and economic policies will be adopted that encourage private firms to create jobs and invest in the applications and physical facilities that comprise the infrastructure. The Federal government will assist industry, labor, academia, and state and local governments in developing the information resources and applications needed to maximize the potential of those underlying facilities. Moreover, and perhaps most importantly, the NII initiative will help educate and train our people so that they are prepared not only to contribute to the further growth of the NII, but also to understand and enjoy fully the services and capabilities that it will make available.

III. Need for Government Action To Complement
Private Sector Leadership

The foregoing discussion of the transforming potential of the NII should not obscure a fundamental fact—the private sector is already developing and deploying such an infrastructure today. The United States communications system—the conduit through which most information is accessed or distributed—is second to none in speed, capacity, and reliability. Each year the information resources, both hardware and software, available to most Americans are substantially more extensive and more powerful than the previous year.

The private sector will lead the deployment of the NII. In recent years, U.S. companies have invested more than $50 billion annually in telecommunications infrastructure—and that figure does not account for the vast investments made by firms in related industries, such as computers. In contrast, the Administration's ambitious agenda for investment in critical NII projects (including computing) amounts to $1–2 billion annually. Nonetheless, while the private sector role in NII development will predominate, the government has an essential role to play. In particular, carefully crafted government action can complement and enhance the benefits of these private sector initiatives. Accordingly, the Administration's NII initiative will be guided by the following nine principles and goals, which are discussed in more detail below:

1) Promote private sector investment, through tax and regulatory policies that encourage innovation and promote long-term investment, as well as wise procurement of services.

2) Extend the "universal service" concept to ensure that information resources are available to all at affordable prices. Because information means empowerment, the government has a duty to ensure that all Americans have access to the resources of the Information Age.

3) Act as catalyst to promote technological innovation and new applications. Commit important government research programs and grants to help the private sector develop and demonstrate technologies needed for the NII.

4) Promote seamless, interactive, user-driven operation of the NII. As the NII evolves into a "network of networks," government will ensure that users can transfer information across networks easily and efficiently.

5) Ensure information security and network reliability. The NII must be trustworthy and secure, protecting the privacy of its users. Government action will also aim to ensure that the overall system remains reliable, quickly repairable in the event of a failure and, perhaps most importantly, easy to use.

6) Improve management of the radio frequency spectrum, an increasingly critical resource.

7) Protect intellectual property rights. The Administration will investigate how to strengthen domestic copyright laws and international intellectual property treaties to prevent piracy and to protect the integrity of intellectual property.

8) Coordinate with other levels of government and with other nations. Because information crosses state, regional, and national boundaries, coordination is important to avoid unnecessary obstacles and to prevent unfair policies that handicap U.S. industry.

9) Provide access to government information and improve government procurement. As described in the *National Performance Review,* the Administration will seek to ensure that Federal agencies, in concert with state and local governments, use the NII

to expand the information available to the public, so that the immense reservoir of government information is available to the public easily and equitably. Additionally, Federal procurement policies for telecommunications and information services and equipment will be designed to promote important technical developments for the NII and to provide attractive incentives for the private sector to contribute to NII development.

IV. Managing Change/Forging Partnerships

We will help to build a partnership of business, labor, academia, the public, and government that is committed to deployment of an advanced, rapid, powerful infrastructure accessible and accountable to all Americans.

Forging this partnership will require extensive intergovernmental coordination to ensure that Administration, Congressional, state and local government policy regarding the NII is consistent, coherent, and timely. It also requires the development of strong working alliances among industry groups and between government and the businesses responsible for creating and operating the NII. Finally, close cooperation will be needed between government, users, service providers, and public interest groups to ensure that the NII develops in a way that benefits the American people.

Specifically, the Administration will:

1) Establish an interagency Information Infrastructure Task Force. The President has convened a Federal inter-agency "Information Infrastructure Task Force" (IITF) that will work with Congress and the private sector to propose the policies and initiatives needed to accelerate deployment of a National Information Infrastructure. Activities of the IITF include coordinating government efforts in NII applications, linking government applications to the private sector, resolving outstanding disputes, and implementing Administration policies. Chaired by Secretary of Commerce Ron Brown and composed of high-level Federal agency representatives, the IITF's three committees focus on telecommunications policy, information policy, and applications.

2) Establish a private sector Advisory Council on the National Information Infrastructure. To facilitate meaningful private sector participation in the IITF's deliberations, the President will sign an Executive Order creating the "United States Advisory Council on the National Information Infrastructure" to advise

the IITF on matters relating to the development of the NII. The Council will consist of 25 members, who will be named by the Secretary of Commerce by December 1993. Nominations will be solicited from a variety of NII constituencies and interested parties. The IITF and its committees also will use other mechanisms to solicit public comment to ensure that it hears the views of all interested parties.

3) Strengthen and streamline Federal communications and information policy-making agencies. In order to implement the ambitious agenda outlined in this document, the federal agencies most directly responsible for the evolution of the NII (such as NTIA [National Telecommunications and Information Administration], the Office of Information and Regulatory Affairs at OMB [Office of Management and Budget], and the FCC) must be properly structured and adequately staffed to address many new and difficult policy issues. The Administration intends to ensure that these agencies have the intellectual and material resources they need. In addition, in accord with the Vice President's *National Performance Review*, these agencies will make the organizational and procedural changes needed to most effectively contribute to the NII initiative.

V. Principles and Goals for Government Action

The Task Force currently is undertaking a wide-ranging examination of all issues relevant to the timely development and growth of the National Information Infrastructure. Specific principles and goals in areas where government action is warranted have already been identified and work has begun on the following matters:

1) Promote private sector investment. One of the most effective ways to promote investments in our nation's information infrastructure is to introduce or further expand competition in communications and information markets. Vibrant competition in these markets will spur our economic growth, create new businesses and benefit U.S. consumers.

To realize this vision, however, policy changes will be necessary:

• *Action:* Passage of communications reform legislation. The Administration will work with Congress to pass legislation by the end of 1994 that will increase competition and ensure universal access in communications market—particularly those, such as the

cable television and local telephone markets that have been dominated by monopolies. Such legislation will explicitly promote private sector infrastructive investment—both by companies already
in the market and those seeking entry.

• *Action:* Revision of tax policies. Tax policies are important
determinants of the amount of private sector investment in the
NII. The President has signed into law tax incentives for private
sector investment in R&D and new business formation, including
a three-year extension of the R&D credit and a target capital
gains reduction for investments in small businesses. Both of these
tax incentives will help spur the private sector investment needed
to develop the NII.

2) Extend the "Universal Service" concept to ensure that information resources are available to all at affordable prices. The
Communications Act of 1934 articulated in general terms a national goal of "Universal Service" for telephones—widespread
availability of a basic communications service at affordable rates.
A major objective in developing the NII will be to extend the
Universal Service concept to the information needs of the American people in the 21st Century. As a matter of fundamental fairness, this nation cannot accept a division of our people among
telecommunications or information "haves" and "have-nots." The
Administration is committed to developing a broad, modern concept of Universal Service—one that would emphasize giving all
Americans who desire it easy, affordable access to advanced communications and information services, regardless of income, disability, or location.

Devising and attaining a new goal for expanded Universal
Service is consistent with efforts to spur infrastructure development by increasing competition in communications and information markets. As noted above, competition can make low cost,
high quality services and equipment widely available. Policies promoting greater competition in combination with targeted support for disadvantaged users or especially high cost or rural areas
would advance both rapid infrastructure modernization and expanded Universal Service.

• *Action:* Develop a New Concept of Universal Service. To
gather information on the best characteristics of an expanded
concept of Universal Service, the Commerce Department's National
Telecommunications and Information Administration (NTIA) will
hold a series of public hearings on Universal Service and the NII,

beginning by December 1993. The Administration will make a special effort to hear from public interest groups. Building on the knowledge gained from these activities, the IITF will work with the Advisory Council on the National Information Infrastructure, as well as with state regulatory commissions, to determine how the Universal Service concept should be applied in the 21st Century.

3) Promote technological innovation and new applications. Government regulatory, antitrust, tax, and intellectual property policies all affect the level and timing of new offerings in services and equipment—including the technology base that generates innovations for the marketplace. But technological innovations ultimately depend upon purposeful investment in research and development, by both the private sector and government. R&D investment helps firms to create better products and services at lower costs.

As noted in the Administration's February 22, 1993 technology policy statement: "We are moving to accelerate the development of technologies critical for long-term growth but not receiving adequate support from private firms, either because the returns are too distant or because the level of funding required is too great for individual firms to bear." Government research support already has helped create basic information technologies in computing, networking and electronics. We will support further NII-related research and technology development through research partnerships and other mechanisms to accelerate technologies where market mechanisms do not adequately reflect the nation's return on investment. In particular, these government research and funding programs will focus on the development of beneficial public applications in the fields of education, health care, manufacturing, and provision of government services.

• *Action:* Continue the High-Performance Computing and Communications Program. Established by the High-Performance Computing Act of 1991, the HPCC Program funds R&D designed to create more powerful computers, faster computer networks, and more sophisticated software. In addition, the HPCC Program is providing scientists and engineers with the tools and training they need to solve "Grand Challenges," research problems—like designing new drugs—that cannot be solved without the most powerful computers. The Administration has requested $1 billion for the HPCC Program in fiscal year 1994, and is in the process of forming a "High-Performance Comput-ing Advisory Committee," to provide private sector input on the Program.

We have also requested an additional $96 million in the FY [Fiscal Year] 1994 budget to create a new component of the HPCC Program—Information Infrastructure Technologies and Appli-cations (IITA). The Administration is working with Congress to obtain authorization to fund this effort, which will develop and apply high-performance computing and high-speed networking technologies for use in the fields of health care, education, li-braries, manufacturing, and provision of government informa-tion.

• *Action:* Implement the NII Pilot Projects Program. In its FY 94 budget, the Administration has requested funding from the Congress for NII networking pilot and demonstration projects. Under NTIA's direction, this pilot program will provide match-ing grants to state and local governments, health care providers, school districts, libraries, universities, and other non-profit enti-ties. The grants will be awarded after a competitive merit review process and will be used to fund projects to connect institutions to existing networks, enhance communications networks that are currently operational, and permit users to interconnect among different networks. Funded projects will demonstrate the poten-tial of the NII and provide tangible benefits to their communities. Equally important, they will help leverage the resources and cre-ativity of the private sector to devise new applications and uses of the NII. The successes of these pilot projects will create an itera-tive process that will generate more innovative approaches each year.

• *Action:* Inventory NII Applications Projects. Many insights can be gained by sharing information about how government can effectively use the NII. By the end of January 1994, the IITF will complete an inventory of current and planned government activ-ities and will widely disseminate the results through electronic and printed means. An electronic forum is being established to encourage government and private sector contributions and com-ments about government applications projects.

4) Promote seamless, interactive, user-driven operation. Be-cause the NII will be a network of networks, information must be transferable over the disparate networks easily, accurately, and without compromising the content of the messages. Moreover, the NII will be of maximum value to users if it is sufficiently

"open" and interactive so that users can develop new services and applications or exchange information among themselves, without waiting for services to be offered by the firms that operate the NII. In this way, users will develop new "electronic communities" and share knowledge and experiences that can improve the way that they learn, work, play, and participate in the American democracy.

To assure interoperability and openness of the many components of an efficient, high-capacity NII, standards for voice, video, data, and multi-media services must be developed. Those standards also must be compatible with the large installed base of communications technologies, and flexible and adaptable enough to meet user needs at affordable costs. The United States has long relied on a consensus-based, voluntary standards-setting process in communications. Particularly in the area of information and communications technology, where product cycles are often measured in months, not years, the standards process is critical and has not always worked to speed technological innovation and serve end-users well. Government can catalyze this industry-driven process by participating more actively in private-sector standards-writing bodies and by working with industry to address strategic technical barriers to interoperability and adoption of new technologies.

To increase the likelihood that the NII will be both interactive and, to a large extent, user-driven, government also must reform regulations and policies that may inadvertently hamper the development of interactive applications. For example, government regulations concerning the lack of reimbursement of health care procedures may deter the growth of distance medicine applications.

• *Action:* Review and clarify the standards process to speed NII applications. By October 15, 1993 the Commerce Department's National Institute for Standards and Technology (NIST) will establish a panel and work with other appropriate agencies to review the government's involvement in establishing network requirements and standards with domestic and international partners. The panel, with input from the private sector and other levels of government, will consider the role of the government in the standards process and will identify opportunities for accelerating the deployment of the NII.

• *Action:* Review and reform government regulations that impede development of interactive services and applications. The

Administration will work closely with the private sector, as well as state and local governments, to identify government policies and regulations that may hinder the growth of interactive services and applications. The IITF will determine how those regulations should be changed.

5) Ensure information security and network reliability. The trustworthiness and security of communications channels and networks are essential to the success of the NII. Users must be assured that information transmitted over the infrastructure will go when and where it is intended to go. Electronic information systems can create new vulnerabilities. For example, electronic files can be broken into and copied from remote locations, and cellular phone conversations can be monitored easily. Yet these same systems, if properly designed, can offer greater security than less advanced communications channels.

Through the use of information systems, gathering, sending, and receiving a wide variety of personal information is now simple, quick, and relatively inexpensive. The use of information technologies to access, modify, revise, repackage, and resell information can benefit individuals, but unauthorized use can encroach on their privacy. While media reports often emphasize the role of modern information technology in invading privacy, technology advances and enhanced management oversight also offer the opportunity for privacy protection. This protection is especially important to businesses that increasingly transmit sensitive proprietary data through electronic means. In a climate of tough global competitiveness to gain market advantage, the confidentiality of this information can spell the difference between business success or failure.

In addition, it is essential that the Federal government work with the communications industry to reduce the vulnerability of the nation's information infrastructure. The NII must be designed and managed in a way that minimizes the impact of accident or sabotage. The system must also continue to function in the event of attack or catastrophic natural disaster.

• *Action:* Review privacy concerns of the NII. The IITF has developed a work plan to investigate what policies are necessary to ensure individual privacy, while recognizing the legitimate societal needs for information, including those of law enforcement. The IITF has also developed a work plan to investigate how the government will ensure that the infrastructure's operations are compatible with the legitimate privacy interests of its users.

• *Action:* Review of encryption technology. In April, the President announced a thorough review of Federal policies on encryption technology. In addition, Federal agencies are working with industry to develop new technologies that protect the privacy of citizens, while enabling law enforcement agencies to continue to use court-authorized wiretaps to fight terrorism, drug rings, organized crime, and corruption. Federal agencies are working with industry to develop encryption hardware and software that can be used for this application.

• *Action:* Work with industry to increase network reliability. The National Communications System brings together 23 Federal agencies with industry to reduce the vulnerability of the nation's telecommunications systems to accident, sabotage, natural disaster, or military attack. And the Federal Communications Commission has an industry and user Network Reliability Council to advise it on ensuring the reliability of the nation's commercial telecommunications networks. These efforts are increasingly important as the threat posed by terrorism and computing hacking grows. The NCS will continue its work and will coordinate with the IITF. In addition, the National Security Telecommunications Advisory Committee, which advises the President in coordination with the NCS, as well as the FCC's Network Reliability Council, will coordinate with and complement the work of the Advisory Council on the National Information Infrastructure.

6) Improve management of the radio frequency spectrum. Many of the dramatic changes expected from the development of the information infrastructure will grow out of advances in wireless technologies. The ability to access the resources of the NII at any time, from anywhere in the country, will be constrained, however, if there is inadequate spectrum available. To ensure that spectrum scarcity does not impede the development of the NII, the Administration places a high priority on streamlining its procedures for the allocation and use of this valuable resource.

• *Action:* Streamline allocation and use of spectrum. The Administration is working with Congress to fully implement the spectrum management provisions of the Omnibus Budget and Reconciliation Act of 1993, to streamline government use of spectrum and to get spectrum to the public efficiently. These provisions will provide greater flexibility in spectrum allocation, including increased sharing of spectrum between private sector and government users, increased flexibility in technical and service standards, and increased choices for licensees in employing their assigned spectrum.

• *Action:* Promote market principles in spectrum distribution.

Further, the Administration will continue to support policies that place a greater reliance on market principles in distributing spectrum, particularly in the assignment process, as a superior way to apportion this scarce resource among the widely differing wireless services that will be a part of the NII. At the same time, the Administration will develop policies to ensure that entrepreneurs and small, rural, minority- and women-owned businesses are able to participate in spectrum auctions.

7) Protect intellectual property rights. Development of an advanced information infrastructure will create unprecedented market opportunities and new challenges for our world-preeminent media and information industries. The broad public interest in promoting the dissemination of information to our citizens must be balanced with the need to ensure the integrity of intellectual property rights and copyrights in information and entertainment products. This protection is crucial if these products—whether in the form of text, images, computer programs, databases, video or sound recordings, or multimedia formats—are to move in commerce using the full capability of the NII.

• *Action:* Examine the adequacy of copyright laws. The IITF will investigate how to strengthen domestic copyright laws and international intellectual property treaties to prevent piracy and to protect the integrity of intellectual property. To ensure broad access to information via the NII, the IITF will study how traditional concepts of fair use should apply with respect to new media and new works.

• *Action:* Explore ways to identify and reimburse copyright owners. The IITF will explore the need for standards for the identification of copyright ownership of information products in election systems (e.g., electronic headers, labels or signature techniques). The Task Force will also evaluate the need to develop an efficient system for the identification, licensing, and use of work, and for the payment of royalties for copyrighted products delivered or made available over electronic information systems.

8) Coordinate with other levels of governmental and with other bodies.

A.) Domestic. Many of the firms that will likely participate in the NII are now subject to regulation by Federal, state, and local government agencies. If the information infrastructure is to develop quickly and coherently, there must be close coordination among the various government entities, particularly with respect to regulatory policy. It is crucial that all government bodies—

particularly Congress, the FCC, the Administration, and state and local governments—work cooperatively to forge regulatory principles that will promote deployment of the NII.

• *Action:* Seek ways to improve coordination with state and local officials. The IITF will meet with state and local officials to discuss policy issues related to development of the NII. The Task Force will also seek input from the private sector and non-federal agencies as it devises proposals for regulatory reform. The Administration is committed to working closely with state and local governments in developing its telecommunications policies.

B.) International. The NII also will develop in the context of evolving global networks. Because customers typically demand that U.S. communications providers offer services on a global basis, it is critical that the infrastructure within this country can meet international, as well as domestic, requirements.

• *Action:* Open up overseas markets. The Administration has shown its willingness to work directly on behalf of U.S. firms to ensure that they have an equal opportunity to export telecommunications-related goods and services to potential overseas customers. For example, the Commerce Department is developing new export control policies governing computers and telecommunications equipment manufactured by U.S. firms. These changes will remove export restrictions on many of these products and permit U.S. manufacturers to enter new markets not previously available to them. The Administration will continue to work to pen overseas markets for U.S. services and products.

• *Action:* Eliminate barriers caused by incompatible standards. Equally important is the need to avoid trade barriers raised by incompatible U.S. and foreign standards or—more subtly—between the methods used to test conformance to standards. Through its participation in international standards committees, the Administration is working to eliminate or avert such barriers.

• *Action:* Examine international and U.S. trade regulations. The IITF will coordinate the Administration's examination of policy issues related to the delivery of telecommunications services to and from the U.S., including claims by some U.S. companies that regulatory practices in foreign countries—including denial of market access for U.S. carriers and the imposition of excessive charges for completing calls from the United States—are harming the competitiveness of the industry and the costs charged to U.S. customers for service. The IITF also will reexamine U.S. regulation of international telecommunications services.

9) Provide access to government information and improve government procurement. Thomas Jefferson said that information is the currency of democracy. Federal agencies are among the most prolific collectors and generators of information that is useful and valuable to citizens and business. Improvement of the nation's information infrastructure provides a tremendous opportunity to improve the delivery of government information to the taxpayers who paid for its collection; to provide it equitably, at a fair price, as efficiently as possible.

The Federal government is improving every step of the process of information collection, manipulation, and dissemination. The Administration is funding research programs that will improve the software used for browsing, searching, describing, organizing, and managing information. But it is committed as well to applying those tools to the distribution of information that can be useful to the public in their various roles as teachers, researchers, businesspeople, consumers, etc.

The key questions that must be addressed are: What information does the public want? What information is in electronic form? By what means can it be distributed? How can all Americans have access to it? A secondary question is: How can government itself improve through better information management?

• *Action:* Improve the accessibility of government information. IITF working groups will carefully consider the problems associated with making government information broadly accessible to the public electronically. Additionally, several inter-agency efforts have been started to ensure that the right information is stored and available. Finally, to help the public find government information, an inter-agency project has been formed to develop a virtual card catalogue that will indicate the availability of government information in whatever form it takes.

• *Action:* Upgrade the infrastructure for the delivery of government information. The Federal government has already taken a number of steps to promote wider distribution of its public reports. Legislation has been enacted to improve electronic dissemination of government document by the Government Printing Office. A number of Federal agencies have moved aggressively to convert their public information into electronic form and disseminate it over the Internet, where it will be available to many more people than have previously had access to such information. In the future, substantial improvements will be made to "Fed-World," an electronic bulletin board established by the Department of Commerce's National Technical Information Service (NTIS), which links the public with more than 100 Federal bulletin boards and information centers. These improvements will enhance FedWorld's ability to distribute to the public scientific, technical, and business-related information generated by the U.S. Government and other sources. Finally, a conference will be held in the Fall of 1993 to begin teaching Federal employees how they can use these distribution mechanisms.

• *Action:* Enhance citizen access to government information. In June 1993, OMB prescribed new policies pertaining to the acquisition, use, and distribution of government information by Federal agencies. Among other things, the policies mandate that, in distributing information to the public, Federal agencies should recoup only those costs associated with the dissemination of that information, not with its creation or collection. Moreover, a number of inter-agency efforts are under way to afford greater public access to government information. One project seeks to turn thousands of local and field offices of various Federal agencies into Interactive Citizen Participation Centers, at which citizens can communicate with the public affairs departments of all Federal agencies.

• *Action:* Strengthen inter-agency coordination through the use of electronic mail. To implement the *National Performance Review*'s recommendation on expanded use of electronic mail within the Federal government, an inter-agency coordinating body has been established to incorporate electronic mail into the daily work environment of Federal workers. The group is also sponsoring three pilot projects to expand connectivity that will build a body of experience that other Federal agencies can draw on when they begin to use electronic mail.

• *Action:* Reform the Federal procurement process to make government a leading-edge technology adopter. The Federal government is the largest single buyer of high technology products. The government has played a key role in developing emerging markets for advanced technologies of military significance; it can be similarly effective for civilian technologies. The Administration will implement the procurement policy reforms set forth in the *National Performance Review.*

VI. America's Destiny Is Linked to our Information Infrastructure

The principles and goals outlined in this document provide a blueprint for government action on the NII. Applying them will ensure that government provides constructive assistance to U.S. industry, labor, academia and private citizens as they develop, deploy and use the infrastructure.

The potential benefits for the nation are immense. The NII will enable U.S. firms to compete and win in the global economy, generating good jobs for the American people and economic growth for the nation. As importantly, the NII promises to transform the lives of the American people. It can ameliorate the constraints of geography and economic status, and give all Americans a fair opportunity to go as far as their talents and ambitions will take them.

Benefits and Applications of the National Information Infrastructure

The development of the National Information Infrastructure is not an end in itself; it is a means by which the United States can achieve a broad range of economic and social goals. Although the NII is not a "silver bullet" for all of the problems we face, it can make an important contribution to our most pressing economic and social challenges.

This infrastructure can be used by all Americans, not just by scientists and engineers. As entrepreneurs, factory workers, doctors, teachers, federal employees, and citizens, Americans can harness this technology to:

• Create jobs, spur growth, and foster U.S. technological leadership.

• Reduce health care costs while increasing the quality of service in underserved areas.

• Deliver higher-quality, lower-cost government services.

• Prepare our children for the fast-paced workplace of the 21st century.

• Build a more open and participatory democracy at all levels of government.

This is not a far-fetched prediction. As shown below, our current information infrastructure is already making a difference in the lives of ordinary Americans, and we have just begun to tap its potential.

Economic Benefits

The National Information Infrastructure will help create high-wage jobs, stimulate economic growth, enable new products and services, and strengthen America's technological leadership. Whole new industries will be created, and the infrastructure will be used in ways we can only begin to imagine. Below are some of the potential benefits to the U.S. economy.

1. Increased Economic Growth and Productivity

• The Computer Systems Policy Project estimates that the NII will "create as much as $300 billion annually in new sales across a range of industries."
• The Economic Strategy Institute concluded that accelerated deployment of the NII would increase GDP by $194 billion.
• $321 billion to GNP by the year 2007, and increase productivity by 20 to 40 percent.

2. Job Creation

Although there are no definitive estimates for the total number of U.S. jobs the deployment of the NII will create, it is clear that it has the potential to create hundreds of thousands of jobs. For example:

Industry experts believe that the Personal Communications Services industry, a new family of wireless services, could create as many as 300,000 jobs in the next 10–15 years. The development of this industry will be accelerated by the Emerging Telecommunications Technology Act, which was signed by President Clinton as part of the budget package.

3. Technological Leadership

The NII will serve as the driver for a wide variety of technologies, such as semiconductors, high-speed networking, advanced displays, software, and human/computer interfaces such as speech recognition.

This technology will be used to create exciting new products and services, strengthening U.S. leadership in the electronics and information technology sector. For example, experts envision the production of powerful computers that will be held in the palm of our hand, "as mobile as a watch and as personal as a wallet, . . . [they] will recognize speech, navigate streets, take notes, keep schedules, collect mail, manage money, open the door and start the car, among other computer functions we cannot imagine today."

4. Regional, State, and Local Economic Development

In today's knowledge-based, global economy in which capital and technology are increasingly mobile, the quality of America's information infrastructure will help determine whether companies invest here or overseas. States and regions increasingly recognize that development of their information infrastructure is key to creating jobs and attracting new businesses.

• In May 1993, Governor Jim Hunt announced the creation of the North Carolina Information Highway, a network of fiber optics and advanced switches capable of transmitting the entire 33-volume Encyclopedia Britannica in 4.7 seconds. This network, which will be deployed in cooperation with BellSouth, GTE, and Carolina Telephone, is a key element of North Carolina's economic development strategy.

• In California's Silicon Valley, academics, business executives, government officials, and private citizens are working together to build an "advanced information infrastructure and the collective ability to use it." A non-profit organization, Smart Valley Inc., will help develop the information infrastructure and its applications. Many business applications are envisioned, including desktop videoconferencing, rapid delivery of parts designs to fabrication shops, design of chips on remote supercomputers, electronic commerce, and telecommuting.

• The Council of Great Lakes Governors has developed a regional telecommunications initiative, which includes creating an open data network as a first step towards creation of a Great Lakes Information Highway, promoting access in rural areas, developing a set of telecommunications service goals and a time table for achieving them, and developing a computerized inventory of each state's advanced telecommunications infrastructure.

5. Electronic Commerce

Electronic commerce (e.g., on-line parts catalogues, multimedia mail, electronic payment, brokering services, collaborative engineering) can dramatically reduce the time required to design, manufacture, and market new products. "Time to market" is a critical success favor in today's global marketplace. Electronic commerce will also strengthen the relationships between manufacturer, suppliers, and joint developers. In today's marketplace, it is not unusual to have 12 or more companies collaborating to develop and manufacture new products.

Health Care

The NII can help solve America's health care crisis. The Clinton Administration is committed to health care reform that will ensure that Americans will never again lose their health care coverage and that controls skyrocketing health care costs. The costs of doing nothing are prohibitive:

• Since 1980, our nation's health care costs have quadrupled. Between 1980 and 1992, health expenditures shot up from 9 percent to 14 percent of GDP; under current policies, they will hit 19 percent by the year 2000. Health care cost increases will eat up more than half of the new federal revenue expected over the next four years.

• Twenty-five cents out of every dollar on a hospital bill goes to administrative costs and does not buy any patient care. The number of health care administrators is increasing four times faster than the number of doctors.

These problems will not be solved without comprehensive health care reform. Better use of information technology and the development of health care applications for the NII, however, can make an important contribution to reform. Experts estimate that telecommunications applications could reduce health care costs by $36 to $100 billion each year while improving quality and increasing access. Below are some of the existing and potential applications:

• Telemedicine: By using telemedicine, doctors and other care givers can consult with specialists thousands of miles away; continually upgrade their education and skills; and share medical records and x-rays. *Example:* In Texas, over 70 hospitals, primarily in rural areas, have been forced to close since 1984. The Texas Telemedicine Project in Austin, Texas offers interactive video consultation to primary care physicians in rural hospitals as a way of alleviating the shortage of specialists in rural areas. This trial is increasing the quality of care in rural areas and providing at least 14 percent savings by cutting patient transfer costs and provider travel.

• Unified Electronic Claims: More than 4 billion health care claims are submitted annually from health care providers to reimbursement organizations such as insurance companies, Medicare, Medicaid, and HMOs. Moreover, there are 1500 different insurance companies in the United States using many different claims forms. The administrative costs of the U.S. health care system could be dramatically reduced by moving towards standardized electronic submission and processing of claims.

• Personal Health Information Systems: The United States can use computers and networks to promote self care and prevention by making health care information available 24 hours a day in a form that aids decision making. Most people do not have the tools necessary to become an active and informed participant in their own health care. As a result, far too many people (estimates range from 50 to 80 percent) entering the health care system do not really need a physician's care. Many improperly use the system by, for example, using the emergency room for a cold or back strain. Many of those who end up with serious health problems enter the health care system too late, and thus require more extensive and costly therapy. Michael McDonald, chairman of the Communications and Computer Applications in Public Health (CCAPH), estimates that even if personal health information systems were used only 25 to 35 percent of the time, $40 to $60 billion could be saved. *Example:* InterPractice Systems, a joint venture of Harvard Community Health Plan in Boston and Electronic Data Systems, has placed terminals in the homes of heavy users of health care, such as the elderly, pregnant women, and families with young children. Based on a patient's symptoms and their medical history, an electronic advice system makes recommendations to HCHP's members about using self care, talking with a doctor, or scheduling an appointment. In one instance, "an 11-year-old who regularly played with the terminal heard his father complain one day of chest pains and turned to the system for help; it diagnosed the symptoms as a probable heart attack. The diagnosis was correct."

• Computer-Based Patient Records: The Institute of Medicine has concluded that Computer-Based Patient Records are critical to improving the quality and reducing the cost of health care. Currently: 11 percent of laboratory tests must be re-ordered because of lost results; 30 percent of the time, the treatment ordered is not documented at all; 40 percent of the time a diagnosis isn't recorded; and 30 percent of the time a medical record is completely unavailable during patient visits.

Civic Networking Technology in the Public Interest

The benefits of the NII extend far beyond economic growth. As the Center for Civic Networking observed: "A country that works smarter; enjoys efficient, less costly government, guided by a well-informed citizenry; that produces high quality jobs and educated citizens to fill them; that paves a road away from poverty; that promotes life long learning, public life and the cultural life of our communities. This is the promise of the National Information Infrastructure."

The NII could be used to create an "electronic commons" and promote the public interest in the following ways:

• Community Access Networks: Grass-roots networks are springing up all over the country, providing citizens with a wide range of information services. The National Information Infrastructure should expand a citizen's capacity for action in local institutions, as it must honor regional differences and the cultural diversity of America's heritage.

Example 1: The Heartland FreeNet in Peoria, Illinois provides a wide range of community information to the citizens of Central Illinois 24 hours a day. Topics covered include 113 areas of social services; a year long community calendar; the American Red Cross; current listings from the Illinois Job Service; resources for local businesses; and local government information. Experts in all fields from law to the Red Cross to chemical dependency volunteer their time and expertise to answer questions anonymously asked by the public.

Example 2: The Big Sky Telegraph began operation in 1988 as an electronic bulletin board system linking Montana's 114 one-room schools to each other and to Western Montana College. Today, the Big Sky Telegraph enables the formation of "virtual communities"—linking schools, libraries, county extension services, women's centers, and hospitals. Montana's high-school students learning Russian can now communicate with Russian students, and science students are participating in a course on "chaos theory" offered by MIT.

• Dissemination of government information: The free flow of information between the government and the public is essential to a democratic society. Improvements in the National Information Infrastructure provide a tremendous opportunity to improve the delivery of government information to the taxpayers who paid for its collection; to provide it equitably, at a fair price, as equitably as possible. *Example:* Some of the most powerful examples of the power inherent in information collection and dissemination come from the experience of Federal agencies. For example, the Emergency Planning and Community Right-to-Know Act of 1986 established a Toxic Release Inventory (TRI), which required industries to report their estimated total releases of toxic chemicals to the environment. The Environmental Protection Agency has used a variety of means for making the data available to the public, including a collaborative effort involving the agency, the nonprofit community, and philanthropy. This effort involved making the TRI available through an online service called RTK NET (the Right-to-Know Computer Network), operated by OMB Watch and Unison Institute. As a result of the TRI program, EPA and industry developed the "33/50" program, in which CEOs set a goal of reducing their pollution by 33 percent by 1992 and 50 percent by 1995. Because of RTK NET's success, EPA is seeking to expand the information available on the service.

• Universal access: The NII must be used to bring Americans together, as opposed to allowing a further polarization between information "haves" and "have nots." *Example:* As part of a recent cable franchise negotiation, fiber optic cable was deployed in Harlem, where 40 percent of the residents live below the poverty line. New York City is exploring the use of interactive video conferencing between community rooms in housing projects and government offices, schools, and New York corporations. These facilities could be used to teach parenting to teenage mothers, and promote mentoring programs between inner city youth and employees of New York corporations.

Research

One of the central objectives of the High Performance Computing and Communications Initiative (HPCCI) is to increase the productivity of the research community and enable scientists and engineers to tackle "Grand Challenges," such as forecasting the weather, building more energy-efficient cars, designing life-saving drugs, and understanding how galaxies are formed.

As a result of advances in computing and networking technologies promoted by the HPCCI, America's scientists and engineers (and their colleagues and peers around the world) are able to solve fundamental problems that would have been impossible to solve in the past. U.S. researchers will continue to benefit from the HPCCI and the emerging National Information Infrastructure. Below are just a few of the ways in which this technology is being used by U.S. researchers:

• Solving grand challenges: As a result of investments in high performance computers, software, and high-speed networks, researchers have access to more and more computational resources. As a result, scientists and engineers have been able to more accurately model the Earth's climate; design and simulate next-generation aircraft (the High Speed Civil Transport); improve detection of breast cancer by turning two-dimensional MRI images into three-dimensional views; and enhance the recovery of oil and gas from America's existing reservoirs.

• Enabling remote access to scientific instruments. Because of advancements in networks and visualization software, scientists can control and share remote electron microscopes, radio telescopes, and other scientific instruments.

• Supporting scientific collaboration: The Internet has allowed scientists in the United States and around the world to access databases, share documents, and communicate with colleagues. For example, one computer language was developed by 60 people in industry, government and academia over a period of 3 years with only two days of face-to-face meetings. Instead, project participants sent 3,000 e mail messages to each other, dramatically reducing the time required to develop the language. As scientific research becomes increasingly complex and interdisciplinary, scientists see the need to develop "collaboratories," centers without walls in which "the nations' researchers can perform their research without regard to geographical location— interacting with colleagues, access instrumentation, sharing data and computational resources, [and] accessing information in digital libraries."

Life-Long Learning

Increasingly, what we earn depends on what we learn, Americans must be well-educated and well-trained if we are to compete internationally and enjoy a healthy democracy. The magnitude of the challenge we face is well-known:

• 25 percent of students nationwide no longer complete high-school, a figure which rises to 57 percent in some large cities.

• Currently, 90 million adults in the United States do not have the literacy skills they need to function in our increasingly complex society.

The Clinton Administration has set ambitious national goals for lifelong learning. The "Goals 2000: Educate America Act" would make six education goals part of national policy: 90 percent high school graduation rate; U.S. dominance in math and science; total adult literacy; safe and drug-free schools; increased competency in challenging subjects; and having every child enter school "ready to learn." Secretary of Labor Robert Reich also has emphasized the need to move towards "new work." New work requires problem-solving as opposed to rote repetition, upgrading worker skills, and empowering front-line workers to continuously improve products and services. All of the Administration's policy initiatives (national skill standards, school-to-work transition, training for displaced workers) are aimed at promoting the transition towards high-wage, higher-value "new work."

Although technology alone can not fix what is wrong with America's education and training system, the NII can help. Studies have shown that computer-based instruction is cost-effective, enabling 30% more learning in 40% less time at 30% less cost. *Fortune* recently reported that: "From Harlem to Honolulu, electronic networks are sparking the kind of excitement not seen in America's classrooms since the space race . . . In scores of programs and pilot projects, networks are changing the way teachers teach and students learn."

The United States has just begun to exploit the educational applications of computers and networks. Students and teachers can use the NII to promote collaborative learning between students, teachers, and experts; access-on-line "digital libraries"; and take "virtual" field trips to museums and science exhibits without leaving the classroom.

Example 1: Headquartered in Cambridge, Massachusetts and funded by the National Science Foundation, the Global Laboratory Project links students from over 101 schools in 27 states and 17 foreign countries, including Japan, Saudi Arabia, Russia and Argentina. All over the world, students establish environmental monitoring stations to study climate change, monitor pollutants such as pesticides and heavy metals, and measure ultraviolet radiation. Students share their data over the Global Lab telecommunications network with each other and with scientists to make comparisons, conduct analyses, and gain a global perspective on environmental problems.

Example 2: In Texas, the Texas Education Network (TE-NET) now serves over 25,000 educators, and is making the resources of the Internet available to classrooms. One Texas educator from a small school district described the impact it was having on the learning experiences of children:

The smaller districts can now access NASA, leave messages for the astronauts, browse around in libraries larger than ever they will ever be able to visit, discuss the Superconducting Supercollider project with the physicist in charge, discuss world ecology with students in countries around the world, read world and national news that appears in newspapers that are not available in their small towns, work on projects as equals and collaborators with those in urban areas, and change the way they feel about the size of their world. This will create students that we could not create otherwise. This is a new education and instruction.

As computers become more powerful and less expensive, students may eventually carry hand-held, computer-based "intelligent tutors," or learn in elaborate simulated environments. One expert predicted the following educational use of virtual reality:

Imagine a biology student entering an immersive virtual laboratory environment that includes simulated molecules. The learner can pick up two molecules and attempt to fit them together, exploring docking sites. In addition to the three-dimensional images in the head-mounted display, the gesture gloves on his hands press back to provide feedback to his sense of touch. Alternatively, the student can expand a molecule to the size of a large building and fly around in it, examining the internal structure.

Creating a Government That Works Better & Costs Less

The Vice President Gore's *National Performance Review* (NPR) provides a bold vision of a federal government which is effective, efficient and responsive. Moving from red tape to results will require sweeping changes: emphasizing accountability for achieving results as opposed to following rules; putting customers first; empowering employees; and reengineering how government agencies do their work. As part of this vision, the NPR emphasizes the importance of information technology as a tool for reinventing government: "With computers and telecommunications, we need not do things as we have in the past. We can design a customer-driven electronic government that operates in ways that, 10 years ago, the most visionary planner could not have imagined."

The NPR has identified a number of ways in which "electronic government" can improve the quality of government services while cutting costs, some of which are described below:

• Develop a nationwide system to deliver government benefits electronically: The government can cut costs through "electronic benefit transfer" for programs such as federal retirement, social security, unemployment insurance, AFDC, and food stamps. For example, 3 billion Food Stamps are printed and distributed to over 10 million households. Estimates suggest that $1 billion could be saved over five years once electronic benefits for food stamps is fully implemented.

• Develop integrated electronic access to government information and services: Currently, citizen access to federal government information is uncoordinated and not customer-friendly. Electronic kiosks and computer bulletin boards can result in quick response, complete information, and an end to telephone tag. *Example: Info/California* is a network of kiosks in places like libraries and shopping malls. Californians can use these touch-screen computers to renew vehicle registration, register for employment openings, and get information on 90 different subjects, such as applying for student loans or resolving tenant-landlord disputes. These kiosks have reduced the cost of job-match services from $150 to $40 per person.

• Establish a national law enforcement/public safety network: Whether responding to natural or technological disasters, or performing search and rescue or interdiction activities, federal, state, and local law enforcement and public safety workers must be able to communicate with each other effectively, efficiently, and securely. Currently, federal, state and local law enforcement agencies have radio systems which can not communicate with each other because they occupy different parts of the spectrum.

• Demonstrate and provide governmentwide electronic mail: Government-wide e-mail can provide rapid communications among individuals and groups, break down barriers to information flows between and within agencies, allow better management of complex interagency projects, and permit more communication between government officials and the public.

THE HISTORY OF THE FUTURE[2]

Who Are They?

Ben Barker: senior vice president and chief technology officer at Bolt, Beranek and Newman (BBN). In 1969, he designed hardware interfaces for the Arpanet.

Roland F. Bryan: founder, president and chief executive officer of ACC Systems in Santa Barbara, Calif. Bryan was principal investigator at the University of California at Santa Barbara, one of the first Arpanet sites.

Stephen Crocker: vice president at Trusted Information Systems, Inc. A graduate student at UCLA in 1969, Crocker helped design the original suite of protocols for the Arpanet.

Robert Kahn: founder and president of the Corp. for National Research Initiatives. An Arpanet pioneer at BBN in the late 1960s, Kahn was an Internet architect and co-inventor of TCP/IP while at the Advanced Research Projects Agency (ARPA) in the 1970s.

Leonard Kleinrock: chairman of the Computer Science Department at UCLA. He developed many of the principles of packet switching in the early 1960s.

Severo Ornstein: retired. At BBN in 1969, he had responsibility for packet switch hardware design. He founded Computer Professionals for Social Responsibility.

Lawrence G. Roberts: president of ATM Systems, a division of Connectware, Inc. He managed development of the Arpanet at ARPA in the late 1960s and early 1970s.

Barry D. Wessler: CEO of Plexsys International Corp. A member of the Arpanet development team at ARPA in the late 1960s.

The Interview

One August day in 1968 an unusual requested arrived on the desk of Frank Heart, a manager at Bolt Beranek and Newman,

[2]Article by Gary H. Anthes, senior editor, from *Computerworld* 28:101–104 O3 '94. Copyright © 1994 by Computerworld, Inc. Reprinted with permission.

Inc., a high technology consulting firm in Cambridge, Massachusetts. It asked for a proposal for the design of a network, based on packet switching, that would connect widely dispersed computers in the U.S. Department of Defense. Heart handed the document to colleague Severo Ornstein and asked for his comments. "The next morning I came in and threw it back on Heart's desk," Ornstein recalls. "I said, 'Sure we could build such a thing, but I don't see why anybody would want it.' It was one of the biggest bloopers ever."

But build it they did. The result was the Arpanet, forerunner of today's global Internet. Twenty-five years later, Bolt Beranek and Newman sponsored a bash at which Ornstein and more than a dozen of the pioneers who built the original network gathered to celebrate its 25th anniversary. *Computerworld*'s Gary Anthes met with some of them at the event, called "The History of the Future," in Boston last month and asked them what we might expect from the Internet of the future. Here's what they said.

Computerworld: What is the future of the Internet? Will it evolve into the so-called "information superhighway?"

Kleinrock: The Internet may well be part of the information superhighway but not nearly all of it. The Internet lacks a number of needed features: a proper security framework, multimedia and a much richer set of qualities of service. Also, middleware is lacking significantly—accounting, billing, name servers, directories and so forth. But these can be added to the Internet incrementally.

Roberts: The Internet will be upgraded to ATM (Asynchronous Transfer Mode) as the base network to support the increased bandwidth. Today's voice net supports 600G bits, and the nation's data net will grow to 3,000G bits by 2020. Putting ATM under the Internet is very easy due to layered protocols and will be done within two years.

Wessler: There is a risk that the current Internet is overhyped for its current range of information services. I expect some dissatisfaction will result when other commercial services, such as America On-Line, provide a more reliable information source.

But I am confident that 10 years from now we will still use the Internet. What else will be around in 10 years is the insight that makes millionaires.

Computerworld: How do you see the Internet evolving for commercial use?

Crocker: The network will be the medium of choice for communication within a single company. The network will also be used for interenterprise and customer-to-merchant interactions. Some of these will involve delivery of goods and services directly over the Internet; other uses will be in support of goods and services delivered conventionally.

Roberts: The corporate decision today should be: Forget building your own network. The Internet is by far the best buy for a commercial user. It offers the largest network; it has the lowest cost.

Uses will be all voice, data and video communications including the listing of all products and services. These listings—not advertisements—will totally change the way industry and the public search for and buy products.

There will be a huge increase in video on the network. In the corporation, the emphasis will be on video messaging. Computers are currently used for two things: computing and nonreal-time messaging. In the future, they will be used for a third thing: real-time communications.

Barker: In three to five years, there will be millions of organizations, mostly small commercial organizations, doing their mainline business over the Internet as naturally as they use the fax today.

In a couple of years, it will be the default expectation that the little restaurant on the corner will have an [Internet directory listing]. As the technology evolves to the point that this can be used to place take-out orders or make reservations, such connectivity will become a prerequisite to survival. The same argument applies to most any business. Add security, credit-card charging and the L. L. Bean catalog, and voila—electronic commerce.

"Yellow Pages" type advertising will be a very effective way of reaching prospects. For example, all those who sell widgets can list their up-to-the-minute pricing for various sizes and quantities of widgets. Those who want to buy widgets can find the best price or submit an offer at some lower price, much as the stock market works today, but based on a software package running on an inexpensive workstation connected anywhere on the Internet.

Temporary labor markets will emerge on the same basis. As corporations continue to downsize and move toward "virtual" corporations, more and more of the work force will contract on a job basis using this sort of electronic market.

Computerworld: Will commercial users, including advertisers, harm the Internet or strengthen it?

Roberts: Commercial users, putting their product information on-line, will greatly strengthen the Internet. Users who send junk mail hurt it but are easily taken care of since return hate mail is easy.
Wessler: Advertising agencies have some very creative people. Eventually they will adapt to the 'net culture and find ways of getting the message through. Thank goodness it probably won't take the form of TV advertising.

Computerworld: Many would-be commercial users avoid the Internet because of security concerns. Are those concerns well-founded?

Roberts: No. Security is a problem, but firewalls and source veri-fication using public key [encryption] techniques will take care of this issue. The need is greater than the risk.
Barker: Security concerns on the Internet are painfully real. Un-fortunately, too many of the Internet access service providers sim-ply provide a port and leave it up to the user to deal with security issues. That may have made sense in connecting a student's PC, for which network security is not a significant concern, but is totally unacceptable for a hospital or a law firm with sensitive information on their networks.

There are solutions. A variety of firewall offerings are avail-able today, and improved offerings will be appearing. Privacy-enhanced mail offerings are also available to carry messages se-curely across the 'net and to verify the authenticity of the sender.

But none of these technologies is adequate to address the problem. Professional analysis is required to understand users' technical and business environments and determine the appro-priate security approaches.

Computerworld: What are the most pressing technical issues facing the Internet over the next two to five years?

Kleinrock: Open access is the most pressing issue.
Crocker: The transition to the next generation [Internet Proto-col] may be the dominant issue during this time. Part of the

design of the new protocol includes attention to security, mobility, real time and multicast, so there are really several different capabilities wrapped up in this transition. Substantial evolution of products, services and organizations will be required.

Kahn: It's not clear in the National Information Infrastructure there's going to be anyone around who knows enough about all the pieces to make something work or, if something goes wrong, to fix it. The challenge is how to prevent that scenario from becoming the showstopper.

Barker: All aspects of the information superhighway, whether it's 500-channel TV, movies on demand, interactive TV, multimedia applications on the Internet, require a great deal more bandwidth and switching capacity than the current infrastructure can support.

There is a stunning consensus that cell-switching, embodied in the emerging ATM standards, is the required infrastructure for this revolution. It is emerging as the appropriate backbone technology to support a variety of user services such as frame relay. Once corporations are connected to ATM backbones for inexpensive broadband data services, the [private branch exchange] vendors will provide ATM interfaces, allowing corporate voice traffic to transition. As Internet applications, cable and video-on-demand and telephone services all transition to ATM networks, the distinction between them disappears.

Bryan: In order of importance: protection of resources from external access and destruction; security and privacy of information; methodology to increase bandwidth to accommodate growth; elimination of unwanted traffic or intrusion; and keeping the costs down.

Computerworld: What are the most pressing business issues facing the Internet over the next two to five years?

Barker: Too many Internet access providers are providing service which does not meet the needs of the new wave of incoming users in two key areas: help in getting connected and diagnosing problems once connected. As a result, too many of the people getting connected tell horror stories of how difficult it was, of how far short of their expectations it fell and of security breach nightmares. Once connected, most service providers are unable to diagnose users' problems that fall outside of the provider's own network. This level of support is clearly inadequate for the kind of mission-critical commerce that the Internet will be carrying over the coming few years. The situation has to change.

Kahn: Protection of intellectual property is key. Companies won't try selling [electronic products] until they understand how they can survive in that world. If you get something over the Internet, how do you know that the person who gave it to you has a right to it? How do you know it's the real thing? If you scan in a photograph and use it in your newsletter, how do you know you are not going to be sued for $1 million by someone saying you didn't have permission to use it? These are really big-ticket items and serious questions.

Computerworld: What are the most pressing social issues facing the Internet over the next two to five years?

Ornstein: I'd like to lift us out of the warm bath of self-congratulation in which we have been wallowing and speculate about the future. In my bleaker view, what was once our little pride and joy will be taken over by commercial institutions that have little interest in the kind of interpersonal and intergroup communication that has thus far dominated network usage. Commercial exploitation of all sorts will be forced into every nook and cranny, just as it is on today's television.
Crocker: The network makes it possible to have complex relationships with individuals and groups of people all over the globe. The workplace and even the home may not be the focal point of one's social interactions. Virtual corporations will come into existence on a regular basis. None of these changes will be trouble-free.
Roberts: The network eliminates the need for big organizations. Individuals can get on, create information and sell it without the need for any company to support them. This totally changes the options for retired people and those who hate working for someone else. This has a major impact on the structure of the information industry, including newspapers, etc.
Barker: The fact that the Internet is also used for activities inappropriate for kids, such as the exchange of pornography. It is a statistically minor issue, and technical improvements will help, but ultimately the responsibility for control rests with parents and teachers. The principal risk is that the issue will receive undue attention in the press and stimulate technophobic politicians to impose draconian restrictions on Internet access.
Bryan: One aspect that might curtail the magic of the Internet is if some regulatory group selects the wrong way to get rid of

unwanted traffic. The Internet grew because it was an open and available resource, albeit mostly available to the "insiders" until recently. Now, if not carefully done, we could put so much of a damper on the overall service as to make it difficult to use.

Computerworld: What role should the government play in the rollout of the information superhighway?

Kleinrock: The government can help encourage the Open Data Network by providing various incentives, be they tax incentives, spectrum use, rights of way, depreciation schedules or their own purchasing policies.

Ornstein: The government is clearly going to have to step in in some regulatory fashion. If it's timid regulation, as in television, it's not going to be very effective. If the government addresses it more as it does telephone communications, then it can be more in the public interest. If not the Federal Communications Commission, some equivalent kind of organization could help impose some order in the public interest, rather than turning it into a free-for-all in the open market.

Barker: The absence of regulation has been a key reason for the creative energy and rapid advancement which has characterized the Internet. If the government moves to regulate it in response to the competitive environment brought on by the success of the Internet, this dynamic energy will be lost.

A MAGNA CARTA FOR THE KNOWLEDGE AGE[3]

I

The central event of the 20th century is the overthrow of matter. In technology, economics, and the politics of nations, wealth—in the form of physical resources—has been losing value and signifi-

[3]Article by Esther Dyson, George Gilder, Jay Keyworth, and Alvin Toffler. From *New Perspectives Quarterly* 11:26–37 Fall '94. Copyright © 1994 by *New Perspectives Quarterly*. Reprinted with permission.

cance. The powers of mind are everywhere ascendant over the brute force of things.

In a First Wave economy, land and farm labor are the main "factors of production." In a Second Wave economy, the land remains valuable while the labor becomes massified around machines and larger industries. In a Third Wave economy, the central resource—a single phrase broadly encompassing data, information, images, symbols, culture, ideology, and values—is actionable knowledge.

The industrial age is not fully over. In fact, classic Second Wave sectors (oil, steel, auto-production) have learned how to benefit from Third Wave technological breakthroughs—just as the First Wave agricultural productivity benefited exponentially from the Second Wave farm-mechanization.

But the Third Wave, and the Knowledge Age it has opened, will not realize its potential unless it adds social and political dominance to its accelerating technological and economic strength. This means repealing Second Wave laws and retiring Second Wave attitudes. It also demands of leaders of the advanced democracies a special responsibility—to facilitate, hasten, and explain the transition.

As humankind explores this new electronic frontier of knowledge, it must confront again the most profound questions of how to organize itself for the common good. The meaning of freedom, structures of self-government, definition of property, nature of competition, conditions for cooperation, sense of community and nature of progress will each be redefined for the Knowledge Age—just as they were redefined for a new age of industry some 250 years ago.

What our 20th-century countrymen came to think of as the American dream and what resonant thinkers referred to as the promise of American life or the American Idea emerged from the turmoil of 19th-century industrialization. Now it is our turn: The knowledge revolution and the Third Wave of historical change summon us to renew the dream and enhance the promise.

The Nature of Cyberspace

The Internet—the huge (2.2 million computers), global (135 countries), rapidly growing (10–15 percent a month) network that has captured the American imagination—is only a tiny part of cyberspace. So just what is cyberspace?

More ecosystem than machine, cyberspace is a bioelectronic environment that is literally universal: It exists everywhere there are telephone wires, coaxial cables, fiber-optic lines or electromagnetic waves.

This environment is inhabited by knowledge, including incorrect ideas, existing in electronic form. It is connected to the physical environment by portals which allow people to see what is inside, to put knowledge in, to alter it, and to take knowledge out. Some of these portals are one-way (e.g. television receivers and television transmitters); others are two-way (e.g. telephones, computer modems).

Most of the knowledge in cyberspace lives the most temporary (or so we think) existence: Your voice, on a telephone wire or microwave, travels through space at the speed of light, reaches the ear of your listener, and is gone forever.

But people are increasingly building cyberspatial warehouses of data, knowledge, information and misinformation in digital form, the ones and zeros of binary computer code. The storehouses themselves display a physical form (discs, tapes, CD-ROMs) but what they contain is accessible only to those with the right kind of portal and the right kind of key.

The key is software, a special form of electronic knowledge that allows people to navigate through the cyberspace environment and make its contents understandable to the human senses in the form of written language, pictures and sound.

People are adding to cyberspace—creating it, defining it, expanding it—at a rate that is already explosive and getting faster. Faster computers, cheaper means of electronic storage, improved software and more capable communications channels (satellites, fiber-optic lines)—each of these factors independently add to cyberspace. But the real explosion comes from the combination of all of them, working together in ways we still do not understand.

The bioelectronic frontier is an appropriate metaphor for what is happening in cyberspace, calling to mind as it does the spirit of invention and discovery that led ancient mariners to explore the world, generations of pioneers to tame the American continent and, more recently, to man's first exploration of outerspace.

But the exploration of cyberspace brings both greater opportunity, and in some ways more difficult challenges, than any previous human adventure.

Cyberspace is the land of knowledge, and the exploration of

that land can be a civilization's truest, highest calling. The opportunity is now before us to empower every person to pursue that calling in his or her own way.

The challenge is as daunting as the opportunity is great. The Third Wave has profound implications for the nature and meaning of property, of the marketplace, of community and of individual freedom. As it emerges, it shapes new codes of behavior that move each organism and institution—family, neighborhood, church group, company, government, nation—inexorably beyond standardization and centralization, as well as beyond the materialist's obsession with energy, money and control.

Turning the economics of mass-production inside out, new information technologies are driving the financial costs of diversity—both product and personal—down toward zero, "demassifying" our institutions and our culture. Accelerating demassification creates the potential for vastly increased human freedom.

It also spells the death of the central institutional paradigm of modern life, the bureaucratic organization. Governments, including the American government, are the last great redoubt of bureaucratic power on the face of the planet, and for them the coming change will be profound and probably traumatic.

In this context, the one metaphor that is perhaps least helpful in thinking about cyberspace is—unhappily—the one that has gained the most currency: The Information Superhighway. Can you imagine a phrase less descriptive of the nature of cyberspace, or more misleading in thinking about its implications? Consider the following set of polarities:

Information Superhighway	vs.	Cyberspace
Limited Matter	vs.	Unlimited Knowledge
Centralized	vs.	Decentralized
Moving on a grid	vs.	Moving in space
Government ownership	vs.	A vast array of ownerships
Bureaucracy	vs.	Empowerment
Efficient but not hospitable	vs.	Hospitable if you customize it

Withstand the elements	vs.	Flow, float and fine-tune
Unions and contractors	vs.	Associations and volunteers
Liberation from First Wave	vs.	Liberation from Second Wave
Culmination of Second Wave	vs.	Riding the Third Wave

"The highway analogy is all wrong," explained Peter Huber in *Forbes* this Spring, "for reasons rooted in basic economics. Solid things obey immutable laws of conservation—what goes south on the highway must go back north, or you end up with a mountain of cars in Miami. By the same token, production and consumption must balance. The average Joe can consume only as much wheat as the average Jane can grow. Information is completely different. It can be replicated at almost no cost—so every individual can (in theory) consume society's entire output. Rich and poor alike, we all run information deficits. We all take in more than we put out."

The Nature and Ownership of Property

Clear and enforceable property rights are essential for markets to work. Defining them is a central function of government. But to create the new cyberspace environment is to create new property—that is, new means of creating goods (including ideas) that serve people.

The property that makes up cyberspace comes in several forms: Wires, coaxial cable, computers and other hardware; the electromagnetic spectrum; and intellectual property—the knowledge that dwells in and defines cyberspace.

In each of these areas, two questions must be answered. First, what does ownership mean? What is the nature of the property itself, and what does it mean to own it? Second, once we understand what ownership means, who is the owner? At the level of first principles, should ownership be public (i.e. government) or private (i.e. individuals)?

The answers to these two questions will set the basic terms upon which America and the world will enter the Third Wave. For the most part, however, these questions are not yet even being asked. Instead, at least in America, governments are attempting to take Second Wave concepts of property and ownership and apply them to the Third Wave. Or they are ignoring the problem altogether.

For example, a great deal of attention has been focused recently on the nature of intellectual property—i.e. the fact that knowledge is what economists call a public good and thus requires special treatment in the form of copyright and patent protection.

Major changes in US copyright and patent law during the past two decades have broadened these protections to incorporate electronic property. In essence, these reforms have attempted to take a body of law that originated in the 15th century, with Gutenberg's invention of the printing press, and apply it to the electronically stored and transmitted knowledge of the Third Wave.

A more sophisticated approach starts with recognizing how the Third Wave has fundamentally altered the nature of knowledge as a good and that the operative effect is not technology per se (the shift from printed books to electronic storage and retrieval systems), but rather the shift from a mass-production, mass-media, mass-culture civilization to a demassified civilization.

The big change, in other words, is the demassification of actionable knowledge.

The dominant form of new knowledge in the Third Wave is perishable, transient and customized: The right information, combined with the right software and presentation, at precisely the right time. Unlike the mass knowledge of the Second Wave— public good knowledge that was useful to everyone because most people's information needs were standardized—Third Wave customized knowledge is by nature a private good.

If this analysis is correct, copyright and patent protection of knowledge (or at least many forms of it) may no longer be necessary. In fact, the marketplace may already be creating vehicles to compensate creators of customized knowledge outside the cumbersome copyright/patent process, as suggested by John Perry Barlow:

One existing model for the future conveyance of intellectual property is real-time performance, a medium currently used only in theater, music, lectures, stand-up comedy and pedagogy. I believe the concept of performance will expand to include most of the information economy, from multicasted soap operas to stock analysis. In these instances, commercial exchange will be more like ticket sales to a continuous show than the purchase of discrete bundles of that which is being shown. The other model, of course, is service. The entire professional class—doctors, lawyers, consultants, architects, etc.—are already being paid directly for their intellectual property. Who needs a copyright when you're on a retainer?

Copyright, patent and intellectual property represent only a few of the rights issues now at hand. Here are some of the others:

• Ownership of the electromagnetic spectrum, traditionally considered to be public property is now being auctioned by the Federal Communications Commission to private companies. But is it public property? Is the very limited bundle of rights sold in those auctions really property, or more in the nature of a use permit—the right to use a part of the spectrum for a limited time, for limited purposes? In either case, are the rights being auctioned defined in a way that makes technological sense?

• Ownership over the infrastructure of wires, coaxial cable and fiber-optic lines that are such prominent features in the geography of cyberspace is today much less clear than might be imagined. Regulation, especially price regulation, of this property can be tantamount to confiscation; as America's cable operators recently learned when the Federal government imposed price limits on them and effectively confiscated billions of their net worth. Whatever one's stance on the FCC's decision and the law behind it, there is no disagreeing with the proposition that one's ownership of a good is less meaningful when the government can step in, at will, and dramatically reduce its value.

The nature of capital in the Third Wave—tangible capital as well as intangible—is its depreciation in real value much faster than industrial-age capital—driven, if nothing else, by Moore's Law, which states that the processing power of the microchip doubles at least every 18 months. Yet accounting and tax regulations still require property to be depreciated over periods as long as 30 years. The result is a heavy bias in favor of heavy industry and against nimble, fast-moving baby businesses.

Who will define the nature of cyberspace property rights, and how? How can we strike a balance between interoperable open systems and protection of property?

The Nature of the Marketplace

Inexpensive knowledge destroys economies-of-scale. Customized knowledge permits just-in-time production for an ever rising number of goods. Technological progress creates new means of serving old markets, turning one-time monopolies into competitive battlegrounds.

These phenomena are altering the nature of the marketplace, not just for information technology but for all goods and materials, shipping and services. In cyberspace itself, market after market is being transformed by technological progress from a natural monopoly to one in which competition is the rule. Three recent examples:

• The market for mail has been made competitive by the development of fax machines and overnight delivery—even though the private express statutes that technically grant the US Postal Service a monopoly over mail delivery remain in place.

• During the past 20 years, the market for television has been transformed from one in which there were at most a few broadcast TV stations to one in which consumers can choose among broadcast, cable and satellite services.

• The market for local telephone services, until recently a monopoly based on twisted-pair copper cables, is rapidly being made competitive by the advent of wireless service and the entry of cable television into voice communication. In England, Mexico, New Zealand and a host of developing countries, government restrictions preventing such competition have already been removed and consumers actually have the freedom to choose.

The advent of new technology and new products creates the potential for dynamic competition—competition between and among technologies and industries, each seeking to find the best way of serving customers' needs. Dynamic competition is different from static competition, in which many providers compete to sell essentially similar products at the lowest price.

Static competition is good, because it forces costs and prices to the lowest levels possible for a given product. Dynamic competition is better, because it allows competing technologies and new products to challenge the old ones and, if they really are better, to replace them. Static competition might lead to faster and stronger horses. Dynamic competition gives us the automobile.

Such dynamic competition—the essence of what Austrian economist Joseph Schumpeter called creative destruction—creates winners and losers on a massive scale. New technologies can render instantly obsolete billions of dollars of embedded infrastructure, accumulated over decades. The transformation of the US computer industry since 1980 is a case in point.

In 1980, everyone knew who led in computer technology. Apart from the minicomputer boom, mainframe computers were the market, and America's dominance was largely based upon the position of a dominant vendor—IBM, with over 50 percent of world market share.

Then the personal-computing industry exploded, leaving older-style, big-business-focused computing with a stagnant, piece of a burgeoning total market. As IBM lost market share, many people became convinced that America had lost the ability to compete. By the mid-1980s, such alarmism had reached from Washington all the way into the heart of Silicon Valley.

But the real story was the renaissance of American business and technological leadership. In the transition from mainframes to PCs, a vast new market was created. This market was characterized by dynamic competition consisting of easy access and low barriers to entry. Start-ups by the dozens took on the larger established companies—and won.

After a decade of angst, the surprising outcome is that America is not only competitive internationally, but, by any measurable standard, America dominates the growth sectors in world economics—telecommunications, microelectronics, computer networking (or connected computing) and software systems and applications.

The reason for America's victory in the computer wars of the 1980s is that dynamic competition was allowed to occur in an area so breakneck and pell-mell that government would've had a hard time controlling it even had it been paying attention. The challenge for policy in the 1990s is to permit, even encourage, dynamic competition in every aspect of the cyberspace marketplace.

II

The Nature of Freedom

Overseas friends of America sometimes point out that the US Constitution is unique—because it states explicitly that power resides with the people, who delegate it to the government, rather than the other way around.

This idea—central to our free society—was the result of more than 150 years of intellectual and political ferment, from the Mayflower Compact to the US Constitution, as explorers struggled to establish the terms under which they would tame a new frontier.

And as America continued to explore new frontiers—from
the Northwest Territory to the Oklahoma land-rush—it consistently returned to this fundamental principle of rights, reaffirm-
ing, time after time, that power resides with the people.

Cyberspace is the latest American frontier. As this and other
societies make ever deeper forays into it, the proposition that
ownership of this frontier resides first with the people is central to
achieving its true potential.

To some people, that statement will seem melodramatic.
America, after all, remains a land of individual freedom, and this
freedom clearly extends to cyberspace. How else to explain the
uniquely American phenomenon of the hacker, who ignored every social pressure and violated every rule to develop a set of skills
through an early and intense exposure to low-cost, ubiquitous
computing.

Those skills eventually made him or her highly marketable,
whether in developing applications-software or implementing
networks. The hacker became a technician, an inventor and, in
case after case, a creator of new wealth in the form of the baby
businesses that have given America the lead in cyberspatial exploration and settlement.

It is hard to imagine hackers surviving, let alone thriving, in
the more formalized and regulated democracies of Europe and
Japan. In America, they've become vital for economic growth and
trade leadership. Why? Because Americans still celebrate individuality over conformity, reward achievement over consensus and
militantly protect the right to be different.

But the need to affirm the basic principles of freedom is real.
Such an affirmation is needed in part because we are entering
new territory, where there are as yet no rules—just as there were
no rules on the American continent in 1620, or in the Northwest
Territory in 1787.

Centuries later, an affirmation of freedom—by this document and similar efforts—is needed for a second reason: We are
at the end of a century dominated by the mass institutions of the
industrial age. The industrial age encouraged conformity and
relied on standardization. And the institutions of the day—
corporate and government bureaucracies, huge civilian and
military administrations, schools of all types—reflected these pri-
orities. Individual liberty suffered—sometimes only a little,
sometimes a lot:

In a Second Wave world, it might make sense for government

to insist on the right to peer into every computer by requiring that each contain a special clipper chip.

In a Second Wave world, it might make sense for government to assume ownership over the broadcast spectrum and demand massive payments from citizens for the right to use it.

In a Second Wave world, it might make sense for government to prohibit entrepreneurs from entering new markets and providing new services.

And, in a Second Wave world, dominated by a few old-fashioned, one-way media networks it might even make sense for government to influence which political viewpoints would be carried over the airwaves.

All of these interventions might have made sense in a Second Wave world, where standardization dominated and where it was assumed that the scarcity of knowledge (plus a scarcity of telecommunications capacity) made bureaucracies and other elites better able to make decisions than the average person.

But, whether they made sense before or not, these and literally thousands of other infringements on individual rights now taken for granted make no sense at all in the Third Wave.

For a century, those who lean ideologically in favor of freedom have found themselves at war not only with their ideological opponents, but with a time in history when the value of conformity was at its peak. However desirable as an ideal, individual freedom often seemed impractical. The mass institutions of the Second Wave required us to give up freedom in order for the system to work.

The coming of the Third Wave turns that equation inside-out. The complexity of Third Wave society is too great for any centrally planned bureaucracy to manage. Demassification, customization, individuality, freedom—these are the keys to success for Third Wave civilization.

The Essence of Community

If the transition to the Third Wave is so positive, why are we experiencing so much anxiety? Why are the statistics of social decay at or near all-time highs? Why does cyberspatial rapture strike millions of prosperous Westerners as lifestyle rupture? Why do the principles that have held us together as a nation seem no longer sufficient—or even wrong?

The incoherence of political life is mirrored in disintegrating personalities. Psychotherapists and gurus do a land-office business, as people wander aimlessly amid competing therapies. People slip into cults and covens or, alternatively, into a pathological privatism, convinced that reality is absurd, insane or meaningless. If things are so good, why do we feel so bad?

In part, this is why: Because we constitute the final generation of an old civilization and, at the very same time, the first generation of a new one. Much of our personal confusion and social disorientation is traceable to the conflict within us and within our political institutions—between the dying Second Wave civilization and the emergent Third Wave civilization thundering in to take its place.

Second Wave ideologues routinely lament the breakup of mass society. Rather than seeing this enriched diversity as an opportunity for human development, they attack it as fragmentation and balkanization. But to reconstitute democracy in Third Wave terms, we need to jettison the frightening but false assumption that more diversity automatically brings more tension and conflict in society.

Indeed, the exact reverse can be true: If 100 people all desperately want the same brass ring, they may be forced to fight for it. On the other hand, if each of the 100 has a different objective, it is far more rewarding for them to trade, cooperate, and form symbiotic relationships. Given appropriate social arrangements, diversity can make for a secure and stable civilization.

No one knows what the Third Wave communities of the future will look like, or where demassification will ultimately lead. It is clear, however, that cyberspace will play an important role knitting together the diverse communities of tomorrow, facilitating the creation of electronic neighborhoods bound together not by geography but by shared interests.

Socially, putting advanced computing power in the hands of entire populations will alleviate pressure on highways, reduce air pollution, allow people to live further away from crowded or dangerous urban areas, and expand family time.

The late Phil Salin offered this perspective: "[B]y 2000, multiple cyberspaces will have emerged, diverse and increasingly rich. Contrary to naïve views, these cyberspaces will not all be the same, and they will not all be open to the general public. The global network is a connected platform for a collection of diverse communities, but only a loose, heterogeneous community itself. Just as access to homes, offices, churches and department stores is controlled by their owners or managers, most virtual locations will exist as distinct places of private property.

"But unlike the private property of today," Salin continued, "the potential variations on design and prevailing customs will explode, because many variations can be implemented cheaply in software. And the 'externalities' associated with variations can drop; what happens in one cyberspace can be kept from affecting other cyberspaces."

Cyberspace is a wonderful pluralistic word to open more minds to the Third Wave's civilizing potential. Rather than being a centrifugal force helping to tear society apart, cyberspace can be one of the main forms of glue holding together an increasingly free and diverse society.

The Role of Government

Eventually, the Third Wave will affect virtually everything government does. The most pressing need, however, is to revamp the policies and programs that are slowing the creation of cyberspace. Second Wave programs for Second Wave industries— the status quo for the status quo—will do little damage in the short run. It is efforts of governments to apply Second Wave modus operandi to the fast-moving, decentralized creatures of the Third Wave that is the real threat to progress. Indeed, if there is to be an industrial policy for the knowledge age it should focus on removing barriers to competition and massively deregulating the fast-growing telecommunications and computing industries.

One further point should be made at the outset: Government should be as strong and as big as it needs to be to accomplish its central functions effectively and efficiently. The reality is that a Third Wave government will be vastly smaller (perhaps by 50 percent or more) than the current one—this is an inevitable implication of the transition from the centralized power structures of the industrial age to the dispersed, decentralized institutions of the Third. But smaller government does not imply weak government; nor does arguing for smaller government require being against government for narrowly ideological reasons.

Indeed, the transition from the Second Wave to the Third Wave will require a level of government activity not seen since the New Deal. Here are five proposals to back up the point:

A. The Path to Interactive Multimedia Access

The Jeffersonian Vision offered by Mitch Kapor and Jerry Berman has propelled the Electronic Frontier Foundation's (EFF) campaign for an open platform telecom architecture:

The amount of electronic material the superhighway can carry is dizzying, compared to the relatively narrow range of broadcast TV and the limited number of cable channels. Properly constructed and regulated, it could be open to all who wish to speak, publish and communicate. None of the interactive services will be possible, however, if we have an eight-lane data superhighway rushing into every home and only a narrow footpath coming back out. Instead of settling for a multimedia version of the same entertainment that is increasingly dissatisfying on today's TV, we need a superhighway that encourages the production and distribution of a broader, more diverse range of programming.

The question is: What role should government play in bringing this vision to reality? But also: Will incentives for the openly-accessible national multimedia network envisioned by EFF harm the rights of those now constructing thousands of non-open local area networks?

These days, interactive multimedia is the daily servant only of avant-garde firms and other elites. But the same thing could have been said about word-processors 12 years ago, or phone-line networks six years ago. Today we have, in effect, universal access to personal computing—which no political coalition ever subsidized or "planned." And America's networking menu is in a hyper-growth phase. Whereas the accessing software cost $50 two years ago, today the same companies hand it out free—to get more people on-line.

This egalitarian explosion has occurred in large measure because government has stayed out of these markets, letting personal computing take over while mainframes rot (almost literally) in warehouses, and allowing (no doubt more by omission that commission) computer networks to grow, free of the kinds of regulatory restraints that affect phones, broadcast and cable.

All of which leaves reducing barriers to entry and innovation as the only effective near-term path to universal access. In fact, it can be argued that a near-term national interactive multimedia network is impossible unless regulators permit much greater collaboration between the cable industry and phone companies. The latter's huge fiber resources (nine times as extensive as industry fiber and rising rapidly) could be joined with the huge asset of 57 million broadband links (i.e. into homes now receiving cable-TV service) to produce a new kind of national network—multimedia, interactive and (as costs fall) increasingly accessible to Americans of modest means.

That is why obstructing such collaboration—in the cause of forcing a competition between the cable and phone industries—is socially elitist. To the extent it prevents collaboration between the cable industry and the phone companies, present federal policy actually thwarts the administration's own goals of access and empowerment.

The other major effect of prohibiting the manifest destiny of cable preserves the broadcast (or narrowband) television model. In fact, stopping an interactive multimedia network perpetuates control by system owners and operators.

When the federal government prohibits the interconnection of conduits, it creates a world of bandwidth scarcity, where the owner of the conduit not only can but must control access to it. Thus the owner of the conduit also shapes the content. It really doesn't matter who the owner is. Bandwidth scarcity will require the managers of the network to determine the video programming on it. The answer is true bandwidth abundance.

Since cable is everywhere, particularly within cities, that would allow a closing of the gap between the knowledge rich and knowledge poor. Cable's broadband "pipes" already touch almost two-thirds of American households (and are easily accessible to another one-fourth). The phone companies have broadband fiber. A hybrid network—coax plus fiber—is the best means to the next generation of cyberspace expansion. What if this choice is blocked?

In that case, what might be called cyberspace democracy will be confined to the computer industry, where it will arise from the Internet over the years, led by corporate and suburban/exurban interests. While not a technological calamity, this might be a social pervasion equivalent to what Japan Inc. did to its middle and lower classes for decades: Make them pay 50 percent more for the same quality vehicles that were gobbling up export markets.

Here's the parallel: If Washington forces the phone companies and cable operators to develop supplementary and duplicative networks, most other advanced industrial countries will attain cyberspace democracy—via an interactive multimedia open platform—before America does, despite this nation's technological dominance.

Not only that, but the long-time alliance of East Coast broad-

casters and Hollywood glitterati will have a new lease on life: If
their one-way video empires win new protection, millions of
Americans will be deprived of the tools to help build a new interactive multimedia culture.

A contrived competition between phone companies and cable
operators will not deliver the two-way, multimedia and more civilized telesociety Kapor and Berman sketch. Nor is it enough to
simply get the government out of the way. Real issues of antitrust
must be addressed, and no sensible framework exists today for
addressing them. Creating the conditions for universal access to
interactive multimedia will require a fundamental rethinking of
government policy.

B. Promoting Dynamic Competition

Technological progress is turning the telecommunications
marketplace from one characterized by economies of scale and
natural monopolies into a prototypical competitive market. The
challenge for government is to encourage this shift—to create the
circumstances under which new competitors and new technologies will challenge the natural monopolies of the past.

Price-and-entry regulation makes sense for natural monopolies. The tradeoff is a straightforward one: The monopolist sub-
mits to price regulation by the state, in return for an exclusive
franchise on the market.

But what happens when it becomes economically desirable to
have more than one provider in a market? The continuation of
regulation under these circumstances stops progress in its tracks.
It prevents new entrants from introducing new technologies and
new products, while depriving the regulated monopolist of any
incentive to do so on its own.

Price-and-entry regulation, in short, is the antithesis of dynamic competition.

The alternative to regulation is antitrust. Antitrust law is designed to prevent the acts and practices that can lead to the creation of new monopolies, or harm consumers by forcing up
prices, limiting access to competing products or reducing service
quality. Antitrust law is the means by which America has, for over
120 years, fostered competition in markets where many providers
can and should compete.

The market for telecommunications services—telephone,
cable, satellite, wireless—is now such a market. The implication of

this simple fact is also simple, and price/entry regulation of telecommunications services—by state and local governments as well as the Federal government—should therefore be replaced by antitrust law as rapidly as possible.

This transition will not be simple, and it should not be instantaneous. If antitrust is to be seriously applied to telecommunications, some government agencies (e.g. the Justice Department's Antitrust Division) will need new types of expertise. And investors in regulated monopolies should be permitted time to re-evaluate their investments given the changing nature of the legal conditions in which these firms will operate—a luxury not afforded the cable industry in recent years.

This said, two additional points are important. First, delaying implementation is different from delaying enactment. The latter should be immediate, even if the former is not. Secondly, there should be no half steps. Moving from a regulated environment to a competitive one is—to borrow a cliché—like changing from driving on the left side of the road to driving on the right: You cannot do it gradually.

C. DEFINING AND ASSIGNING PROPERTY RIGHTS

In 1964, libertarian icon Ayn Rand wrote:

It is the proper task of government to protect individual rights and, as part of it, formulate the laws by which these rights are to be implemented and adjudicated. It is the government's responsibility to define the application of individual rights to a given sphere of activity—to define (i.e. to identify), not create, invent, donate, or expropriate. The question of defining the application of property rights has arisen frequently, in the wake of oil rights, vertical space rights, etc. In most cases, the American government has been guided by the proper principle: It sought to protect all the individual rights involved, not to abrogate them.

Defining property rights in cyberspace is perhaps the single most urgent and important task for government information policy. Doing so will be a complex task, and each key area—the electromagnetic spectrum, intellectual property, cyberspace itself (including the right to privacy)—involves unique challenges. The important points here are:

First, this is a central task of government. A Third Wave government will understand the importance and urgency of this undertaking and begin seriously to address it; to fail to do so is to perpetuate the politics and policy of the Second Wave.

Second, the key principle of ownership by the people—private ownership—should govern every deliberation. Government does not own cyberspace, the people do.

Third, clarity is essential. Ambiguous property rights are an invitation to litigation, channeling energy into courtrooms that serve no customers and create no wealth. From patent and copyright systems for software, to challenges over the ownership and use of spectrum, the present system is failing in this simple regard.

The source of America's historic economic success can, in case after case, be traced to our wisdom in creating and allocating clear, enforceable property rights. The creation and exploration of cyberspace requires that wisdom be recalled and reaffirmed.

D. Creating Pro-Third-Wave Tax and Accounting Rules

We need a whole set of new ways of accounting, both at the level of the enterprise, and of the economy.

GDP and other popular numbers do nothing to clarify the magic and muscle of information technology. The government has not been very good at measuring service-sector output, and almost all institutions are incredibly bad at measuring the productivity of information. Economists are stuck with a set of tools designed during, or as a result of, the 1930s. So they have been measuring less and less important variables with greater and greater precision.

At the level of the enterprise, obsolete accounting procedures cause us to systematically overvalue physical assets (i.e. property) and undervalue human-resource assets and intellectual assets. So, if you are an inspired young entrepreneur looking to start a software company, or a service company of some kind, and it is heavily information-intensive, you will have a harder time raising capital than the guy next door who wants to put in a set of beat-up old machines to participate in a topped-out industry.

On the tax side, the same thing is true. The tax code always reflects the varying lobbying pressures brought to bear on government. And the existing tax code was brought into being by traditional manufacturing enterprises and the allied forces that arose during the assembly line's heyday.

The computer industry correctly complains that half its product is depreciated in six months or less—yet it cannot depreciate it for tax purposes. The US semiconductor industry faces five-year depreciation timetables for products that have three-year lives (in contrast to Japan, where chipmakers can write off their fabrication plants in one year). Overall, the tax advantage remains with the long, rather than the short, product life-cycle, even though the latter is where all design and manufacturing are trending.

It is vital that accounting and tax policies—both those promulgated by private-sector regulators like the Financial Accounting Standards Board and those promulgated by the government at the IRS and elsewhere—start to reflect the shortened capital life-cycles of the Knowledge Age, and the increasing role of intangible capital as wealth.

E. Creating a Third Wave Government

Going beyond cyberspace policy per se, government must remake itself and redefine its relationship to the society at large. No single set of policy changes can create a future-friendly government. But there are some yardsticks we can apply to policy proposals. Among them:

• Is it based on the factory model, i.e. on standardization, routine and mass-production? If so, it is a Second Wave policy. Third Wave policies encourage uniqueness.

• Does it centralize control? Second Wave policies centralize power in bureaucratic institutions; Third Wave policies work to spread power—to empower those closest to the decision.

• Does it encourage geographic concentration? Second Wave policies encourage people to congregate physically; Third Wave policies permit people to work at home, and to live wherever they choose.

• Is it based on the idea of mass culture—of everyone watching the same sitcoms on television—or does it permit, even encourage, diversity within a broad framework of shared values? Third Wave policies will help transform diversity from a threat into an array of opportunities.

A serious effort to apply these tests to every area of government activity—from the defense and intelligence community to health care and education—would ultimately produce a complete transformation of government as we know it.

III.

Grasping the Future

The conflict between Second Wave and Third Wave group-
ings is the central political tension cutting through our society
today. The more basic political question is not who controls the
last days of industrial society, but who shapes the new civilization
rapidly rising to replace it. Who, in other words, will shape the
nature of cyberspace and its impact on our lives and institutions?

Living on the edge of the Third Wave, we are witnessing a
battle not so much over the nature of the future—for the Third
Wave will arrive—but over the nature of the transition.

On one side of this battle are the partisans of the industrial
past. On the other are growing millions who recognize that the
world's most urgent problems can no longer be resolved within
the massified frameworks we have inherited.

The Third Wave sector includes not only high-flying computer
and electronics firms and biotech start-ups; it embraces advanced,
information-driven manufacturing in every industry. It includes
the increasingly data-drenched services—finance, software, entertainment, the media, advanced communications, medical services, consulting, training and learning. The people in this sector
will soon be the dominant constituency in American politics.

And all of those confront a set of constituencies made fright-
ened and defensive by their mainly Second Wave habits and
locales: Command-and-control regulators, elected officials, political opinion-molders, philosophers mired in materialism, traditional interest groups, some broadcasters and newspapers—and
every major institution (including corporations) that believes its
future is best served by preserving the past.

For the time being, the entrenched powers of the Second
Wave dominate Washington and the statehouses—a fact nowhere
more apparent than in the 1991 infrastructure bill: Over $100
billion for steel and cement, versus one lone billion for electronic
infrastructure. Putting aside the question of whether the government should be building electronic infrastructure in the first
place, the allocation of funding in that bill shows the Second Wave
swamping the Third.

Only one political struggle so far contradicts the landscape
offered in this document, but it is a big one: Passage of the North
American Free Trade Agreement last November. This contest

carried both sides beyond partisanship, beyond regionalism, and—after one climactic debate on CNN—beyond personality. The pro-NAFTA coalition opted to serve the opportunity instead of the problem, and the future as opposed to the past. That's why it constitutes a standout model for the likely development of a Third Wave political dialectic.

But a mass movement for cyberspace is still hard to see. Unlike the masses during the industrial age, this rising Third Wave constituency is highly diverse. Like the economic sectors it serves, it is demassified—composed of individuals who prize their differences. This very heterogeneity contributes to its lack of political awareness. It is far harder to unify than the masses of the past.

Yet there are key themes on which this constituency-to-come can agree. To start with, liberation from Second Wave rules, regulations, taxes and laws laid in place to serve the smokestack barons and bureaucrats of the past. Next, of course, must come the creation of a new civilization, founded in the eternal truths of the American Idea.

It is time to embrace these challenges, to grasp the future and pull ourselves forward. If we do so, we will indeed renew the American Dream and enhance the promise of American life.

II. ECONOMIC AND BUSINESS ASPECTS

EDITOR'S INTRODUCTION

Business and consumer spending on high-technology products has accounted for approximately 38% of U.S. economic growth since 1990. This section focuses on the economic consequences of the information revolution. The first article, "Digital Juggernaut," reprinted from *Business Week,* analyzes the burgeoning information sector of the American economy.

The next article, from *Fortune,* examines the mixed effects of the on-line revolution on the retail industry. The following piece, from *Common Cause Magazine* asks "If This Is the Information Superhighway, Where Are the Rest Stops?" and goes on to discuss the ramifications of telecommunications on the American consumer. Finally, an article from *Freedom Forum* probes the economic and technological impact of the information revolution on media and news organizations.

THE DIGITAL JUGGERNAUT[1]

In every era, there is a group of industries that sets the pace for the rest of the economy. A century ago, the railroads were America's growth engine. In the postwar decades, manufacturing was the key to U.S. prosperity. During the 1980s, the driving forces of expansion were booming service industries such as health care, legal services, and retailing: All told, during that decade, the service sector accounted for practically all of the growth in jobs and corporate profits. Economists began to speak of the U.S. shift from a manufacturing to a service economy.

[1]Article by Michael J. Mandel, staff writer, from *Business Week* (special issue on the Information Revolution) 22–27 My 18 '94. Copyright ©1994 by McGraw-Hill, Inc. Reprinted with permission.

Yet for all the vitality of services, many skeptics did not see how they could make the economy thrive over the long term. In fact, the shift seemed like a giant step backward, since service jobs paid lower wages on average than manufacturing and had significantly slower productivity growth. Moreover, services such as medical care and retailing were much harder to export than manufactured goods. The worry was that if the U.S. lost its manufacturing industries, it would have a difficult time selling enough services abroad to pay for its imports of cars, consumer electronics, and other goods.

Fear not: Like adolescence, the service economy has turned out to be a temporary stage. Far more than most people realize, economic growth is now being driven not by services, but by the computer, software, and telecommunications industries. Indeed, according to the Commerce Dept., business and consumer spending on high-tech equipment accounts for some 38% of economic growth since 1990.

What's more, government statistics underplay the evolution of the information economy. Industries that depend on processing and moving information—such as financial services and entertainment—are prospering. And companies in every industry are using information technology to reengineer themselves and become more competitive. In short, "the role of information is transforming the nature of economy," says Kenneth J. Arrow, a Nobel prizewinning economist at Stanford University.

In this regard, at least, the U.S. is leading the way for the rest of the world. Europe is deregulating its telecommunications industry in order to create jobs and stimulate development. Japan is mounting an intense effort to narrow the considerable edge the U.S. has built over the decade in personal-computer and network use. Even developing countries such as China, Hungary, and Thailand are investing heavily in state-of-the-art communications systems in an effort to leapfrog their way to prosperity.

America remains way ahead, however. And it's the place where the consequences of the new economy are first showing up. To a large degree, the news is turning out to be good. For one thing, unlike most services, information products such as software and entertainment can be easily exported. And whereas productivity in the service sector grew slowly, investment in information technology is boosting productivity across the economy.

Beyond that, the effect on work is less harmful than once feared. Far from becoming low-paid burger-flippers, the quintessential job of the service sector, many Americans are turning into computer jocks. Economic studies show that their wages are on the rise as a result. For example, earnings for male computer programmers have risen by 12% since 1990, compared with 6% for all male workers. For female computer programmers, the pay gains have been even bigger: a 21% rise since 1990, vs. 13% for all female workers.

The drawback is that along with the winners, there will temporarily be lots of losers. Higher productivity has led to big layoffs at many companies, especially in the telecommunications industry. Elsewhere, meanwhile, advancing technology is favoring skilled workers over unskilled, increasing the inequality in wages.

For better or for worse, this transformation is occurring at an astonishing rate. Look at business investment. Measured in inflation-adjusted dollars, computers and other information technology now make up nearly half of all business spending on equipment—and that doesn't include the billions that companies spend on software and programmers each year. Meanwhile, business spending on industrial machinery, which traditionally has been the guts of manufacturing, has fallen as a share of equipment investment from 32% in 1975 to only 18% in 1993.

At the same time, information technology and services are helping to drive the continuing export boom. The aircraft industry is often held up as the shining star among U.S. exporters. Yet America's overseas sales of information-technology equipment in 1993 were $62 billion, far more than the $33 billion in overseas aircraft sales. The U.S. is also the world's largest exporter of software, a fact that doesn't show up in the government's numbers. In 1993, major U.S. software companies sold $2.5 billion worth of personal computer programs in Western Europe, Asia, and Latin America, according to the Software Publishers Assn. Microsoft Corp. alone derives some 55% of its revenues from overseas sales.

The U.S. also is running a huge $3 billion trade surplus in computer-related services, such as data processing and information databases. It's nearly as easy now to send information to Europe or Japan as to the next state or across the hall. For example, Mead Data Central Inc., the company that runs the Lexis and Nexis services, which contain legal news and general news respectively, also has databases on French and British law that lawyers in those countries use. The location of these databases: Dayton, Ohio.

Coming improvements in overseas communications will even make it possible to export such services as medical care. By this coming summer, doctors across sparsely populated South Dakota will be able to use a statewide telecommunications network to consult with specialists hundreds of miles away. The same expertise could be transmitted to Asia or Latin America just as easily. "The information economy can breed a healthy economy because a lot of its services are exportable," says George Bennett, chairman of Symmetrix, a technology consulting firm.

Two other positive byproducts of the Information Age are greater efficiency and lower prices. During much of the 1980s, economists worried that they could not find any impact of computers on productivity. But more recent research shows that investments in computers are worthwhile. Economists Erik Brynjolfsson and Lorin Hitt of the Massachusetts Institute of Technology surveyed 400 large companies to gauge the effect of technology on output per employee. They found that the return on investment in information systems exceeded 50%. "And most of these benefits are being passed on to consumers in the form of lower prices," says Brynjolfsson.

In fact, the productivity surge of the last two years—when nonfarm output per worker rose by 4.9%, its biggest two-year jump since 1976—may reflect the efforts of U.S. companies to finally take full advantage of the huge sums they've spent purchasing information technology. "If I put technology in and nothing changes, and then later a business gets in a crunch and discovers that it can cut out all the middle management, what made it possible?" asks Raymond Perry, chief information officer at Avon Products Inc. "Well, probably the technology did. It's just that we weren't ready to take the people out until a later point in time."

Even the recent productivity numbers probably far understate the critical role of information technology and services in driving growth. To put it simply: Government statistics track goods and jobs, not flows of information. That means the U.S. has a large and vibrant "ghost economy" that traditional economic indicators don't measure. Take the communications sector, which includes the telephone, broadcasting, and cable industries. According to government figures, communications is only 3.1% of the economy, up from 2.8% in 1984, at the time of the AT&T divestiture. Over the same period, minutes of telephone use—a key number tracked by the Federal Communications Commission—has grown only slightly faster than the overall economy.

Yet a closer look shows that the official statistics ignore many of the changes of the past decade. For one, a much greater percentage of the calls over the phone network are faxes and computer data going back and forth, rather than people talking. As much as 10% to 20% of the traffic across the AT&T long-distance network may be data, estimates Frank Ianna, the company's general manager for network services. That's up from 7% to 10% a few years ago. And because of time and language differences, about half of international calls are data, not voice.

These fax and computer messages pack a lot more data into a minute than they used to. Over the past few years, for example, the speed of a typical modem—which is used to transfer information between computers over phone lines—has quadrupled. That means the amount of information being pumped through the system has gone through the roof. The point is this: If the output of the communications sector is measured in terms of data transferred instead of the number of minutes it's in use, it would show far more dramatic growth than the published numbers indicate.

Prices in the communications sector have also likely fallen much more sharply than the government numbers show. According to the Bureau of Labor Statistics, the producer price index for interstate telephone service has risen by 2.4% over the past five years. Yet this figure doesn't take into account the discount calling plans that most long-distance companies now offer. Nor does it adequately track the cost and use of leased lines. The BLS hopes to remedy some of these problems with a new index for telephone prices, perhaps by January.

The information economy also has a much larger productive capacity than the current government statistics indicate. For the moment, the main measure of how close the economy is to its maximum operating rate is the Federal Reserve's industrial capacity utilization number. While this includes utilities that sell electricity and natural gas, it leaves out telecommunications. That means there is no good measure of the amount of spare capacity in the U.S. telecom network. That's an important omission, since many businesses have become increasingly dependent on reliable—and widely available—communications services.

Even the investment boom of the past few years understates the true value of the spending on information technology. According to Commerce Dept. figures, investment in communications equipment has barely risen since 1990. What these numbers don't say is that for the same price, companies have been able to buy vastly more sophisticated switching gear and other telecommunications equipment, with new capabilities such as call forwarding.

Beyond those hidden by the measurement problems, there are some fundamental differences between the information economy and its predecessors. In the past, technological improvements such as railroads, auto plants, and steel mills required vast amounts of capital. But because the price of information technology continues to drop so quickly, companies can spend less to get healthy improvements in productivity and quality. Indeed, in recent years, the productivity of capital—defined as the amount of output produced per dollar of plant and equipment—has gone up for the first time in the postwar era. "As the U.S. becomes an information-oriented economy," says William Sterling, an economist at Merrill Lynch & Co., "you may have less need for capital than you have in the past."

For example, phone companies are able to boost the carrying capacity of their existing fiber-optic cables by simply upgrading the electronics at either end. That means they can add to capacity without having to go through the expensive process of digging up old cables and installing new ones.

Even connecting all of the nation's homes to the Information Superhighway may cost less than expected. In California, Pacific Telesis Group and AT&T are estimating that it will cost an average of $800 to wire each of 1.5 million homes with a combined fiber-optic/coaxial cable network that can carry the most advanced services. That compares with $1,600 for the electronics and labor needed to run a fiber cable all the way to the home. "The fiber-only estimates were scaring everybody off," says Robert Clark, vice-president for marketing and sales at AT&T Network Systems. "We've been able to see another way of getting all the services."

If these lower estimates turn out to be right, it won't come as a total surprise: On a comparable basis, the price of information-technology equipment has dropped by 23% over the past five years, according to Commerce Dept. numbers. This trend, if it continues, will have important implications for interest rates. If companies need to borrow less money to finance their investment in high-tech equipment, that will keep overall rates lower than they would have been otherwise. And that will benefit homeowners, the government, and other borrowers.

Still, there's the matter of those losers from the shift to the information economy. At the top of the list are the workers who have lost their jobs as companies reengineer their businesses. The reduction in staff can be enormous. At USAir Inc., 650 people were once needed in the revenue accounting department. Now that much of the process has been automated, only 350 people are needed to do the work, says Senior Vice-President and CFO John W. Harper. And at many companies, the downsizing isn't over. "Where will all these people be employed?" asks Lester Thurow, an economics professor at MIT and former dean of the university's Sloan School of Management. "It's not at all obvious."

Ironically, some of the biggest staff reductions have come at computer and telephone companies, which are at the heart of the information economy. Competitive pressures play a role, but these cuts are being driven mainly by technological advances that let the phone companies, for example, do with fewer operators, maintenance people, and other workers. NYNEX Corp., which supplies local phone service in New England and New York, announced plans last January to pare its workforce by 22%, or 17,000 people, by the end of 1996. Overall, employment in the telephone and computer manufacturing industries has already dropped by 154,000 since 1988, with more cuts to come.

Also at sea in the information economy are unskilled workers and people who can't keep up with technology. Indeed, recent studies suggest a hefty payoff for workers who feel at home in the digital world. Princeton University economist Alan B. Krueger estimates that people who use computers at work earn 10% to 15% more than colleagues in similar occupations who do not use computers. Says Lawrence Katz, chief economist at the Labor Dept.: "There is very strong evidence that people who work with computers earn higher wages."

Still, even if some people are being left behind, the information economy is creating thousands of new businesses and jobs. For example, the Home Shopping Network—which sells jewelry and other merchandise on cable TV—has grown to employ some 5,000 people, up from 600 in 1985. At the other end of the spectrum are startups such as SandPoint Corp., a Cambridge (Mass.) maker of software that helps people track down information in databases. Over the past year, SandPoint has grown from 15 to 32 employees, and it's still expanding. Overall, the number of jobs in the software, data processing, and information retrieval industries has risen by 31% since 1988, and these industries now employ more people than the auto industry.

Besides creating jobs, the information economy may even make it a bit easier to match workers to existing jobs. The Online Career Center, based in Indianapolis, provides job and resumé listings on the Internet. Since it went online in June, 1993, observes Director William Warren, it has become one of the most popular databases on the system, with 13,000 to 14,000 job openings listed and nearly as many resumés. Ultimately, nationwide listing services such as this could make labor markets more efficient and help lower unemployment.

The effects of the information economy are even reaching into rural areas by shifting development away from congested urban regions. With more and more parts of the country having access to high-capacity telecommunications, companies can now put jobs such as order-taking in remote locations without losing touch with the rest of the business. "What telecommunications allows you to do is put the right facilities with the right labor," notes Ken Kuhl, a consultant with Moran, Stahl & Boyer, a business relocation firm.

Technological advances will have an even more profound impact on the vitality of rural areas by bringing big-city services and amenities to small towns. For example, the telecommunications network operated by the state of South Dakota enables rural schools to offer Spanish classes via interactive TV—something they would never have been able to do on their own. The information revolution, says South Dakota Governor Walter D. Miller, "is going to change the face of South Dakota as much as rural electrification did."

That's an apt parallel. Just as the U.S. economy today would be unthinkable without electricity, so will tomorrow's economy be spurred by the free flow of information. Judging by the explosive growth of information technology so far, the juice is only starting to flow.

WILL THE INFORMATION
SUPERHIGHWAY BE THE DEATH
OF RETAILING?[2]

Bill Gates, billionaire chairman of Microsoft and semipro visionary, leans forward to describe the future of shopping: "You're watching *Seinfeld* on TV, and you like the jacket he's wearing. You click on it with your remote control. The show pauses and a Windows-style drop-down menu appears at the top of the screen, asking if you want to buy it. You click on 'yes.' The next menu offers you a choice of colors; you click on black. Another menu lists your credit cards, asking which one you'll use for this purchase. Click on MasterCard or whatever. Which address should the jacket go to, your office or your home or your cabin? Click on one address and you're done—the menus disappear and *Seinfeld* picks up where it left off.

"Just as you'll already have taught the computer about your credit cards and addresses, you will have had your body measured by a 3-D version of supermarket scanners, so the system will know your exact sizes. And it will send the data electronically to a factory, where robots will custom-tailor the jacket to your measurements. An overnight courier service will deliver it to your door the next morning. And because this system cuts out so many middlemen, the jacket will cost 40% less than the off-the-rack version you'd find in a department store."

As Gates readily admits, that particular future may never arrive. But with cable TV and telephone companies, including US West, Time Warner, and Bell Atlantic, investing billions to provide America's neighborhoods with two-way data communications, interactive shopping of some kind is inevitable. After all, interactive shopping is just a high-tech extension of direct marketing, the familiar practice of selling to consumers through such media as catalogues and TV shopping channels instead of stores.

Once wires carrying two-way TV signals reach most U.S. households, direct marketers will be able to deliver their pitches on demand, using a rich electronic palette of text, video, and

[2]Article by Stratford Sherman, staff writer, from *Fortune* 129:98 Ap 18 '94. Copyright © 1994 by Time Inc. Reprinted with permission.

sound. Consumers will gain the power to browse databases filled with everything from movies to videogames to product information, and will also be able to transmit their orders instantly.

By promising customers more convenience and merchants greater efficiency, interactivity could revitalize the troubled retailing sector. "When we make it *really* interactive, shopping in the home will dwarf revenues from entertainment," predicts Sol Trujillo, CEO of US West Marketing Resources, a subsidiary of the Bell operating company, which says it will invest $12.5 billion on its part of the information superhighway. Last year Americans spent almost $60 billion through catalogues, TV shopping channels, and other direct-marketing alternatives. That's only 2.8% of the nation's $2.1-trillion-a-year retail marketplace, which includes supermarkets, mall outlets, car dealerships, department stores, warehouse clubs, boutiques, and much more. Merchants and technologists expect conventional retailing to hold steady or contract slightly over the decade as the industry's shakeout continues, while technocharged direct marketing surges to capture some 15% of total sales. That would make the new business one of the world's biggest, with annual revenues of well over $300 billion.

But your guess may be as good as any expert's. Screenwriter William Goldman's famous summation of the movie business— "Nobody knows anything"—increasingly applies to the twilight zone where telecommunications, computing, entertainment, and merchandising converge. Says Duncan Davidson of Gemini Consulting, an adviser to big technology companies: "There just isn't much information available yet. That's what makes this situation so much fun. All great technologies, from the railroads on, start with a mania. There's no other way to open up new markets." Consumers, who haven't been given much chance to express their opinions, will ultimately decide what kind of electronic shopping makes sense.

The timing and force of the onslaught will depend on the speed with which the information superhighway—the infobahn, as it's being called this month—gets built, and how it is designed. A decade or more may pass before even the needed networks or wireless links are in place. The main hurdle is financial: Building the infobahn could cost at least $100 billion, and telephone and cable companies must find business justifications for the stupendous investment.

Despite the fancy name, the infobahn is simply a network, like AT&T's long-distance phone system. This one is defined by fiber-optic cables and high-capacity switches and computers that can carry video, audio, and data signals into and out of our homes. Two-way video is the technology that gets merchants cranked up. American adults already devote more time to TV than anything but work and sleep, an average of 4½ hours daily. Interactivity could intensify TV's appeal. As Spencer Sherman, 7, says, "Computers are better than TV because you can control what you see."

Hidden behind tomorrow's TV screens will be tremendous computational power that will let viewers search through vast databases by answering multiple-choice questions and pointing and clicking with a remote control. Potentially, such systems could automatically comparison-shop for us, popping up the names of merchants offering the mix of price, quality, and service that most closely matches our needs.

To shop the way Bill Gates imagines, consumers will probably have to use a specially designed remote control to let the system know what they want. Once they master the on-screen "user inter-face" that translates their instructions into commands computers understand, they will be able to pluck other sorts of data from the network and gain access to whatever information businesses of-fer, including details about products. For business, the hard part is designing interactive systems complex enough to give consum-ers a wide range of choice yet simple enough to operate with a beer in one hand.

What will get people to learn the necessary skills? Richard Notebaert, CEO of Ameritech, the Bell operating company based in Chicago, says many will learn on the job: "Air conditioning started in office buildings. So did cellular phones, VCRs, and PCs. Once people get used to a new technology at work, they want it at home." Some interactive-shopping enthusiasts think new forms of entertainment will entice consumers. Most appealing may be video on demand: the ability, for a fee, to call up a movie or TV show at any time.

Douglas Briggs, head of electronic retailing for QVC, the popular TV shopping channel, can't wait for truly interactive shopping to arrive: "We're constrained now by the fact that we can show only one product at a time on TV. This is interactivity in its crudest form. Once the customer has control, our business will explode." QVC's enormously profitable main channel is nothing more than an ordinary cable TV program in which announcers hype jewelry, clothes, and housewares, plus the 800 number that will send it all home to you. The company is now converting its separate fashion channel into a testing ground for still more selling shows. This summer, rival Home Shopping Network is adding a second channel in which the sales pitches will be set in a mock shopping mall. MTV Networks and others are developing shop-a-thon channels too. None of these channels give viewers control over what they see when.

In a truly interactive system, product pitches could be recorded in advance and stored, much like voice-mail messages today, in powerful central computers called servers. Then anyone interested in, say, rodeo belt buckles with cubic-zirconia adornments could zip straight to the relevant video. Interactive video is a medium made for merchandising. Want to see how those Eddie Bauer waders look on Cindy Crawford? Just click. In the market for a vintage El Camino like Bill Clinton owned in the 1970s? Click and ye shall find.

Lots of retailers are watching the action from the sidelines. Some, including Leslie Wexner, chairman of the Limited, are technology-savvy but see little point in rushing into a marketplace that hasn't yet been defined. Others, including CEO Richard Sharp of Circuit City Stores, which sells electronic products and appliances, believe their wares will always sell best in conventional stores. The wisest of the doubters are participating in small-scale experiments that enable them to master new technology while monitoring the infobahn's progress. One such is Andy McKenna, senior vice president of Home Depot. Says he: "What's amazing to me is that in many cases this technology is a solution looking for a problem. The fundamental question we haven't answered is, What does the consumer really want?"

The diverse enterprises contributing to the infobahn's design—Bell operating companies, cable TV operators, PC software companies, and Hollywood studios, among others—fall into two opposing camps, whose philosophical differences have enormous financial and technical implications. Call them Suits and Surfers. The Surfers are mostly wonks at companies such as Microsoft, Hewlett-Packard, and AT&T, who expect the market for interactive technologies to develop much as the personal computer business did. Having themselves felt the transforming power of PCs and access to information-packed databases, they want to deliver the experience to the masses.

Surfers don't pretend to know what people will want to do with their interactive TVs, but they're less fearful than the Suits of exposing consumers to technological complexity. They figure that if the consumer is in the driver's seat with a souped-up TV and broad access to a world of computerized content via networks, interesting products and services will arise spontaneously and lots of people will get rich. That's how things work in the PC market, with software developers and hardware designers introducing an endless stream of new products.

The Suits can be found mostly at the phone and cable TV companies that intend to finance and build the new networks. Facing little competition in local markets, these corporations are not used to taking cues from customers or to providing network access to other businesses without charge. Says Richard Bodman, chief of strategy for AT&T: "Anybody who's investing billions of dollars is looking at control of access. Control is what's driving people into spending the money."

That attitude is pushing cable and phone companies to design electronic Disneylands, self-contained cyberspace theme parks that keep things controllable by limiting consumer choice. Two key experimental systems now under construction follow that model: one by Viacom in Castro Valley, California, and one by Time Warner (parent of the publisher of *Fortune*) in Orlando.

The test that emphasizes shopping is Time Warner's. It will offer access only to selected retailers, such as Spiegel and Eddie Bauer; the stores' on-line databases will provide a small fraction of the choices available in their regular inventories. If the experience of the on-line services CompuServe and Prodigy is any guide, Time Warner won't permit automated comparison-shopping, partly because merchants fear it might transform their wares into commodities.

Although the user interfaces in these and other experiments vary enormously, all sacrifice power for simplicity. The first step is replacing the computer and keyboard with the more familiar TV and remote control. That decision has a cost: Users who cannot type in their choices are forced to select items from menus. Locating a particular product—a purple cashmere turtleneck sweater, say, under $90—amid huge volumes of information can require laborious plodding through a series of menus nested within one another like Russian dolls. An extreme example is the Media Objects interface designed by Oracle, a leading maker of database software. Its remote control has only one button for data entry. By the time you'd clicked through enough multiple-choice menus to reach your sweater, your thumb might be blistered.

A more robust system may soon be found on Time Warner's experimental network in Orlando. Although the company refuses to comment, *The Hollywood Reporter* estimates that it will spend $750 million to wire just 4,000 homes. Even adjusting for Tinseltown exaggeration, the experiment is pricey. The system includes a whiz-bang network with true video on demand, computer circuitry by Silicon Graphics atop every TV, and user interfaces that present choices in innovative ways. In one variation, the system allows viewers to "fly" over and down into a futuristic 3-D metropolis in which buildings represent choices such as movies, a news service, or shopping. The cost of this system can be expected to plunge, but the distance between the $187,500 per home that Time Warner is said to be investing and the $101.06 per annum that the average American adult spends on cable TV suggests the scope of the challenge ahead.

To many Surfers, even Time Warner's system seems pathetically constricted, since it ignores some of the technology's most interesting possibilities. Says Robert Frankenberg, a Hewlett-Packard vice president: "I think some of the first interactive systems will not work out well, and then the market will open up to entrepreneurs doing cool stuff."

Reaching for a way to explain what's cool, Surfers often point to the Internet, the loose confederation of computer networks that links some 20 million computer users around the world. Anyone connected to the Internet can share files and E-mail with anyone else. By offering open access to mind-boggling amounts of information from university libraries, government files, and millions of other users, the Internet has fostered an on-line community whose members enjoy sharing information freely. Surfers see such unrestricted traffic in ideas as a powerful force for social good; to some, it's almost a religion. But you don't need to be a fanatic to sense the essential strength of their point of view: a commitment to letting people choose what they want. That's customer focus—precisely what's required to make any kind of merchandising successful.

Traditional retailers beware. The most radical thing interactive systems could do is whet consumers' appetites for the sort of customized products and services that Microsoft's Gates has envisioned. Let ordinary shoppers sift through the product information in databases. Give nontechies access to electronic bulletin boards where people pool their knowledge by candidly discussing their experiences with products. Do that, and watch the mystery and cachet of smoke-and-mirrors merchandising evaporate. Products get clearly differentiated by quality, price, and details of delivery, while selling becomes an auction. Says Gates: "There will be an efficiency in this marketplace that people have to wrap their minds around."

The requirements for this Tomorrowland would be vast: a universal network linking homes and businesses to thousands of databases, technical standards enabling all the different computers to understand one another, interfaces that help ordinary users define their needs easily and precisely, and software that can find what users are seeking amid countless terabytes of computer files. All this would require much more computer processing and data transmission per transaction, which could translate into up-front costs even higher than Time Warner's.

But the costliest systems of all will be those that fail to give customers what they want. "In the long term the consumers will win because they have all the money," says Steven Johnson, who studies interactivity for Andersen Consulting. Nicholas Donatiello Jr., CEO of Odyssey, a San Francisco research firm, recently completed a study of consumer attitudes about interactive systems. He warns that if the first systems are ill-conceived, consumers could lose interest in the whole idea. "It's much more important to be right than to be first. If errors delay widespread adoption in this market, the cost will be enormous."

Back here in Todayland, interactive shopping is still dismayingly primitive. The major innovations propelling direct marketing's growth are 800 numbers, overnight delivery services, and TV shopping channels—brilliant concepts all, but light-years removed from technology's leading edge. Most consumers make their purchases in ways that are more primitive still. Data from the Direct Marketing Association reveal that people place most of their orders by mail, not phone, and usually pay by cash, check, or money order, not credit card.

Sales of computer programs via electronic catalogues on compact disks amounted to less than $10 million last year, according to Mark Bronder, CEO of InfoNow, a pioneer in that business. Out of nearly 100 million U.S. households, one-third of which own PCs, only seven million people subscribe to interactive services such as CompuServe, Prodigy, and America On-line (most

Internet users don't connect from home). Prodigy, which is owned by IBM and Sears Roebuck, was conceived as an arena for information, communication, and direct selling. But after investing nearly $1 billion, the partners concluded that subscribers prefer exchanging messages to shopping on-line.

That will change as interactive merchants demonstrate compelling advantages to consumers. Says Nathan Myhrvold, a bearded former protégé of physicist Stephen Hawking who is Microsoft's senior vice president for advanced technology: "In the early stages of bootstrapping something new, it's very important to have a unique sales proposition. One of the most effective is a lower price."

Pointing the way is CUC International, a company in Stamford, Connecticut, whose Comp-U-Card shopping service produces annual revenues of some $850 million. The company's primary mission is not to sell goods but to provide the information people need to comparison-shop. CUC maintains databases with detailed information on some 250,000 products, such as cars, TV sets, and air conditioners. In return for a $49 annual fee, each of the service's 30 million subscribers gets unlimited access to the information—usually by dialing an 800 number and speaking to a human being who consults the computer database. Those who wish to order products through CUC can do so by phone or computer; the company relays the order to the manufacturer. Says CEO Walter Forbes: "This is virtual-reality inventory. We stock nothing, but we sell everything." CUC is participating in several interactive tests, including Viacom's in Castro Valley, and plans to adapt to new merchandising media as they arise.

For most retailers, who make money by selling products, not information, interactivity may not produce big cost savings. Consider the case of conventional direct marketers, who devote some 25% of their revenues to costs like printing and postage for catalogues. Interactive networks could help cut such expenses, but the cost of making glitzy product videos could eat up the difference. For now, companies participating in such tests as the Orlando project may economize by using still photos and footage left over from commercials. Once interactive marketing becomes a business, though, viewers accustomed to Hollywood production values surely will expect better.

Interactive shopping won't revolutionize retailing overnight. It will probably take hold first in niches such as recorded music and software, which can be delivered via digital transmission, and personal computers, which often sell through direct marketing. Anything that is merchandized by TV or catalogue today could be sold interactively tomorrow.

Despite the high cost and uncertainties, retailers have powerful incentives to embrace the new medium. While available store space in the U.S. has increased 4% per year on average since 1987, merchants' sales per square foot declined at an annual rate of almost 3%. As much as one-third of the country's retailing space may be superfluous. Dan Nordstrom, 31, head of the direct-sales division of Nordstrom, the Seattle-based chain famed for personal services, sees an added imperative: "People's time seems to be increasingly constrained. They need to do more of their shopping from home."

The segments of retailing that are thriving are those most in touch with a timeless truth: Success in business comes from giving customers what they want. The understanding that people like saving money has propelled warehouse stores such as Sam's Club into a $33-billion-a-year business. When the infobahn starts to deliver the combination of ease of use and buying power that shoppers crave, it too will take off. Says Stanley Marcus, 88, the brilliant merchandiser who built Neiman Marcus: "You lose everything if you don't think like the customer. If customers don't want to get off their butts and go to your stores, you've got to go to them."

IF THIS IS THE INFORMATION SUPERHIGHWAY, WHERE ARE THE REST STOPS?[3]

It's hard to say when it happened exactly, but at some point around Halloween things started moving very quickly on the telecommunications front.

Suddenly, what was once a fanciful vision of the distant future—when Americans would be able to communicate with

[3]Article by Deborah Baldwin, editor, from *Common Cause Magazine* 20:17+ Spring '94. Copyright © 1994 by Common Cause. Reprinted with permission.

their appliances via cell phone and carry on conversations with their loved ones via computer—became as immediate as next season's sitcoms.

Things were already getting out of hand for those of us who had held onto record players during the ascendance of CDs, stubbornly refusing to invest in new consumer electronics "until things settle down." By the close of 1993, everything from pencils and postal carriers to Blockbuster and the Big Three networks began to look suspiciously out of date.

Meanwhile we were inundated with the details of the Viacom-QVC battle for Paramount—or was it the other way around?—as Bell Atlantic, a formerly reputable phone company, got hitched to cable behemoth Tele-Communications Inc. (TCI) in a $32 million ceremony. It was hard to know what to think, much less what to do, about all this merger mania beyond contemplating a future in which the number of info-phone-tainment-TV-companies-with-shopping-networks would be down to two.

As if all this weren't bad enough, computer hackers—known in some circles as mouse potatoes—got sex appeal. It was hard to keep dismissing people who whiled away their time at the keyboard (what—didn't they have jobs? couldn't they get dates?) when their hero Bill Gates was the richest man in America. Gone were the days when the electronically challenged could feign politeness as discussions turned to modems, megabytes and ROMS vs. RAMs. Maybe most Americans would rather have lower monthly utility rates, safer schools and a new washing machine than a connection to global E-mail, but the Information Age had arrived, and the media brought the message forth in a tsunami of articles about the Internet, a loose network of computers that until recently was of concern only to science nerds, academics and computer junkies. Today, according to countless breathless accounts commissioned by editors clearly concerned about how all this may affect their profession, the number of Americans with access to the Internet is 15 million—and climbing.

The lonely crowd's worst fears about the electronic frontier—where citizens will be able to hook themselves up to a life-support system consisting of television, telephone and computer, and never have to leave the house in order to work, shop or even vote—were about to become reality. And inevitably, in a town where the term policy wonk was invented, fascination with things electronic took hold like the latest strain of Asian flu. As Information Superhighway hysteria spread down Pennsylvania Avenue, you could almost hear humming in the air: It's the dawning of a new era in communications law! Don't miss this opportunity to participate in the latest policy debate! Say "goodbye" to old-fashioned representative democracy—"hello" to Virtual Government!

Hey—be the first person in your political coalition to host an Internet news group!

"When I started in 1990, there were damn few people working on this," says Jamie Love, who in three short years has established himself as Ralph Nader's telecommunications policy guru and Internet gadfly. Nowadays, when Love drops by meetings of public interest types who want to join in the telecommunications fun, there are so many Johnny Come Latelys he can barely find a chair.

Part of the attraction is the prospect of participating in a bleeding-edge campaign that has none of the baggage of such aging issues as saving the spotted owl, reforming federal prisons and making automobiles more energy efficient. The revolution in telecommunications is all new and it's all up for grabs.

And before long, a growing chorus of advocates says, it will be too late for the public interest community to try to influence telecommunications policy—to make interactive TV channels available, for example, for democratic discourse and the like. Already, money from cable, broadcast, telephone, home shopping and Hollywood is pouring through Congress like Mississippi River floodwaters—at the rate of about $10 million in 1991–92, according to one analysis. And the raw economic power of media chieftains like John Malone, the zillionaire co-founder of TCI, coupled with their dazzling appeal in a city better known for pushing paper than global vision, is threatening to turn policymakers into whimpering schoolchildren.

Still, if Wall Street barons are on the edges of their seats awaiting some signal from the marketplace about what Americans really want (video-porn delivered by phone? a hair-care channel?), Washington's public interest community is at a similar turning point. Many groups have heard the call. But it's one thing to have a passionate interest in telecommunications policy. It's another to develop a grassroots Information Superhighway lobbying group—and raise enough money to keep it going.

There's No Escaping Now

In case you're still at the stage I was four months ago— curious about the Information Superhighway but genuinely worried about having to program anything more complicated than a VCR—here's what all the hype is about. It's been about 10 years since the PC and Mac turned typewriters into landfill; a new kind of computerized communications will similarly eclipse the telephone. It will tie our computers at home and work to the outside world, enabling us to plunder the world's entertainment and information resources at the push of a button.

After we get all our other work done, of course.

In the beginning was the Internet, a network of computer networks tied together by high-speed wire. Devised by the Pentagon as a way to protect the flow of military information during a nuclear holocaust, the Internet was embraced early on by academic researchers, who soon learned to use it to open up the electronic card catalogues at other colleges, communicate with colleagues in faraway places (exchanging dissertations became popular) and bellyache about tenure. Anyone with a modem and a subscription to a local Internet exchange can also communicate by E-mail—a cheap, convenient alternative to having to rummage for stamp and envelope or wait for discount phone rates to apply. You type your message, fire it off and wait for the inevitable snappy comeback, which will be typed at the sender's convenience and read at yours—making the notion of human beings walking from house to house to deliver mail as quaint as ice wagons. The Internet also offers the possibility of conversations with like-minded souls (there are new groups devoted to every imaginable topic, from Iran-contra to Jerry Seinfeld) and access to umpteen kinds of information that have been dumped onto the system.

"It's hard to get a good conceptual understanding" of all this, concedes Jim Keller, formerly with Sprint and now with the industry-funded Information Infrastructure Project at Harvard's Kennedy School. With the superhighway, it would be possible to distribute video and other media and—assuming the highway going out of your house were as big as the one coming in—an opportunity to broadcast everything from political diatribes to home video.

Other useful functions: When dinner debates erupted over who was the winning pitcher in the last game of the World Series in 1950, you'd be able to stroll over to the keyboard and call up a sports almanac. Endless amounts of information about political candidates and causes could be yours: no more wading through prime time in search of an engaging critique of the gubernatorial incumbent's voting record. Tired of having to recycle those unread sections of the paper piling up in the living room? Drop your subscription and read only what you want on a computer screen. Can't decide whether to vacation in Egypt? Ask the computer to put you in touch with people who've been there. And let's not mention buying stuff and renting videos without having to drive to the mall.

No one's foolish enough, however, to assume that the John Malones of the world will go out of their way to provide services that don't automatically make money—things like the local equivalent of C-SPAN, for example. Cable TV companies didn't think up community access stations on their own, and they're not likely to sweat about electronic democracy unless someone makes them. Same applies to the phone companies that are so anxious to build Information Superhighway on-ramps everywhere: The only reason they charge relatively low rates for basic service now is because regulators set the prices. Let 'em loose so they can start delivering video by phone, and they'll charge what the market will bear.

Enter the media reform movement, which began in the early 1970s as an effort to advance such things as the Fairness Doctrine (a requirement that broadcasters give time to both sides of a political debate) and equal time (access to the airwaves for opposing candidates). The 1980s were a bad time for media reform— "from my perspective, it was devastating," says Andrew Blau, coordinator of the Benton Foundation's Communications Policy Project—because the buzzwords changed from "public" and "access" to "deregulation," the latter responsible for the untrammeled growth of cable TV—not to mention cable TV rates.

Then, in the 1990s, something funny happened. Deregulation backlash led to a sweeping new cable TV law. And a fascination with reform arose outside Washington, in Cambridge and Silicon Valley, where traditionally libertarian computer users started worrying about government policies affecting privacy and access—about big government using the new technology to simultaneously learn more about its citizens and tell them less. A bit of the industry's technological know-how and money was grafted onto the media reform movement's thinning stalks, creating a strange new progressive-libertarian hybrid.

Attempting to take root under the Information Superhighway's grow lights today are a handful of groups, ranging from Ralph Nader's tiny Taxpayer Assets Project to the brash Electronic Frontier Foundation, which was bankrolled by the inventor of Lotus software. There's the 20-year-old Media Access Project—

still lobbying to bring back the Fairness Doctrine—and the Consumer Federation of America, which wants to protect consumers from gouging by the regional Bell operating companies, or RBOCs (pronounced Are Box), which are anxious to get into fancy new lines of work like video. Add the 14-year-old Benton Foundation, the two-year-old Center for Media Evaluation and the nascent Center for Civic Networking . . . plus the ACLU, whose former Washington director is now director of the Electronic Frontier Foundation, the Center for Policy Alternatives and Computer Professionals for Social Responsibility. Also active are the librarians—yes, the librarians—who have provided the contemporary media reform movement with some of its few female leaders. (As a showcase for brainy, techie types, telecommunications boasts a large number of fast-thinking, faster-talking men, who compete to see who gets the most invites to testify on Capitol Hill and who has greater impact at the White House.)

Galvanizing this eclectic group is the sheer size and political clout of the opposition, a composite of media-communications-entertainment interests about as consumer-friendly as the Terminator. The RBOCs alone—collectively, individually—comprise a fantastic political force both in Washington and locally, where they badger regulators for rate hikes and sweet-talk about getting schools and hospitals onto the highway.

"It's just huge," says Gene Kimmelman, formerly with the Consumer Federation of America and now an aide to Sen. Howard Metzenbaum (D-Ohio). "In one year the seven [RBOCs] put together $22 million" to lobby in Washington—"and that doesn't include public relations." Kimmelman counts the number of phone company lobbyists in Washington in "the hundreds," and reminds his caller of where the money came from to pay their hourly fees: Thanks to consumers, the phone companies already have a $90-billion-a-year operating cash flow.

Some of that money helped the U.S. Telephone Association snap up top Clinton aide Roy Neel for a reported $500,000 salary and brought Peter Knight—a former top Senate aide to Vice President Albert Gore—to Bell Atlantic's account at one prestigious law firm and Clinton campaign adviser Thomas Casey to its account at another. Virtually every major Washington firm works in some way for the telecommunications industry, says Kimmelman, with phone company money providing a significant part of the business.

"When you talk about the phone companies you are talking

about political power unlike any other," says Nick Johnson, a consumer advocate who served on the Federal Communications Commission (FCC) in the early '70s. Pointing to the Bell Atlantic-TCI merger, Johnson anticipates "absolutely overpowering" political pressure on Washington to let the Big Guys run the Superhighway anyway they want.

What way is anybody's guess at this point, because no one knows for sure how the highway will shape up. (Well, a few things are certain: People want to be able to put their videos on hold when they go to the bathroom, and they like to order things over the phone.) So what brings the Big Guys to Washington? A desire for carte blanche—for the right to compete in a new era of hands-off government as they keep splitting like amoebas, mating like rabbits and cashing in like casinos. The RBOCs, with control of local phone service, want access to money-making long-distance services now dominated by AT&T, Sprint and MCI—and vice versa; the cable companies want access to money-making phone services—and vice versa; the entertainment giants want to cut deals with the most lucrative producers—and vice versa; and everybody wants the right to merge with everybody else without having bothersome antitrust lawyers breathing down their necks. "The thing that frightens me most is the merger mania," Rutgers University political scientist Benjamin Barber said in a November speech.

Not Tonight, I Have a Headache

But if the looming threat of a vertically integrated, shared telecommunications monopoly leaves you longing for an evening with Jane Austen, this is no time to look the other way. Public interest advocates believe there's a way to harness all this new technology for the betterment of democracy, and no better time than now to press the communications industry for concessions like toll-free on-ramps for everyone, starting with schools and libraries—which might prefer some new books and lighting fixtures but would probably settle for a bank of Macs.

Advance thinkers have been gathering not only on the Internet but at a series of in-person conferences designed to raise consciousness and engender hobnobbing. At a January confab in Arlington, Va., hosted by Vanderbilt University's Freedom Forum First Amendment Center and the National Emergency Civil Liberties Foundation, a rapt audience was treated to an hour-long rain dance by Sun Microsystems' technical wizard John Gage, who traced electronic communications back to the invention of speech (60,000 years ago), the written word (6,000 years ago), the printing press (600 years ago), TV (60 years ago) and user-friendly Internet software (last July) while explaining how quickly new technology was overtaking society's ability to cope with it.

Panelists from groups like the ACLU and EFF tackled issues of privacy and civil rights, while members of the audience argued over whether Ross Perot-style electronic town meetings would improve democracy or turn it into mob rule. "It sounds creepy," opined panelist David Burnham, author of *The Rise of the Computer State*, while others spoke forcefully about energizing the public.

If it's unclear whether the Information Superhighway will improve the political process, at a minimum keyboards and modems will speed things up. And activists like Jamie Love firmly believe that when they aren't busy watching TV, shopping at home and firing off E-mail, Americans will want to use the new technology to, say, debate the issues with their fellow "netizens," download government information on myriad topics, let their voices be heard at the local school board and seek out information about those who are willing to leave the house long enough to run for office.

"In 1991 I started posting notices [about telecommunications policy] on the Internet," Love says of his earliest experiments in desktop lobbying, "and all of a sudden we were reaching 10,000 people"—at virtually no cost. In sharp contrast to the customary ways of Washington, lobbying on the Internet proved amazingly, well, democratic and, Love says, gave "a tiny group like ours an opportunity to shape the debate." Today, thanks to his persevering presence on the Internet (and in-your-face style of politicking), he gets invited to gather around the table with Al Gore and telecommunications industry CEOs.

"In Washington what's 'politically possible' dominates the debate," Love says, while Internet users have higher expectations. Meanwhile there are no letterheads, pinstriped suits or other visual cues to give weight to one side—"it all looks the same, so the only thing that matters is the merit of your argument."

Love's major coup, the culmination of a three-year battle with the Securities and Exchange Commission, will give the public access to valuable financial databases at the SEC that had been controlled by Mead Data Central, which makes available on-line everything from *The Journal of Injectable Drugs* to *Common Cause Magazine*—at gulpingly high rates.

A different kind of electronic lobbying campaign unfolded in California last year when Jim Warren, a retired computer entrepreneur, saw a way to make state legislation (both enacted and proposed) available on-line. Operating out of his home on a redwood-covered ridge 30 miles south of San Francisco, Warren posted a call to action to Internet users, who responded with enough mail to California lawmakers to move the necessary legislation forward. "According to the author of the bill, the on-line activism was instrumental," Warren says in a phone interview conducted as he watches out his window for forest fires.

"There is a heavy push in the information on-line industry to privatize access to government records," Warren says, adding that until now an electronic copy of all California state statutes would have cost $200,000.

Warren traces his politicization to 1990, when questions of privacy and government raids on computer hackers compelled a number of formerly apolitical computer mavens to get organized. "I actually believe that constitutional stuff," he says with a laugh when asked why he got involved. Warren predicts that within a year no serious candidate will be able to campaign without the Internet—something President Clinton clearly has taken to heart with the installation of a hookup at the White House.

The Los Angeles-based Center for Government Studies has devised an experimental "Interactive Multimedia Political Communications Project" aimed at helping citizens dial up everything from 30-second political spots to lengthy speeches, press conferences and candidate biographies. The project is designed to let people get past paid political advertising and ultimately participate in a kind of electronic balloting system. Envisioning an America that makes fans of representative government cringe, the center's Tracy Westen says, "In 100, or maybe 50, years, elected officials will be honorary. . . . We'll have Virtual Government."

Who knows how quickly the average information-overloaded citizen will leap at the opportunity to dial up next year's version of "The Man From Hope." At the same time, there's ample evidence that the mouse potatoes currently cruising the Internet are an especially opinionated, information-hungry bunch who don't mind speaking their minds (and speaking . . . and speaking). Wild debates over public policy issues go on for days and weeks on the Internet, which has generated its own informal etiquette and even, in the manner of Personals ads, its own acronyms. One of my favorites is IMHO—"in my humble opinion"—a useful euphemism for "you nut."

In communities where computers are old hat, citizens already are experimenting with electronic lobbying. Computer Professionals for Social Responsibility is setting up an interactive network in Seattle, home of Boeing. And Santa Monica, Calif., has such advanced computer communications that the homeless recently used terminals installed at libraries and other public places to lobby for shower facilities, bathrooms, a laundromat and lockers so they could get cleaned up for job interviews. Now people who can't afford housing on their own are using the terminals to find roommates, and donated computer equipment is being used to train the unemployed for jobs, says local activist Michelle Wittig.

In Government They Distrust

Santa Monica aside, right now the average electronic lobbyist is less likely to be one of the homeless than one of the computer gentry—folks who joined the electronic revolution years ago as the first ones on their block to buy a modem, who already enjoy access to the Internet through either an academic institution or a monthly subscription to a local network, who've conveniently forgotten the tens of millions of dollars the government has invested in creating the Internet and who don't understand what all the fuss is about in Washington.

Asked how he harnesses the Internet constituency to fight for changes in Congress, Danny Weitzner, who lobbies for the Electronic Frontier Foundation, responds, "That's an interesting issue. . . . In terms of our supporters, a lot are skeptical when we talk about the need to legislate. They say, 'Ah—the government is just going to screw it up again.'"

At issue are two major bills, one introduced by House Judiciary Committee Chair Jack Brooks (D-Texas) and House Energy and Commerce Committee Chair John Dingell (D-Mich.), which would set the terms for RBOCs wanting entree into long-distance service, the other an ambitious rewrite of the 1934 Communications Act introduced by Rep. Edward Markey (D-Mass.), chair of the telecommunications subcommittee. In exchange for allowing phone companies to get into video delivery, and cable companies to get into phone service, the bill would encourage a system of universal (everyone can get it) access to the Information Superhighway and direct the FCC to figure out a way to bring about an "open platform"—a way for anyone to distribute information as well as receive it.

Another provision in the Markey bill would bar companies from owning both the local cable TV franchise and local phone service, a measure meant to protect the public from a media takeover by the 21st century equivalent of the Rockefellers. The provision lapses after five years, an arrangement Jamie Love rejects as a sellout and the Media Access Project's Andrew Jay Schwartzman compares to "coitus interruptus—just when things get going, it ends."

Because the bill contains affordable service and open platform provisions, however, it has won the endorsement of the Electronic Frontier Foundation (EFF), which takes some pride in the fact that it is a pragmatic, coalition-building group with good political connections and few delusions about who really controls the telecommunications debate. (Hint: It's not Ralph Nader.)

Co-founded by Mitchell Kapor, who bagged multimillions as a founder of the Lotus Development Corp. before dropping out and getting political, EFF has described itself as "a public interest organization dedicated to realizing the democratic potential of new computer and communications media." In political circles, EFF likes to play mainstream to Jamie Love's gadfly extremism.

Asked about the debate within the public interest Telecommunications Policy Roundtable over the Markey bill, EFF Executive Director Jerry Berman says, "We believe Markey is the vehicle [for negotiating]. The idea that we should go off and build a perfect bill is just wrongheaded. We've got to make common cause [with the Big Guys]."

Love, who dismisses all of Congress as a tool of special interests, naturally disagrees, and he just can't resist taking potshots at EFF, arguing that it is accommodating because it too takes money from such industry giants as AT&T, Bell Atlantic, MCI, Apple and IBM. Perched on a broken chair in a warehouse labyrinth that appears to be crammed with all the paper ever generated by Nader's Center for the Study of Responsive Law, Love takes the purist's position. He can afford to, as his two-person staff, which gets slim funding from the center and a few foundations, is perennially broke.

EFF, in contrast, recently opened smart offices in downtown Washington, where a staff of 11 uses state-of-the-art equipment to debate the big issues and keep track of its appointments on Capitol Hill. "We do not shade our positions," says Berman, referring to the flap over EFF's funding. "We take them and try to build coalitions behind them." Groups that rely on foundation money, he suggests, aren't as credible as those that depend on support from the real world of business and commerce.

Like some members of Congress, Berman suggests that contributions from lots of sources tend to cancel themselves out, and lots of contributions represent, in classic checkbook democracy fashion, lots of constituents. Clearly annoyed by ongoing debate on the Internet about EFF's politics, he continues, "I've been in the public interest community for many years, when I could have been with [the fat cat lawyer-lobbying firm] Covington and Burling, and I resent the implication that as an individual or organization we've been paid off." When it is suggested that the problem may be one of having to mingle in the corporate world, he responds, "I don't know where else to mingle!"

One alternative is to build a membership of small contributors, something EFF has toyed with doing. But that's an expensive endeavor, especially if it's done through direct mail, and EFF's efforts to advertise $40 memberships over the Internet have had only limited success. (The foundation has about 1,300 members.) One problem is that "netiquette" discourages requests for money—perhaps because of the Internet's historic ties to high-minded academia, or perhaps because the greatest fear among Internet users is that someday someone will figure out a way to make them pay.

"There's a debate going on among users of the Internet and groups like EFF about whether the Internet should be used to solicit funds; is it such sacrosanct ground that it shouldn't be sullied by commercialism?" says Roger Craver, a public-interest fundraising consultant who does most of his work through conventional snail mail. But the real problem, he believes, isn't netiquette but the nature of the system, which is so large and encompassing that it's impossible for fundraisers to target relatively narrow audiences. "There's the sheer size. . . . You hang out your message and hope someone sees it," he explains. "If you're trying to build membership you need targeting of some sort."

In other words, there is no direct mail fundraising without a List.

That phenomenon is one reason why so much of the public interest activity on the telecommunications front is funded by foundations and corporations: No one's figured out how to do it differently. And it's another reason so much of the lobbying is done by tax-exempt nonprofits like EFF: If EFF were set up only as a lobbying group, it wouldn't be able to take tax-deductible grants.

Andrew Schwartzman of the Media Access Project, which accepts small amounts of industry money, says the debate over funding is misplaced. "We all want the same thing; the question is how we get there." In the meantime, "There is a false sense of urgency: 'The train is leaving the station!" But another year isn't going to make a difference. The technology doesn't even exist yet. Wall Street is pressing this because the big companies want to take advantage before policymakers realize they are giving away the store."

No matter who ends up with the goods, says Schwartzman, "10 years from now you're still going to be looking to Dan Rather and his successors." What matters isn't the Superhighway of the year 2008 but the transition, he argues, and that means fighting for the same old reforms that put people to sleep during the '80s—things like the Fairness Doctrine and rules barring the phone company from controlling the content of the information it carries. By focusing too much on the distant future, he argues, we may end up giving everything to three or four companies. "That will transform the democratic process," he predicts, and not for the better.

INFORMATION SUPERHIGHWAY[4]

The next person who compiles a list of journalism pioneers might want to save a footnote for *New York Times* reporter John Markoff, early cyberscribe.

Fifteen years ago, Markoff was a news-service reporter in Silicon Valley when curiosity caused him to log onto Arpanet, the Pentagon-funded computer network used by elite scientists to swap data. It was an unheard-of audacity, like crashing an ultra-exclusive cocktail party. But Markoff stayed, and he gained entrée to high-powered electronic conversations and contacts unknown

[4]Article from *The Freedom Forum* 4+ My '94. Copyright © 1994 by *The Freedom Forum*. Reprinted with permission.

elsewhere. "I really was the only kid on my block when I started," he said. "I had a window into a world that no one else had."

Markoff has consistently exploited his advantage. In 1988, his on-line sources helped him identify the perpetrator of the worst computer virus epidemic in U.S. history. Robert T. Morris, a 23-year-old Cornell graduate student, had in one night unwittingly caused the failures of more than 6,000 computers at companies, universities and military facilities across the USA. Markoff fingered him on the front page of the Nov. 5 *New York Times*. "Most of my sources are accessible over the 'Net," Markoff said. "I use it as much as my telephone."

Today, millions of people worldwide use Internet, Arpanet's descendant, whose offerings compare to those of a megalopolis. Markoff has seen his edge erode as more reporters mine computer networks for sources, ideas and data. Still, he depends on Internet every day as an essential tool of his trade.

Journalists still waiting for the vaunted information superhighway should know that some competitors already are driving on it. Networks such as Internet and on-line services such as America Online, CompuServe, GEnie and Prodigy are changing the way people work and play.

But as the highway continues to develop, important questions remain for the news industry: What does the information superhighway mean for the future of the news media? Will journalists become obsolete? And what will be the consequences for news consumers?

The Media Convergence

Content—information, entertainment and other services—is the commodity that will be bought, sold and traded along the information superhighway. News organizations are ideally suited to profit and prosper on the highway because they are, in effect, content factories.

Newspapers, particularly, mint enormous quantities of high-quality content every day in the form of news stories. And because people will need old news to give perspective to new news, newspaper libraries are mines of priceless info-ore waiting to be smelted into marketable, digital form.

"It's almost a waste for a newspaper to expend huge resources gathering the news, print it once, then put it away in a box," said Sig Gissler, former editor of *The Milwaukee Journal*. Distributing news electronically on the information superhighway will let savvy news organizations get more bang for their journalistic bucks.

Many newspapers are starting to do just that, among them *USA TODAY, The Washington Post,* the *Atlanta Journal* and *Constitution, The Boston Globe* and the *Albuquerque Journal.*

One year ago, the *San Jose Mercury News* started an on-line service called Mercury Center, which is available to the 700,000 nationwide customers of America Online. "It is not an electronic newspaper. It has no pretensions of that," said Bill Mitchell, director of electronic publishing for the *Mercury News.* "Print is clearly the medium for browsing, to be surprised. But if you're searching for something, then the electronic medium is easier."

Mercury Center customers can: tap into the *Mercury News* electronic newspaper library that dates to June 1985; correspond with *Mercury News* managers; peruse *Mercury News* stories in greater detail; read what's happened since the morning newspaper; read 200 to 300 stories daily that the *Mercury News* has no room for; and access more than a dozen other newspapers.

The point, Mitchell said, is to provide the public the information it wants in any form it wants, all under the *Mercury News'* brand name. The challenge, Mitchell says, is a matter of survival. "There are lots of other people who would love to serve our customers."

That was the idea that drove the Tribune Co. to create Chicago Online and ChicagoLand Television News, a 24-hour news channel that calls for the cooperation of the company's media properties. An unusual feature of CLTV is that reporters and editors from the *Chicago Tribune* appear on camera to discuss stories they've worked on. The TV camera sits just outside the editor's office in the newspaper newsroom.

Such collaboration among print, broadcast and computer media—called media convergence—will be essential if they are to survive, said John Pavlik, associate director/research and technology studies, at The Freedom Forum Media Studies Center.

"Info-niches"

The news product of the information superhighway likely will reflect the convergence of news media—text, audio and video—into a simple package. It will be interactive; consumers will be able to tailor the news to their interests.

The technology of the information superhighway will give

rise to more sophisticated, specialized digital news products that serve increasingly narrow "info-niches" of consumers. Desktop publishing technology has triggered an explosion of specialty publications. On-line services are hosts to hundreds of electronic forums and clubs for nearly every vocation and avocation. On-line micro-publishing will be common on the information super-highway, experts say.

Real-time news services—where the news is constantly up-dated and delivered to customers electronically—also will be commonly available on the information superhighway. The business world has had them for years, but at prices prohibitive for the average consumer.

For example, worldwide subscribers of Bloomberg Business News can—for $1,000 a month—instantly access up-to-the-minute stock-and-bond-market figures in full-color graphics. They also can peruse an endlessly updated menu of the latest world news, classified ads and other features. "It's like having a worldwide news wire on your desk," said Mark Thalhimer, technology manager at The Freedom Forum Media Studies Center.

The news vehicle of the information superhighway will be small in size and flexible in function, according to Roger Fidler of Knight-Ridder's Information Design Lab. Fidler's vision of tomorrow's "newspaper" will be a single flat, lightweight, interactive information screen that displays print, full color video and sound. Its content could be updated as often as desired by plugging the display into an information source.

Journalists Will Be More in Demand

If the information superhighway is good for the news industry, it also is good for journalists. Easier access to data and people empower reporters to file better stories under tighter deadlines than ever before.

Journalists also will not be immune to the trend of telecom-muting—working from home or other remote site without going to the office. "I already work in a virtual newsroom," said Mark-off, who is based in San Francisco. He uses his phone, modem, laptop computer and Internet to report and to communicate with his *New York Times* editors.

Time Associate Editor Philip Elmer-DeWitt recalled looking for information on an encryption chip that intelligence agencies wanted to install in communications devices so they could eaves-

drop on electronic conversations. "But it turns out that every
cryptographer in the world is on Internet," he said. "You can get
stuff straight from the horse's mouth."

That's great if you're sure the horse isn't of a different color.
All the do's and don'ts of smart journalism apply on the information superhighway. The speed of digital communication and the
demand for up-to-the-second news require that journalists more
than ever maintain a solid grounding in journalism ethics and
news judgment. News that is both fast and accurate will be the
credibility standard on the information superhighway.

While future newsrooms may be virtual, the need for journalists on the information superhighway will be real. Yes, the public
will have more information at its fingertips than ever before. But
that information glut will create a critical role for talented people
who can sift, shape and share it.

Ann Brill, a journalism professor at the University of Missou-
ri, who helps run the Digital Missourian project with the *Columbia
Missourian,* said future journalists will need to see news as a
whole—text, audio, video, data—and be able to organize the elements to best serve the user.

Some reporters, armed with portable computers and satellite
telephones, already are filing stories from remote locations such
as Somalia. As the technology becomes more commonly available,
more reporters will be able to work as journalistic nomads, roam-
ing their geographic or electronic communities to cover stories
whenever and wherever they happen.

However, journalists shouldn't get too hung up on how news
and information will be reported or delivered, said Gissler, now a
senior fellow at The Freedom Forum Media Studies Center.
"Most important is having faith in your fundamental function of
gathering and making sense of information."

More Power to the News Consumer

Clearly the greatest beneficiaries of the information superhighway will be media consumers, who will have more control
over more information than ever before. They will be able to
expect more depth and dimensions from news stories. They also
will have the choice to bypass the news media and read, see and
hear much of that information raw.

The interactive media also will let them communicate with
more people, including newsmakers. Citizens can now send

e-mail to the White House. "Instead of 'Big Brother' keeping millions of citizens under continuous electronic surveillance, millions of citizens are keeping 'Big Bubba' in the White House under continuous electronic surveillance," said Larry Grossman, former president of NBC News and PBS. The public, thus empowered, is becoming a fourth branch of government in an "electronic democracy," said Grossman, who is planning what he calls a "cultural C-SPAN" television channel.

News consumers will even become information providers themselves. "With computer networks, anyone with a word processor and a modem can be a publisher," *Time*'s Elmer-DeWitt said. On the *Atlanta Journal* and *Constitution*'s Access Atlanta service, customers can submit their own stories and photographs for publication.

That interactive capability and all that information will be expensive. So far, little thought has been given to the costs of the information superhighway. Will providers pay? Advertisers? Consumers? The recent uproar over cable TV rates showed that there is a limit to what subscribers will pay for news, information and entertainment.

As people become more dependent on the information superhighway to go about their lives, some people could be passed by—because they can't afford to be connected or because companies can't afford to connect them.

Even today's taken-for-granted technologies are not accessible to all Americans. While come communities are hooking up to fiber-optic phone lines, others, particularly rural enclaves such as Hill City, Kan., are still struggling with lead trunk lines four decades old. One Hill City resident complained in *USA TODAY* that the phone company had relegated his town of 1,800 to the "information cowpath."

The USA's biggest cities harbor infoghettoes. Parts of the Bronx still don't have cable, while sections of Queens already are wired for 150 channels. South Central Los Angeles was the last area of the city to receive cable. For already disenfranchised citizens, the coming of the information superhighway means they could be stranded in a social, economic and educational desert.

That's too bad, because the information superhighway has the potential to connect people who are most cut off from society, said Bill Dutton, director of the U.K. Programme on Information Communication Technologies at Brunel University in London.

The city of Santa Monica, Calif., for example, found that

homeless people were frequent registered users of its Public Electronic Network (PEN), whose terminals are available in libraries and other public locations. PEN allowed homeless people to keep in touch with each other, as well as meet other users electronically and face to face, Dutton said. They may have been homeless in real life, but not in cyberspace.

Expect the Unexpected

Universal access to the information superhighway should be a critical public-policy issue. "We have always subsidized low-income groups to give access to the telephone," Dutton said. "The more people connected to any communication network, the more valuable it is."

Likewise, visionary newspapers and other news organizations are realizing that the information superhighway can help them deliver better-quality news to more customers than printing presses and 10-year-olds with bad aim. But experts concede that it is impossible to predict what the information superhighway will really be like.

About 40 years ago, the interstate highway system began giving people a way to travel quickly between major urban centers. But travelers used the highways mainly for local transportation, Gissler said. Today, the only worthy expectation for the information superhighway, he said, is that the consequences will be unexpected.

New York Times reporter Markoff already has moved his beat beyond computers in search of the next cyber frontier. "The basic law of Silicon Valley is that every 18 months, the number of transistors that can be mounted on a chip doubles," he said. "The PC isn't the be all or end all. There will be significant changes. I'm trying to find those things."

III. LEGAL AND LEGISLATIVE ISSUES

EDITOR'S INTRODUCTION

The information superhighway, like the automotive highway, needs administration and regulation. In the first article, from *Issues in Science and Technology,* Rep. Edward J. Markey (D-Mass.) proposes a legislative agenda for telecommunications. The limits of freedom of speech have always been debated, but the complexities of cyberspace have raised even more questions about First Amendment rights. In *U.S. News & World Report,* Vic Sussman explores this conflict. Privacy is another right under attack in the modern electronic age, and the following piece from *Scientific American* details the technological mischief of "wire pirates." Finally, Gary Wolf, writing in *Wired,* chronicles a case over who owns legal information.

A LEGISLATIVE AGENDA FOR TELECOMMUNICATIONS[1]

Federal policy must support the transition to an integrated communications and information infrastructure. Recent headlines tell an exciting story in the communications industry. AT&T Buys McCaw. Time Warner Forms Partnership with US West. IBM and DEC Develop Video Servers. Microsoft in Talks with Cable Giants.

Spurred by the convergence of communications and computer technology, this experiment in recombining corporate DNA to create a new, hardier life-form is leading inexorably toward the creation of a new mega-industry—the information in-

[1]Article by Rep. Edward J. Markey, (D-Massachusetts), chairman of the subcommittee on Telecommunications and Finance of the House Energy and Commerce Committee. From *Issues in Science and Technology* 10:59–64 Fall '93. Copyright © 1993 by the University of Texas at Dallas. Reprinted with permission.

dustry. The integration of computer companies, software houses, telephone and cable companies, manufacturers of wireless gadgets, and others promises to deliver a vast array of new services to consumers and businesses and to change for the better the way we learn, work, and live.

The challenge facing federal policy-makers is to ensure that our communications networks support this rapidly evolving technological transition. We must prevent deficiencies in the communications infrastructure from stalling or derailing the transition. And we must make certain that this transition does not leave behind huge segments of society. In short, our goal is to progress smoothly toward a national communications and information infrastructure that becomes the "electronic superhighway" that our nation can ride into the 21st century.

To accomplish the overarching goal of building a national communications "infostructure," we need to address four separate questions that together add up to a comprehensive view of how our communications network will evolve. Let us review these in turn and then explore how they combine to sketch out a coherent policy.

Identifying Needs

First, how do we ensure that our communications infrastructure serves today's needs as well as tomorrow's visions? This question demands congressional attention because the communications infrastructure is too important to our society to be left to the invisible hand of the marketplace or the quite visible hand of the phone companies.

My goal is to put our nation on a path to a future infrastructure that meets the needs of business users and residential consumers alike. In my opinion, the critical requirements for infrastructure are that it be universally available, reasonably priced, and capable of providing short-term advantages within five years and full advantages within ten years. Virtually everyone agrees that we need a long-term strategy that will result in a system of integrated phone, video, radio, and information services. Where I differ from the popular consensus is in my conviction that we also need a short-term strategy to get us through the transition.

To set us on the path to this future, I propose two concrete steps. First, we must recognize the role that wireless communications will play in the future and make the radio spectrum available for those services. To make certain that future products and services will have the radio spectrum they need, I pushed legislation through the House of Representatives earlier this year that would require the federal government to free up 200 megahertz of radio spectrum now reserved for its own use, mostly by the Pentagon, so that it can be used by private industry. To put this in perspective, the $10-billion cellular industry grew out of a government decision almost 20 years ago to allocate just 50 megahertz of spectrum for use by cellular phones. President Clinton took a giant step toward the wireless future when he signed my bill into law as part of the Omnibus Budget Reconciliation Act.

Second, we as a nation must set measurable goals that will guide future regulatory decisions. One immediate goal that I propose is that all Americans should have access to affordable residential digital service, which will be essential to take advantage of many of the new services being developed. The phone companies have already made extensive investments in digital technology, and with federal leadership it is clearly possible for most households to have access to digital service within three years and for all households to have access within five years.

State utility commissions in Massachusetts and Tennessee, where critical pricing issues have already played out, have found that this service need not be that expensive. In Massachusetts, the telephone company initially proposed to the commission that the charge for home digital service be approximately $45 per month per line with an additional usage charge of 10 cents per minute. If you are a regular user, that would add up to a substantial bill pretty quickly. Thankfully, consumer groups challenged the phone company. They discovered that the actual marginal cost of providing the service was closer to $10 per month per line with a usage cost almost equivalent to the 2 to 3 cents per minute it costs for analog voice traffic. The Massachusetts commission implemented reasonable rates to encourage the use of digital technology.

The numerous new services being promised for the information age will require a robust physical infrastructure. Government should play a limited role in building that infrastructure but a huge role in setting the ground rules and incentives that will govern its construction. The federal government should set goals and facilitate improvements in telecommunications capabilities, set standards for interconnection, interoperability, and access, and fund limited pilot projects to demonstrate how new software applications and communications links can enrich the lives of ordinary Americans. Beyond that, the private sector must be the primary source for meeting our communications and information needs—guided, prodded, and, where necessary, mandated by the federal government.

The reasons behind this view are philosophical as well as practical. From a philosophical perspective, I think that private industry, spurred by competition made possible by government policy and motivated by profits (that is, driven by fear and greed), can do a better job than the federal government at delivering communications and information services. From a practical perspective, I have trouble seeing how even modest visions of a government-funded infrastructure are going to get money in an era of "shared sacrifice." When there is not enough money for AIDS research or housing, and taxes on Social Security are being discussed, I cannot envision a major new government initiative to build communications lines that industry itself is perfectly capable of building.

The "Baby Bells"

Defining the role of the private sector is somewhat complex because of the diverse number of companies who want to own a chunk of the electronic superhighway. Perhaps the toughest job is to determine what role the Regional Bell Operating Companies (RBOCs, or "Baby Bells") will play.

Under the Modified Final Judgment, the consent decree that broke up the Bell System, the RBOCs were prohibited from offering information services, engaging in manufacturing of communications equipment, or providing long-distance service. These line-of-business restrictions were put in place to protect consumers from the type of monopolistic abuses that had led to the government's antitrust suit and were predicated on the RBOCs' monopoly control of the local phone loop.

Pointing to the changes that have occurred in technologies and markets since 1984, the Baby Bells argue that these line-of-business restrictions no longer make sense. They persuaded the courts to lift the restriction on information services two years ago and are pressuring Congress for relief from the other two restrictions.

All of this is background to the second question: Should the RBOCs be allowed to enter the manufacturing or long-distance businesses? It seems to me that the RBOCs have made a good case that they need to be able to collaborate with equipment engineers from other companies and that they need to be in the research stage of product development. Consequently, I think that this restriction should be modified. However, the fact that the Baby Bells need to engage in some manufacturing activities does not obviate the need for appropriate safeguards. And it is over the details of those safeguards that progress has broken down in the past.

On the question of RBOC entry into long distance, I am not persuaded that at the present time it would be good for consumers if the RBOCs were permitted to offer long-distance services. It may be worthwhile to explore whether permitting the RBOCs to offer some aspects of long-distance service—for example, service that is incidental to the offering of an information service or that is used to complete a wireless phone call—could benefit consumers and make telephone-company operations more efficient. But on the larger question of long-distance services, even the Bush Justice Department notified the House Subcommittee on Telecommunications and Finance just last summer that the Baby Bells continue to have monopoly control of the local phone loop and that therefore the potential for discriminatory conduct is too great to risk letting the RBOCs into long-distance services.

This is a dynamic business, however, and that monopoly control can be broken. When the RBOCs no longer control the local phone loop, we will have to ask ourselves whether these restrictions still make sense. Last December, Robert Allen, chairman and CEO of AT&T, making a similar point at a conference in Washington, D.C., addressed the need to develop the "proper metrics" to determine when the RBOCs no longer have such control. I agree with Allen that we need to develop those yardsticks. To free up the RBOCs too soon could result in uneconomic and discriminatory behavior that would be harmful to consumers; but to free up the RBOCs too late could put those companies in an untenable position.

Competition in Local Markets

The matter of phone-company control of the local phone loop brings me to the next question: How will we manage the introduction of competition in the local loop? The premise behind this question is that competition is coming, especially for the larger phone companies. That reality fits the rush of technology development and the clear directives of the Federal Communications Commission (FCC) as well as the demands of the marketplace.

Local-loop competition means that when you pick up the phone you reach the local company of your choice, just as you now do when making a long-distance call. But reaching this goal will take much effort. First and foremost, we must solve the unavoidable problems of universal service and affordable rates. We cannot have a situation in which today's local phone companies are like some public hospitals in urban settings—the uncompensated providers of last resort.

The clearest analogy to this debate is what happened in the early 1980s when MCI was trying to compete against AT&T. At the time, we were told that universal service would be in danger if we promoted competition. And do you know what? Those in Congress and at the FCC took those claims very seriously. In fact, we built a very elaborate structure—including rules governing access fees, subscriber line charges, and other aspects of service—to deal with the changes that were wrought by introducing competition into a previously monopolized service. As part of that process, I learned that you can't wish away real problems. But on the other hand, you cannot let those problems paralyze progress.

The bottom line is that competition is coming, and coming soon, to the local phone loop. The FCC has taken critical steps in promoting competition along the lines of proposals that I outlined over two years ago. Hence, I welcome the FCC's role in this area, but I doubt that the agency has the authority or the scope of vision to construct a whole new policy governing the local phone loop. Consequently, Congress should legislate principles that promote competition and preserve universal service.

What I envision for the future is a network of competing communication networks made seamless and transparent by government standards and operated and maintained by private industry. This competitive marketplace will benefit consumers small and large by yielding better service at lower prices. The phone companies can compete and win in that environment and so can cable companies, wireless companies, long-distance providers, and many others who have the know-how to giver consumers what they want.

Dial-a-TV

The last question facing the communications policymakers is: Should telephone companies be able to provide video programming and enter the cable business in their own service territories?

Telephone companies are generally prohibited from offering video programming to their own subscribers by virtue of the 1984 National Cable Act. However, a lot has changed since 1984. In fact, a lot has changed since 1991, when Congress first considered a cable re-regulation bill. Although many questioned whether we would succeed in that effort, and it took the only override of a President Bush veto to pull it off, the fact is that the cable business is now subject to reasonable rate regulation and rules for program access.

In just the past year, we have witnessed a dizzying array of multimedia deals on top of cable upgrade announcements. We've had TCI with its promise to offer 500 channels, Time Warner and its partnership with US West to build a network offering "switched everything" service (including video-on-demand and long-distance access), and Cox and TCI purchasing Teleport, a major competitor with the local phone companies. These rapid changes in the marketplace and technology mean that it is time to reassess whether the restriction on local phone company participation in the cable market continues to serve the people well, or whether the public could not be better served by more competition. This reassessment is made all the more urgent by a district court decision in August holding the cable/telephone-company restriction unconstitutional.

I propose that local telephone companies be permitted to enter the cable business only in the old-fashioned way—by building a new system. They should not be allowed to enter by buying an existing cable system. The reason for this is simple: The best rationale for lifting the restriction would be to promote competition with cable. Buying an existing system does not change the competitive scenery.

From a consumer perspective, a fundamental difference exists between lifting the cable restriction and lifting the long-distance restriction. The RBOCs and others argue that enabling them to enter the long-distance business will help the telephone companies. If the goal is to help the telephone companies, then the long-distance restriction should be lifted. But make no mistake—only by accepting a trickle-down view of the world can one conclude that lifting the long-distance restriction completely will benefit the infrastructure going to every home in America. In short, permission to enter the long-distance business would enable telephone companies to hold on to large business customers, make some profit, and maybe get better prices for residential customers, but there is no evidence that it would result in additional investment in the communications infrastructure.

On the other hand, if the goal is to help residential and small-business customers get a line into the information age and to encourage robust competition with the cable coaxial wire already coming down the street, then it may make sense to permit telephone companies to offer video programming. The reason is that if the local telephone companies can offer video services, they should have the incentive and the revenue to upgrade their wires, which go into every U.S. home.

To some it is a little scary that the phone company would also be their cable company. A traditional American suspicion of bigness and concentrated power is probably behind this feeling of unease. To address that concern, I think that phone companies getting into the cable business in their service areas should remain common carriers. This does not necessarily mean that the phone companies could not own programming. One need only look for an analogy to the current information-services market, where the RBOCs have an obligation to carry everyone's service but also can provide programming of their own. What it does mean is that the local phone companies, some of which are among the richest companies in our country, will not have a stranglehold over the information and entertainment that goes into the vast majority of homes.

This discussion raises a collateral point: How come these common-carrier obligations in the video programming arena get put upon phone companies and not cable companies? Two comments are in order. First, to the extent that cable companies move out of providing video programming and move into telephone-like service, I think it is clear that they should have common-carrier obligations, meaning that they must provide service to everyone on a nondiscriminatory basis at reasonable rates.

Second, as the cable industry moves from providing 60 channels to 500 channels or to infinite capacity as Time Warner envisions, we should take a fresh look at the question of common-carrier status for video delivery. As cable-system capacity grows, I believe that it takes on the quality of a carrier of communication services. In addition, as the capacity grows in size so does the importance of the industry as a source of information and entertainment. Because of that importance, the nondiscriminatory principle embedded in the common-carrier concept should apply.

Basic Values

The good news from Washington is that everyone wants a national communications infrastructure. The bad news is that no one knows what it means. But whatever specific shape it takes, it must incorporate the values that form the heart of the Communications Act of 1934—universal service and diversity.

Universal service—the notion that all Americans get communications service at affordable rates—must evolve to stay current with the race of technology, or else we will have a world where the children of the well-off have access to the future and the children of the poor are using the equivalent of rotary-dial technology. If we let that happen, we will live in a world of information haves and have-nots, and the American experiment will be on the road to failure.

Diversity has come to mean not just a large number of speakers with open access to a communications network—which is embodied in the principle of common carriage—but also a significant number of providers of communications services. I look forward to a day when there are two wires going down each street and a cheap (and small) satellite dish in each backyard so that consumers have lots of choices. Competition has given us a richer and more robust communications industry, which has benefited consumers. I believe that we should continue to apply the principle of competition to further expand the services offered by the industry.

Looked at individually, these telecommunications policy questions may seem too arcane to be of national significance. But together they will form the basis for a coherent national communications and information infrastructure that will place our nation ahead of the rest of the world.

POLICING CYBERSPACE[2]

If ever a buzzword buzzed too much for traditionbound law enforcement, it's *cybercop*. It kicks up images of the clanking earnestness of a laser-guided RoboCop. Agents snickered when senior instructor Kevin Manson first used the word a couple of years ago at the Federal Law Enforcement Training Center near Brunswick, Ga. Nobody at FLETC laughs much anymore. They are too busy training cybercops. "The day is coming very fast," says FLETC's director, Charles Rinkevich, "when every cop will be issued a badge, a gun and a laptop."

Adding a high-speed modem, cellular phone, cryptography textbooks and a bulletproof vest to that arsenal might also be prudent because "crime involving high technology is going to go off the boards," predicts FBI Special Agent William Tafoya, the man who created the bureau's home page on the Internet, the worldwide computer network. "It won't be long before the bad guys outstrip our ability to keep up with them." These crimes are worrisome precisely because they use the advantages of cyberspace that have made it a revolutionary, liberating form of communication: its ability to link millions of computer and modem owners around the world; its technological breakthroughs, such as digital encoding, that allow average citizens to use sophisticated encryption to protect their data, and its wide-open culture, where cops and other agents of government are more often than not thought to be the enemy.

No one knows exactly how much computer crime there really is, though FLETC's experts agree that the damage starts in the billions of dollars and will surely surge upward. The size and scope of cybercrimes are limited only by the bad guys' imagination, technical skill and gall. But here are the crimes that worry authorities the most:

• White-collar crime. Virtually every white-collar crime has a computer or telecommunications link, says Carlton Fitzpatrick, branch chief of FLETC's Financial Fraud Institute. Sometimes the crimes are simple, such as the case of the bookkeeper at a bicycle store who frequently entered incoming checks as returned

    [2]Article by Vic Sussman, staff writer, from *U.S. News & World Report* 118:55–60
Ja 23 '95. Copyright © 1995 by *U.S. News & World Report*. Reprinted with permission.

merchandise, then cashed the checks. Even more damaging are cases involving skilled computerists. The FBI says that Kevin Mitnick, currently America's most wanted computer criminal, has stolen software from cellular-phone companies, caused millions of dollars in damage to computer operations and boldly tapped FBI agents' calls.

• Theft. Given the expanse of computer networks, even seemingly small crimes can have big payoffs. "Salami slicing," for example, involves a thief who regularly makes electronic transfers of small change from thousands of accounts to his own. Most people don't balance their ledgers to the penny, so the thief makes out, well, like a bandit. A more targeted approach involves pilfering industrial secrets. Last November, someone infiltrated Internet-linked computers owned by General Electric and stole research materials and passwords.

• Stolen services. Swiping and reselling long-distance calling codes is a big business, says Bob Gibbs, a Financial Fraud Institute senior instructor, as is breaking into private phone networks and selling long-distance access. One university discovered this the hard way when its monthly phone bill, a staggering $200,000, arrived in a box instead of an envelope.

• Smuggling. Drug dealers launder their proceeds through cyberspace and use the Internet to relay messages. Moreover, they cover up secret communications by cracking into corporate voice-mail systems and by operating their own cellular-telephone networks.

• Terrorism. Since computers are the nerve centers of the world's financial transactions and communications systems, there are any number of nightmarish possibilities. Authorities especially worry that a cracker—cyberspeak for a malevolent hacker—might penetrate FedWire, the Federal Reserve's electronic funds-transfer system, or vital telephone switching stations. Key New York phone systems did go down temporarily in 1992, and though it has been chalked up to a software problem, some FLETC cybercops still wonder if it didn't involve a cracker testing his muscles.

• Child pornography. There is a lot of it out there. Jefferson County, Ky., police Lt. Bill Baker broke a major kiddie-porn ring in England even though he never left Kentucky. An E-mailed tip from a source in Switzerland led Baker to an Internet site in Birmingham, England. After about three months of investigation that involved downloading 60 pages of file names related to child

porn and 400 images, Baker called on Interpol, New Scotland
Yard and police in Birmingham, who arrested the distributor.

To combat once and future cybercrimes, FLETC's Financial
Fraud Institute conducts some 14 programs, regularly updated
to keep pace with wrinkles in crime. Agents learn how to analyze
evidence, track credit card fraud and apply constitutional search-
and-seizure techniques when they find evidence of crimes on
computer bulletin board systems (BBSs). This is a new world for
law enforcement, says Dan Duncan, a FLETC Legal Division senior instructor, because "cops have always followed a paper trail,
and now there may not be one."

When they start rooting around for crime, new cybercops are
entering a pretty unfriendly environment. Cyberspace, especially
the Internet, is full of those who embrace a frontier culture that is
hostile to authority and fearful that any intrusions of police or
government will destroy their self-regulating world. The clash
between the subculture of computerists and cops often stems
from law enforcement's inexperience. The Internet buzzes with
stories of cops who "arrest the equipment" by barging into BBS
operations to haul off all the electronic gear, as if the machines
possessed criminal minds.

Still, keeping up with wise guys in cyberspace will tax the
imaginations and budgets of law enforcement agencies and put
revolutionary pressures on America's notions of privacy, property
and the limits of free speech. The rights of everyone are at stake.
What follows is a look at perhaps the most crucial issues that will
emerge as a profoundly new chapter in human communication
unravels.

Invasions of Privacy

Once upon a time, only Santa Claus knew whether you had
been good or bad. But jolly supernaturalism has been supplanted
by aggressive data processing: Your chances of finding work, getting a mortgage or qualifying for health insurance may be up for
grabs, because almost anybody with a computer, modem and telephone can surf through cyberspace into the deepest recesses of
your private life. A fairly accurate profile of your financial status,
tastes and credit history can be gleaned from such disparate
things as your ZIP code, Social Security number and records of
credit-card usage.

Even more personal information will be available as commercial transactions increase through online services. And that raises the most pressing cyberspace issues for everyday Americans, says Phil Agre, a communications professor at the University of California at San Diego. Such transactions will increase as the Internet grows more popular. Those records, enriched with demographic information and perhaps Social Security numbers, will be routinely sold to marketers, says Agre. He asks: "Who will have access to the complete transaction data?"

Suppose you have a history of buying junk food or large amounts of over-the-counter drugs. Could an insurance company obtain that information and decide you are a poor health risk? If records showing purchases of cigarettes, liquor and red meat were collated with your medical records, would the picture look even worse? Computer networking and sophisticated data processing are making it easier and cheaper for businesses and the government to collect such personal data, says Esther Dyson, of EDventure Holdings, which observes the computer industry. "It's really simple to call up amazing stuff about anybody," she says.

But legal access to data is only part of the problem. Another difficulty is unauthorized peeking into personal records, which Dyson says occurs with alarming regularity because company safeguards are often laughable. Knowing a person's Social Security number is usually enough to get into medical and financial records. A second problem is that wrong and harmful "facts" can creep into the databases. Malicious tipsters can poison a person's record with innuendo, and it takes much effort to correct the mistake.

In this environment, it is virtually inevitable that Americans will demand stronger privacy protections. The United States has a law barring release of video rental records but no strong laws against scanning personal medical data. "Many European countries have privacy commissions, and they find it strange that we don't," notes Anne Branscomb, author of *Who Owns Information?* and a law professor at the University of Pennsylvania. She urges laws that give citizens the right to control data about themselves.

The new Congress will soon begin deliberations over proposals that would offer privacy protections for Americans' medical, credit and telecommunications data. Similar proposals have not gotten off the ground in previous Congresses, but handicappers say passage of a bill limiting the release of confidential medical records is much more likely in this Congress as is a measure to limit online service providers' ability to sell membership data. The potent telemarketing industry probably has the power, though, to soften a proposal barring the sale of personal data to commercial vendors without a person's consent, according to Evan Hendricks, publishers of the newsletter *Privacy Times*.

Encrypting Data

Cybercops especially worry that outlaws are now able to use powerful cryptography to send and receive uncrackable secret communications. That could make some investigations impossible and create a breed of "crypto-criminals," says FLETC's Manson. But there is widespread agreement across the Internet and among entrepreneurs hoping to do business in cyberspace that cryptography is necessary for privacy in a networked universe.

Besides businesses, which will need cryptography for transmitting sensitive information, the other market for cryptography is the millions who use electronic mail. "Without encryption, E-mail is no more secure than a postcard," says cryptographer Bruce Schneier, author of *E-mail Security: How to Keep Your Electronic Messages Private*. E-mail passes from machine to machine, and many people in the middle can read it. Systems are also vulnerable to break-ins, and passwords are commonly stolen. Some may decide they don't need the high level of privacy cryptography affords, especially given the additional effort encrypting data requires. But as Internet communication becomes common, people will want private contact with business associates, physicians, attorneys, accountants and lovers.

The increasing use of encryption leaves cops in the lurch unless they have a way to break the code. "We are totally, enthusiastically supportive of encryption technology for the public," says Jim Kallstrom, the FBI special agent in charge of the Special Operations Division in the New York office. "We merely think that criminals, terrorists, child abductors, perverts and bombers should not have an environment free from law enforcement or a search warrant. I think most victims of crime agree." Kallstrom sees the Clipper chip—which is supposed to offer phone privacy to consumers while providing police access—as a good way to give the public powerful encryption while still preserving law enforcement's ability to conduct electronic surveillance. The FBI won a round last year when Congress passed the Digital Telephony Act, which requires future telecommunications systems to be accessible to wiretaps. But officials have not persuaded Congress or industry to back Clipper. Many opponents agree with the Electronic Privacy Information Center's Marc Rotenberg, who calls Clipper part of the "Information Snooperhighway."

Law enforcers are also deeply worried about another aspect of cyberspace that offers absolute anonymity to anyone who wants it. Anonymous re-mailers—free E-mail forwarding sites in Europe and elsewhere—can convert return addresses to pseudonyms and render E-mail untraceable. Anonymity is crucial for whistleblowers and people expressing unpopular views against repressive governments, but it raises other problems, says the FBI's Tafoya. Anonymous re-mailers outside the reach of American authorities are being used by electronic vandals to bedevil their victims with threatening messages or "mail bombs" composed of thousands of gibberish messages. They either clog a victim's mailbox or jam his computer system. Child pornographers also use anonymous re-mailers.

The simple truth, though, is that no legislative act can stop the spread of cryptography, according to Lance Hoffman, a computer-security expert and professor at George Washington University. "There are 394 foreign encryption products; over 150 use DES—strong encryption," says Hoffman. "And all are legal to import."

Cryptography will become even more popular once cyber-surfers discover digital cash, which is the electronic equivalent of real money that resides in a computer. David Chaum, the developer of DigiCash, a Dutch-owned company, says his creation combines the benefits of anonymous legal tender with the speed and convenience of online commerce. There is no risky exchange of credit-card information. DigiCash is electronically transferred like actual cash, while powerful cryptography makes it theft- and counterfeit-proof, says Chaum. DigiCash can prevent consumers' names and personal habits from funneling into databases. Schneier thinks the enhanced confidentiality of electronic lucre will be good for society, but suggests that "criminals will love digital cash. Anybody can use it to transfer money for legal or illegal purposes." Many people believe the widespread use of E-cash will be one more aspect of the Internet that erodes the power of central government control.

Freedom of Speech

The advent of space-age telecommunications raises enormous questions about the future of government regulation of media.

Though the First Amendment asserts there should be no law abridging freedom of speech or the press, there have been laws aplenty in the last three generations that regulate speech on new kinds of technology. Different restrictions apply to telephones, radio and TV stations and cable TV. But cyberspace is a convergence of media and the blurring of distinctions between transmission modes. "With the advent of fiber-optic [cables], it is conceivable that a single transmission medium could become the conduit for newspapers, electronic mail, local and network broadcasting, video rentals, cable television and a host of other information services," says Robert Corn-Revere, a former Federal Communications Commission official who now practices First Amendment law. He argues that the day is passing when government can justify licensing and regulating media.

Modern telecommunications knows no borders and has few limits. For the first time in history, almost every recipient of information has the potential to become a publisher of information, says Jonathan Emord, an attorney and author of *Freedom, Technology and the First Amendment*. The liberating potential of that technology is exhilarating as it unleashes information and breaks down communications hierarchies. But it also creates a situation where Americans can be offended or otherwise victimized by information from people sitting at computers in foreign lands beyond the reach of U.S. authorities. "Right now, cyberspace is like a neighborhood without a police department," says FLETC's Fitzpatrick.

One of the most pressing dangers, says Fitzpatrick, is that people bound by hate and racism are no longer separated by time and distance. They can share their frustrations at nightly, computerized meetings. "What some people call hate crimes are going to increase, and the networks are going to feed them," predicts Fitzpatrick. "I believe in the First Amendment. But sometimes it can be a noose society hangs itself with."

Of course, the antidote to offensive speech, noted Supreme Court Justice Louis Brandeis, is *more* speech, and the Internet is still an equal-opportunity soapbox. Messages on public bulletin boards can be challenged and rebutted, which widens debate. Moreover, users can go where they choose on the Internet. So, those offended by discussions are always free to start their own groups.

Of all the material floating between computers, pornography best illustrates the difficulties of trying to apply old rules and laws to cyberspace. Late last year, a jury in Memphis, Tenn., convicted a Milpitas, Calif., couple of violating obscenity laws. Using a computer and modem in Memphis, a postal inspector downloaded pictures from the couple's California-based BBS. The couple were tried in Memphis, and a jury found that the pictures violated local community standards. But the pictures, which existed only as data stored on a hard drive, were voluntarily extracted from a computer sitting in a community where the images were *not* illegal. People create their own communities in cyberspace, based on affinity rather than geography. This means the courts will have to unravel when, where and how potential crimes should be investigated.

Ultimately, there are no easy solutions to such problems because the First Amendment, designed to protect offensive speech, has always cut both ways: It encourages robust and healthy discussion, but it also allows everyone a platform. Mike Godwin, legal counsel for the Electronic Frontier Foundation, which promotes civil liberties in cyberspace, says "I think we're still in the turmoil that comes when a new medium is presented to the public and to the government. There's a tendency to first embrace it and then to fear it. And the question is, how will we respond to the fear?"

Intellectual Property

John Perry Barlow, an Internet visionary, kicked up controversy last year when he suggested in a widely read *Wired* magazine article that traditional notions of copyright were dead in cyberspace. "Digital technology is detaching information from the physical plane," he write, "where property law of all sorts has always found definition." The government's top copyright officer, Marybeth Peters, partially concedes the point, saying, "The Internet is the world's biggest copying machine." But she says that doesn't mean copyright is useless, just that it needs to work differently in a world where "property" is as evanescent as dots of light dancing on a computer screen.

One way, suggests Peters, will be to provide access to data only to those who pay. An example is WestLaw, an online law database. Students use an electronic card that gives them access to the system, and their law school pays the fee. Other information systems now being developed use encryption, selling the access key to users. But once someone gets a first look at data, sound or graphics files, it is easy to make copies—an economic nightmare for software developers.

Ken Wasch, executive director of the Software Publishers Association, says pirated software costs the industry $9 billion a year. The issue is hot enough to spark a U.S.-China trade war. The Clinton administration recently threatened to raise tariffs on some Chinese products unless China stops its global trade in illegally copied CDs, books, movies and computer software.

Wasch believes copyright law is elastic enough to protect material regardless of media, and that software should be protected as a "literary work." But he agrees that some updating is in order: "We don't want to criminalize someone giving a copy to another person." But a recent court case shows how complicated the issues are: Late last month, a U.S. District Court judge in Boston dismissed charges of wire fraud against an MIT student who ran a bulletin board allowing users to extract copies of more than $1 million in software at no charge. While calling the student's actions "heedlessly irresponsible," the judge said the government's charges would make even legitimate copying, such as that done for backup purposes, illegal. Intellectual-property expert Branscomb agrees. "You cannot take an old law intended for telegraphy and telephony and turn it into a mechanism for criminalizing behavior that Congress has not addressed directly," she said.

The only solid protection for ideas flying through cyberspace is their originality and style, which was the point of copyright in the first place, maintains Internet guru Barlow. If you are creative and have something worthwhile to say, the public "will pay to hear your latest thoughts or your latest research. Value comes back to you by increasing your celebrity and people's awareness of your work," he says. Bringing copyright laws crafted in 1787 up to warp speed in cyberspace will be difficult at best, especially on the Net, where information is routinely traded for more information and no money changes hands. Besides, says Barlow, collecting tolls on an information highway is the wrong concept. "The Internet is nothing like a superhighway. It's an organism."

WIRE PIRATES[3]

Someday the Internet may become an information super-highway, but right now it is more like a 19th-century railroad that passes through the badlands of the Old West. As waves of new settlers flock to cyberspace in search of free information or commercial opportunity, they make easy marks for sharpers who play a keyboard as deftly as Billy the Kid ever drew a six-gun. Old hands on the electronic frontier lament both the rising crime rate and the waning of long-established norms of open collaboration.

It is difficult even for those who ply it every day to appreciate how much the Internet depends on collegial trust and mutual forbearance. The 30,000 interconnected networks and 2.5 million or more attached computers that make up the system swap gigabytes of information based on nothing more than a digital handshake with a stranger. (Even estimates of the Internet's size, compiled by SRI International, rely on the cooperation of system administrators around the globe.) Most people know, for example, that electronic-mail messages can be read by many people other than their intended recipients, but they are less aware that e-mail and other communications can be almost tracelessly forged—virtually no one receiving a message over the net can be sure it came from the ostensible sender.

Electronic impersonators can commit slander or solicit criminal acts in someone else's name; they can even masquerade as a trusted colleague to convince someone to reveal sensitive personal or business information. Of those few who know enough to worry about electronic forgeries, even fewer understand how an insidiously coded e-mail message can cause some computers to give the sender almost unlimited access to all the recipient's files. And mail-transfer programs are only one of the wide range of ways that an attacker can gain access to a networked computer. "It's like the Wild West," says Donn B. Parker of SRI: "No laws, rapid growth and enterprise—it's shoot first or be killed."

To understand how the Internet, on which so many base their hopes for education, profit and international competitiveness, came to this pass, it can be instructive to look at the security

[3]Article by Paul Wallich, staff writer, from *Scientific American* 270:90+ Mr '94.

record of other parts of the international communications infrastructure. A computer cracker may become a "phone phreak" to
avoid paying for the long-distance habit that computer intrusion
sometimes requires, or he may take up phone phreaking as a
related hobby (much as a poacher might both hunt and fish). Not
only are some of the players the same, so are many of the basic
design issues. Furthermore, engineers building each new generation of technology appear to make the same mistakes as their
predecessors.

The first, biggest error that designers seem to repeat is adoption of the "security through obscurity" strategy. Time and again,
attempts to keep a system safe by keeping its vulnerabilities secret
have failed. Consider, for example, the running war between
AT&T and the phone phreaks. When hostilities began in the
1960s, phreaks could manipulate with relative ease the long-
distance network in order to make unpaid telephone calls by playing certain tones into the receiver. (One phreak, John Draper, was
known as "Captain Crunch" for his discovery that a modified
cereal-box whistle could make the 2,600-hertz tone required to
unlock a trunk line.) The precise frequencies were "hidden" in
technical manuals and obscure journal articles, but college students and others soon ferreted them out. Phreaks built so-called
black, blue and red boxes to produce the required signals, and a
small cottage industry flourished until the telephone company
adopted methods that were less vulnerable to spoofing through
the telephone mouthpiece.

Telephone credit cards underwent an evolutionary process
that continues today. When the cards were first introduced, recalls Henry M. Kluepfel of Bell Communications Research,
credit-card numbers consisted of a sequence of digits (usually
area code, number and billing office code) followed by a "check
digit" that depended on the other digits. Operators could easily
perform the math to determine whether a particular credit-card
number was valid. And phreaks could easily figure out how to
generate the proper check digit for any given telephone number.
The telephone company had to rely on detecting fraudulent calls
as they occurred, tracking phreaks down and prosecuting them, a
strategy that "never worked in the long term," according to
Kluepfel.

In 1982 AT&T finally put in place a more robust method.
The corporation assigned each card four check digits (the "PIN,"
or personal identification number) that could not be computed

easily from the other 10. A nationwide on-line database made the numbers available to operators so that they could determine whether a card was valid.

Since then, theft of telephone credit-card numbers has become a matter of observation and guile rather than mathematics. "Shoulder surfers" haunt train stations, hotel lobbies, airline terminals and other likely venues. When they see a victim punching in a credit-card number, they transmit it to confederates for widespread use. Kluepfel noted ruefully that his own card was compromised one day in 1993 and used to originate more than 600 international calls in the two minutes before network-security specialists detected and canceled it. "I made a call from a coin phone and shielded the number from the scruffy-looking guy on my left, but I was unaware of the guy in the business suit on my right," he confesses.

Kluepfel cites estimates that stolen calling cards cost long-distance carriers and their customers on the order of half a billion dollars a year. The U.S. Secret Service has placed the total volume of telecommunications fraud at $2.5 billion; industry numbers range from $1 billion to $9 billion.

Somebody Else's Problem

Over the course of a generation, AT&T developed monitoring tools to thwart callers trying to evade toll charges. The corporation also used them to foil individuals who dialed into telephone switching systems to manipulate the facilities directly. Such access let phreaks forward other people's telephones to new locations, route calls around the world or even cut off one another's telephone service. After the Bell system breakup in 1984, however, AT&T was no longer the global policeman of the telecommunications world. In particular, tens of thousand of large and small companies that purchased PBXs (so-called private branch exchanges) to automate their internal telephone networks found themselves the targets of "finger hackers," but they had nothing like AT&T's expertise in self-defense.

The simplest way to commit finger hacking, says Kevin Hanley of AT&T, is "dial 1-800 and seven digits." At the other end of many toll-free lines sits a PBX remote-access unit, a subsystem that permits company employees to call their home office and then dial out from there to any number in the world. Most such units require a security code for outgoing calls, Hanley notes, but sometimes "the chairman doesn't want to remember a password." No one knows precisely what such oversight and self-indulgence cost. Industry estimates for PBX fraud range from a few hundred million to more than a billion dollars a year. "It's a bonehead crime," sneers Mark Abene, a hacker now serving a one-year sentence in federal prison for computer intrusion. (During an interview, Abene sketches out the architecture of digital inter-office signaling systems while complaining about what he considers unwarranted slurs on his character in internal telephone-company memos.)

Nevertheless, relentless trial-and-error dialing is highly profitable. Finger hackers can make tens or hundreds of thousands of dollars in calls before being detected. Most such crimes, Hanley notes, are committed by organized groups of criminals, who may even set up storefronts where they sell long-distance calls at cut price. Customers walk in, pay their money and tell an attendant the number they want to call. Less image-conscious thieves may sell calls out of a corner telephone booth.

Almost all these attacks can be circumvented by configuring a system to block calls to locations where a company does no business and by logging incoming calls to detect attempts at intrusion. Yet many PBX owners are unaware of the danger they face, Hanley says. Even those who do know their peril may not have managers on duty at night or during weekends, when most frauds occur. Of the 40 or 50 attendees at the security seminars that Hanley conducts, only "two or three know how toll fraud works," he asserts: "Maybe 30 or 40 percent know what it is, and that it's a bad thing."

Designers of the next big innovation in telecommunications, the cellular telephone, apparently ignored the lessons that their wire-bound predecessors so painfully learned. Leaving aside the fact that anyone with the right radio receiver can listen in on calls, the units are uniquely vulnerable to toll fraud. Every cellular telephone call begins with a broadcast of the telephone's serial number and billing number. Cellular switches check the pair against a database of working telephones to decide whether a call should go through. Unfortunately, these numbers are also the only information a thief needs to impersonate a legitimate caller.

As early as 1984, communications expert Geoffrey S. Goodfellow (who got his start in the field when he broke into a computer at SRI and ended up with a job offer) wrote an article laying out a road map for cellular-phone fraud; only during the past year or two have thieves used the more sophisticated schemes he outlined. The fundamental problem, Goodfellow asserted, was that cellular-phone engineers underestimated both the technical expertise and the persistence of those who might want to subvert their equipment. He called for immediate replacement of current cellular-phone standards with more secure alternatives, but to little avail.

The simplest attack is known as cloning: reprogramming the serial number and telephone number of a pirate unit to that of a telephone currently in use by a legitimate customer. Although standards call for telephones to be built so that it will be impossible to change a serial number without irreparable damage, some early cellular-phone manufacturers supplied the numbers in a memory chip that could be popped out with a screwdriver. Others now place the information in an electrically programmable chip that can be accessed simply by applying the appropriate voltage to the telephone.

More sophisticated frauds adapt the same circuitry that allows a cellular phone to listen for incoming calls to decode the numbers as they are broadcast. A thief can then replay them to make calls that will be billed to others. The companies that carry cellular-phone traffic—and thus are financially responsible for fraudulent charges—have adopted a number of monitoring techniques to detect illicit calls; in addition, some have set their switching equipment to prevent long-distance cellular traffic to areas of the world where fraudsters often call (the countries that topped one carrier's list early in 1993, for example, were the Dominican Republic, Egypt, Pakistan, India, the former Soviet Union, El Salvador, China, Colombia, Mexico and Ghana).

Instead of just monitoring calling patterns, telecommunications engineers have been working on hardware fixes that could block the vast bulk of fraudulent cellular calls. In the fall of 1993 TRW announced a technique for analyzing the analog transmission "signature" of each telephone and storing it along with the serial number and telephone number. If a unit's serial number and telephone number do not match the signature, it must be fraudulent. Details of the characteristics that make up the signature are, of course, supposed to remain secure to prevent evil-doers from devising countermeasures.

Such measures are a stopgap. The major cellular carriers are already preparing to replace the current analog cellular-phone system with a digital one. Most proposed digital-cellular standards incorporate protocols in which a telephone making an outgoing call must respond to a mathematical challenge based on its serial number and telephone number, rather than disclosing the pair directly. Some units can also encrypt conversations to prevent the new ubiquitous practice of cellular eavesdropping; in some countries this feature has led law-enforcement agencies to oppose their sale.

During the same years that telephone companies were fighting the phone phreaks and cellular-phone architects were designing an estimated billion-dollar annual fraud bill for users and providers of service, computer scientists were laying the foundations of the Internet. Although initial funding came from the Department of Defense's Advanced Research Projects Agency, security was not really a concern, recalls ARPANET veteran David J. Farber, now at the University of Pennsylvania. In the early days, only researchers had access to the net, and they shared a common set of goals and ethics, points out Eugene H. Spafford of Purdue University.

The very nature of Internet transmissions embodies this collegial attitude: data packets are forwarded along network links from one computer to another until they reach their destination. A packet may take a dozen hops or more, and any of the intermediary machines can read its contents. Indeed, many Internet packets start their journeys on a local-area network (LAN), where privacy is even less protected. On a typical LAN, computers broadcast each message to all the other computers attached to the network. Only a gentleman's agreement assures the sender that the recipient and no one else will read the message.

The Cyber-Neighborhood Goes Downhill

A lack of security on the ARPANET did not bother anyone, because that was part of the package, according to Dorothy E. Denning, a professor of computer science at Georgetown University: "The concerns that are arising now wouldn't have been legitimate in the beginning." As the Internet grew, however, the character of its population began changing, and many of the newcomers had little idea of the complex social contract—and the temperamental software—guiding the use of their marvelous new tool.

By 1988, when a rogue program unleashed by Robert T. Morris, Jr., a Cornell graduate student, brought most Internet traffic to a halt for several days, a clear split had developed between the "knows" and the "know-nots." Willis Ware of Rand, one of the deans of computer security, recalls that "there were two classes of people writing messages. The first understood the jargon, what had happened and how, and the second was saying things like, 'What does that word mean?' or 'I don't have the source code for that program, what do I do?'"

Since then, the Internet's vulnerabilities have only gotten worse. Peter G. Neumann of SRI, a security researcher who edits the RISKS Forum, an on-line discussion of computer vulnerabilities, characterizes the situation as "unbelievably bad." Anyone who can scrounge up a computer, a modem and $20 a month in connection fees can have a direct link to the Internet and be subject to break-ins—or launch attacks on others. A few years ago the roster counted established names such as "mit.edu," "stanford.edu" or "ibm.com"; today you are as likely to find "mtv.com" or even "pell.chi.il.us," the nom du net of a battered PC-compatible with a hardware-store brass handle screwed into its case for portability.

Moreover, as the Internet becomes a global entity, U.S. laws become mere local ordinances. In European countries such as the Netherlands, for instance, computer intrusion is not necessarily a crime. Spafford complains—in vain, as he freely admits—of computer science professors who assign their students sites on the Internet to break into and files to bring back as proof that they understand the protocols involved.

Ironically, the more thoroughly computerized and networked an organization is, the more risk it may face when making its initial connections to the outside world. The internal network of a high-technology company may look much like the ARPANET of old—dozens or even hundreds of users, all sharing information freely, making use of data stored on a few central file servers, not even caring which workstation they use to access their files.

As long as such an idyllic little pocket of cyberspace remains isolated, carefree security practices may be defensible. System administrators can safely configure each workstation on their network to allow connections with any other workstation. They can even set up their network file system to export widely used file directories to "world"—allowing everyone to read them—because, after all, the world ends at their corporate boundaries. Indeed, computer companies have made a practice of shipping their wares preconfigured so that each machine automatically shares resources with all its peers.

It does not take much imagination to see what can happen

when such a trusting environment opens its digital doors to the Internet. Suddenly, "world" really means the entire globe, and "any computer on the network" means every computer on *any* network. Files meant to be accessible to colleagues down the hall or in another department can now be reached from Finland or Fiji. What was once a private lane is now a highway open to as much traffic as it can bear.

Dan Farmer of Sun Microsystems and Wietse Venema of the Eindhoven University of Technology report that even some of the most respected domains on the Internet contain computers that are effectively wide open to all comers—the equivalent of a car left unattended with the engine running. A recent security alert from CERT (the Computer Emergency Response Team), a clearinghouse for security-related problems based at Carnegie Mellon University, illustrates the point. The alert disclosed that all Sun workstations with built-in microphones had been preset to give their audio input "world-readable" status. Anyone who could gain network access to such a workstation could listen to conversations nearby.

Another alert warned system administrators that the memory buffers that store images displayed on workstation screens might also be preset to world-readable status, as might those that store characters typed on the keyboard. Patient attackers have watched until someone logged in to a privileged account and then simply read the password out of the computer's memory. Once intruders have gained such "root" access, they can masquerade as any legitimate user and read, alter or delete any files. They can also install programs to help them invade other computers and even modify system logs to erase signs of their intrusion.

Even if newcomers to the net try to secure their systems, they do not always have an easy time finding the information they need. Computer hardware and software vendors are often loath to talk about security problems, Neumann says. And CERT generally issues net-wide advisories only after manufacturers have developed a definitive fix—weeks or months later, or sometimes never. Most advisories do not explain the security flaw in question; instead they name the software and hardware involved and specify the modifications that should be made to reduce the chances of intrusion.

This policy keeps potentially useful information away from those crackers who are not well connected within the illicit community. But it also keeps many novice system administrators in the dark, Neumann complains: "You find out by having a buddy who's a system administrator somewhere else." Neumann estimates that between half and three quarters of the security holes currently known to hackers have yet to be openly acknowledged. "People don't know the risks," Spafford comments. "They know the benefits because people talk about those."

Many of those benefits come from programs such as Gopher, World-Wide Web or Mosaic, which help people navigate through cyberspace in search of information. A single menu selection or click of a mouse may take a researcher from a computer in Minnesota to another in Melbourne or Zurich. Files containing U.S. census data, pictures of the aft plumbing of the space shuttle and lists of British pubs or of artificial-intelligence software are available free for the finding. Such tools, many of them just a gleam in researchers' eyes a few years ago, are drawing tens of thousands of people to the Internet.

Yet that rapid evolution may have leapfrogged steps that could have contributed to security, Spafford notes. Cybersurfers are relying on "the first or second version" of programs originally written to test ideas rather than to provide industrial-strength services.

The popular Gopher program, according to CERT advisories and other sources, has security flaws that make it possible to access not only public files but private ones as well. ("It's only insecure if you configure it wrong," insists Abene, who will return to his job as system administrator for an on-line service in New York City when he is released from prison.) Running Gopher initiates a dialogue between a client program on the user's machine and a Gopher server somewhere on the Internet. The server presents the client with a menu of choices for information, along with a set of "magic cookies"—shorthand specifications for the location of additional information.

If the user wants to delve deeper into a particular subject, the client program sends the server the cookie corresponding to that piece of information. Yet it is relatively easy to modify the cookie so that it specifies the location of information on the server's machine that is supposed to be kept private. An unsuspecting Gopher server will deliver those private files without checking whether the cookie it receives matches one of the items in the menu it presented. Although Gopher servers can readily be confined so that they have access only to public information, by default they have free rein.

By Bits Deceived

Failure to check the propriety of commands is a common oversight—as Othello with Iago, computers on the Internet trust not wisely but too well. E-mail, one of the net's most basic services, sets the tone: an electronic letter consists simply of a text file containing a header specifying the sender, addressee, subject, date and routing information, followed by a blank line and the body of the message. Although mail programs generally fill in the header lines accurately, there is little to prevent a whimsical or malicious person from inserting whatever information they please. A message from "president @whitehouse.gov" could as easily originate from a workstation in Amsterdam as from the Executive Office Building in Washington, D.C. Forging e-mail is "trivial," Farber asserts; what makes such forgeries a problem as the Internet grows is that the incentive for successful forgeries does so, too, as do the dangers of being taken in. Companies and individuals have already begun doing business via e-mail; real money and goods change hands on the basis of electronic promises.

Computer scientists have developed protocols for verifying the source of e-mail messages, but spoofers are also improving their techniques. Correspondence on Usenet discussion groups such as "comp.security.misc" illustrates this coevolution: some security-minded system administrators have advocated the use of "IDENT daemons." If a spoofer connects to a mail server and offers a false identification (the first step in sending a forged message), the mail server can query the IDENT daemon on the spoofer's machine.

Others disparage IDENT; they point out that the name returned by the daemon is only as trustworthy as the computer it runs on. Once hackers have gained control of a machine—either by breaking in or because they own it—they can configure the IDENT daemon to respond to queries with whatever name they please.

Some system administrators are meeting the threat of such deceptions by barring connections to their computers from untrustworthy parts of the Internet. Each range of numbered addresses on the Internet corresponds to a particular organization, or domain, and so it is simple to refuse connections from computers in a domain believed to serve as a vehicle for hackers. Even this step has a countermeasure. Spafford points out that most machines rely on "domain name servers" to translate back and forth between numbered network addresses and domains such as "xerox.com" or "umich.edu." But the name servers are just ordinary computers. They are vulnerable to deception or intrusion, and so the road maps they provide can be rewritten to serve deceitful ends. A cracker can modify the name server's database so that it tells any computer querying it that the address belonging to, say, "evil.vicious.hackers.org" is instead that of "harvard.edu." A computer that accepts connections from Harvard University will then allow the hackers in as well. Indeed, Spafford laments, it is almost impossible for any program to know for sure where the data packets reaching it over the Internet really come from or where the packets it sends out are going.

Another class of security problems comes not from misplaced trust in domain name servers or IDENT daemons but rather from the same versatility that makes networked computers so useful. Perhaps the best example of this is the "sendmail bug," a disastrous loophole that has reappeared time after time in the history of the net.

The bug arises because most mail programs make it possible to route messages not only to users but also directly to particular files or programs. People forward mail, for instance, to a program called vacation, which sends a reply telling correspondents that the intended recipient is out of town. Many people also route mail through filter programs that can forward it to any of several locations depending on sender, subject matter or content.

But this same mechanism can be subverted to send electronic mail to a program that is designed to execute "shell scripts," which consist of a series of commands to perform system functions, such as extracting information from files or deleting all files older than a certain date. This program will then interpret the body of the message as a script and will execute any commands it contains. Those commands could cause a copy of the receiving computer's password file to be sent to an intruder for analysis, fashion a subtle back door for later entry or simply wreak havoc on the recipient's stored data. Mail sent to certain files can have similar effects.

Some fixes for the latest incarnation of the sendmail bug have been published on the Internet and presumably have been implemented by most system administrators who saw them, but many systems remain vulnerable. Furthermore, other programs that process electronic mail contain analogous holes.

Even more ominous is the fact that e-mail is by no means the sole way to plant uncontrolled data in a victim's computer. Steven M. Bellovin, a researcher at Bell Labs, points out that Gopher and other information-retrieval programs also transfer large, potentially ill-identified files. A hacker would have to go to some trouble to set up a corrupt Gopher server and would even have to stock it with useful information to entice people into making connections to it. "I won't be surprised when it starts happening," Bellovin says.

Walls in Cyberspace

If the Internet, storehouse of wonders, is also a no-computer's-land of invisible perils, how should newcomers to cyberspace protect themselves? Security experts agree that the first layer of defense is educating users and system administrators to avoid the particularly stupid mistakes. People still tape passwords to their keyboards or use no password at all for privileged computer accounts. One graduate student, pressed into service as administrator for a cluster of workstations at the University of Michigan, found that a simple password-guessing program could compromise a quarter of her users' accounts. Five of 80 users had chosen their names as passwords. Some administrators have installed programs that reject passwords based on dictionary words or obvious personal identifiers, but their use is far from widespread.

The next level of defense is the so-called fire wall, a computer that protects internal networks from intrusion. Most major companies have long since installed fire walls, and many universities are adopting them as well. Fire walls examine all the packets entering and leaving a domain to limit the kinds of connections that can be made from the Internet at large. They may also restrict the information that can be passed across those connections. "Anyone who would connect a corporate network directly to the Internet should be fired," Farber asserts.

Proposing a fire wall and constructing it are two different matters. Users would like to have access to all possible Internet services. But that desire encounters a harsh reality: "Some things you can't do securely," maintains Marcus J. Ranum of Trusted Information Systems. Ranum, who helped to install the fire wall for "whitehouse.gov," names Gopher and Mosaic as two programs whose trusting nature defies the attempts of a fire wall design to provide safety. In such cases, he argues, security experts must be content to minimize risk rather than eliminate it entirely.

At a bare minimum, a fire wall must pass mail, according to Bellovin (even though mailers may be demonstrably insecure). After that, users want to be able to log in to machines elsewhere on the Internet and to retrieve files from public archive sites or from the directories of colleagues at other institutions.

To perform these functions, AT&T built a fire wall consisting of two dedicated computers: one connected to the Internet and the other connected to the corporation's own network. The external machine examines all incoming traffic and forwards only the "safe" packets to its internal counterpart. In addition, it will accept outgoing traffic only from the internal gateway machine, so an attacker attempting to transfer information illicitly out of AT&T's domain would be unable to do so without subverting the internal gateway. The internal gateway, meanwhile, accepts incoming traffic only from the external one, so that if unauthorized packets do somehow find their way to it, they cannot pass.

Other services are more problematic. Workers would like to be able to log in to their office computers from anywhere on the Internet, for instance. Any intermediate computer relaying traffic over the Internet might have been compromised, however, and could be reading packets (including those containing passwords) as they go by. In fact, in two separate incidents in October 1993, hackers gained access to Panix, a public-access Internet site in New York City, and to BARRNet, an Internet carrier in California, and installed "packet sniffers." These programs watched all the data going by and recorded user names and passwords as people logged in to (at least) hundreds of other computer systems, according to system administrators at Panix.

Such attacks render conventional passwords "obsolete," Ranum asserts. Instead safe connections to machines inside a fire wall require a different kind of authentication mechanism, one that cannot be recorded by a sniffer and then replayed to gain unauthorized access. Two methods are already in limited use: the "one-time" password and "challenge-response."

To use one-time passwords, a worker simply carries a list of them. Reuse indicates that an intrusion attempt is in progress. Challenge-response systems have no list of passwords; instead they require an answer to a random query before allowing access. Most often the query consists of a number that must be mathematically transformed by a secret key known only to authorized users. Most people cannot multiply 100-digit numbers in their heads, so commercial challenge-response equipment usually employs a "cryptographic calculator," primed with the key and activated by a shorter sequence that a person can remember.

Encryption Is Key

If passwords should traverse the Internet only in encrypted form, what about other sensitive information? Standardization efforts for "privacy-enhanced" e-mail have been under way for more than five years, but widespread adoption lies well in the future. "The interoperability problem is nasty," Ware says, unless everyone has software that can handle encrypted messages, it is of little use to anyone.

Encryption could provide not only privacy but authentication as well: messages encoded using so-called public-key ciphers can uniquely identify both recipient and sender. But encryption software in general remains at the center of a storm of political and legal controversy. The U.S. government bars easy export of powerful encoding software even though the same codes are freely available overseas.

Within the U.S., patent rights to public-key encryption are jealously guarded by RSA Data Security, a private firm that licensed the patents from their inventors. Although software employing public-key algorithms has been widely published, most people outside the U.S. government cannot use it without risking an infringement suit.

To complicate matters even further, the government has proposed a different encryption standard, one whose algorithm is secret and whose keys would be held in escrow by law-enforcement agencies. Although many civil libertarians and computer scientists oppose the measure, some industry figures have come out in favor of it. "You can't have absolute privacy," Parker says. "A democracy just can't operate that way."

The question is not whether cyberspace will be subjected to legislation but rather "how and when law and order will be imposed," Parker says. He predicts that the current state of affairs will get much worse before the government steps in "to assure privacy and to protect the rights people do have."

Others do not have Parker's confidence in government intervention. Ranum foresees an Internet made up mostly of private enclaves behind fire walls that he and his colleagues have built.

"There are those who say that fire walls are evil, that they're balkanizing the Internet," he notes, "but brotherly love falls on its face when millions of dollars are involved."

Denning counts herself among the optimists. She lends her support to local security measures, but "I don't lose any sleep over security," she says. Farber, also cautiously optimistic, sees two possible directions for the Internet in the next few years: rapid expansion of existing services, or fundamental reengineering to provide a secure base for the future. He leaves no doubt as to which course he favors. Spafford is like-minded but gloomier. "It's a catch-22," he remarks. "Everyone wants to operate with what exists, but the existing standards are rotten. They're not what you'd want to build on."

Even if computer scientists do redesign the Internet, he points out, putting new standards in place may be impossible because of the enormous investment in old hardware and software. So much of the Internet rests on voluntary cooperation, he observes, that making sweeping changes is almost impossible.

Then again, Ware counters, perhaps piecemeal evolution may be the only possibility. No single organization understands the idea of a national information infrastructure well enough to be put in charge, he contends: "There's no place to go and say, 'Here's the money, work out the problems.' There aren't even three places, and I'm not sure there should be."

In the meantime, the network grows, and people and businesses entrust to it their knowledge, their money and their good names.

WHO OWNS THE LAW?[4]

"The law . . . should surely be accessible at all times and to everyone."— *Franz Kafka*

Who owns the law? If you feel a momentary temptation to raise your hand and chirp, "Hey, this is a democracy; nobody can

---

[4]Article by Gary Wolf, freelance writer, from *Wired* 2:98+ My '94. Copyright © 1994 by Gary Wolf. Reprinted with permission.

own the law," then you should probably sit tight for a minute and wait for the impulse to pass. A private database owner has effectively asserted copyright ownership over thousands of decisions handed down by the circuit and district courts of the United States. If you want to cite these decisions in a legal brief, or include these decisions in an electronic database, you will probably have to traverse this vendor's copyright. And that means you pay. As they say in New Orleans: cha-ching!

Of course, the actual words of legal decisions are public domain. They cannot be copyrighted. What West Publishing of Eagan, Minnesota has managed to acquire is ownership of the quasi-official page numbers of federal decisions. Many judges recommend or demand that lawyers appearing before the court include citations to specific West-owned publications, such as the *Supreme Court Reporter,* the *Federal Reporter, Federal Supplement,* or *Federal Rules Decisions.* Under a copyright claim that has survived at least one challenge in court, other publishers of legal decisions are not permitted to show, in the margins of their books or in the headers of their databases, parallel citations that describe where decisions appear in West-owned books or in the West-owned electronic database, Westlaw. This puts West in the catbird seat: Any publisher is free to compile collections of federal decisions, but without citable page numbers these collections are little more than worthless.

Naturally, West's competitors are irritated. Small-time legal publishers are beginning to come out with relatively inexpensive CD-ROMs containing the historical case law in specific fields, such as telecommunications, or tax law, or employment law. But when it comes to the all-important circuit and district courts of the United States, CD-ROM publishers are holding back, because they can't get access to the page numbers.

Testifying before Congress last year on behalf of the American Association of Law Libraries, Laura Gasaway used a striking metaphor to describe West's tasty data monopoly. "Citations fulfill an infrastructural role in legal circles which is similar to that of currency in a modern society," Gasaway said. "Just as the currency system allows financial transactions to occur, so the system for citing law materials facilitates information exchanges." In other words, control over citations equals control over the circulation of money. In the legal field, West Publishing finds itself in the happy situation of having a license to print cash.

How did this happen? The text of United States law has been

a profitable commodity for West since the end of the last century, when the company began collecting court decisions and reproducing them in a useful, well-arranged format. Many courts came to depend upon West, along with other private companies, to provide them with the authoritative text of the law. Over the last decade, paper databases have begun to be overshadowed by electronic databases, but one of the things the court system has inherited from the old regime of paper-based publishing is this dependence on private enterprise to manage the dissemination of the law. Even government agencies such as the US Department of Justice purchase access to case law in a not-so-open market.

In the past, West's dominance in the area of federal case law had certain advantages. The task of putting an identical set of legal source books in hundreds of thousands of law offices would not have been easily accomplished by a patchy network of small, competing firms, or by the almost completely decentralized fiefdoms of the federal judiciary. Print, however, is no longer the ideal medium for a database, and getting identical case law into the offices of firms across the country no longer requires a well-organized army of typesetters, collators, book salespeople, and messengers. Using online access to simple ASCII files, it ought to be trivial to download cheap, standard, citable electronic texts of US court decisions from anywhere in the world.

Technically, it is trivial, but you still can't do it, at least not cheaply. Although the history of the privatization of the text of the law is complex, the results are simple. Electronic legal databases are available to well-heeled firms and law school students, while the majority of individual users and small businesses cannot gain entry.

Is There No Juris?

James Love is an information activist; he is devoted to liberating data. By last summer, Love was well aware of the problems with electronic access to the law. In July of 1993, Love submitted a petition to Attorney General Janet Reno asking her to allow the general public entry into a little-known Department of Justice database called Juris.

Love, the director of a Ralph Nadarite public interest group called the Taxpayer Assets Project, knew that the obscure database at the Department of Justice could be the key to unlocking the case law monopoly. Juris was publicly owned, and it contained a complete collection of federal case law going back, in some areas, to 1900. If Love could convince the Department of Justice to open the Juris system to users outside the government, it would be a milestone on the road toward information equality. Through Westlaw and its only licensed competitor, Lexis, users pay $200 to $250 for this sort of information. Public access to Juris would make it almost free.

Love's effort did not succeed. Six months into his campaign, it was clear that the public would not get cheap access to Juris. On the other hand, the locked-out citizens were in good company. By December 31, the Department of Justice didn't have access, either. The two dozen or so employees of Juris had been fired or reassigned. The disk drives were silent. The database was dead. The story of how a campaign for access to the law resulted in the destruction of the country's most important publicly owned legal database offers a few clues about the balance of power in the coming information age.

Juris was created in 1971, two years before Lexis and four years before Westlaw. It inherited the electronic records of an experimental Air Force program called FLITE (Finding Legal Information Through Electronics), whose history goes back to the early '60s. During the months before it was shut down, Juris was used by about 15,000 government employees.

Unfortunately, back in 1983 the Department of Justice had grown tired of handling the bothersome data entry and data management tasks for the case law portion of Juris. In a move consistent with the Reagan-era emphasis of privatization, a leading database vendor was hired to take over the job. The vendor was West Publishing. Displaying a remarkable lack of foresight, the Department of Justice neglected to secure the right to reclaim their database should West ever decide not to renew the contract.

Rebecca Finch, the director of Linguistic Data Consortium, a broadly based group of 65 corporations, universities, and government agencies, frequently enters into contracts with large private data vendors. Finch looks back on the Department of Justice's agreement with scorn. "It was a pretty stupid move to negotiate that kind of contract," she says. "We have contracts with news wires and other vendors and sometimes we hear that we have to give the data back when the contract is over. We just say no. Once we pay for it it is ours. Usually when we take this stance we get what we are after."

The Justice Department lawyers were not so tough. Starting

in 1983, the case law portion of the Juris database was leased from West with the understanding that if the data vendor ever withdrew it could take the case law with it. A decade later, when Love pressed his argument for open access, West did exactly that. Soon after the department's budget for the next two years was finalized in Congress, West announced it was pulling out of Juris. This left the department with a gap in its legal records that stretched over ten years.

But West didn't just take the data. They also took their proprietary page-numbering system. Without a budgetary appropriation to reenter the missing data, and without confidence that the data, even if reentered, would be usable to its attorneys, the Department of Justice had no choice but to shut the system down.

Love says the conflict over legal information is the toughest public access battle he has ever seen. The details of the controversy are too complicated for the evening news, and West is probably the most politically influential data vendor in the country. "I think we will win," Love predicts, "but it is a question of when. They've been able to delay this for a long time."

Today, the focus of the public access effort has shifted from lobbying the Department of Justice to suing it. Although the Juris system is dead, the case law has not yet been literally erased, and several Freedom of Information Act (FOIA) requests have been filed asking for parts of the database. A well-known FOIA attorney, William Debrovir, is seeking a court injunction forbidding the Department of Justice from deleting the valuable records until the FOIA requests are resolved.

"There is now no question that machine-readable data are agency records and are subject to FOIA," argues Debrovir. Still, the attorney, who represents not Love's group but another database publisher called Tax Analysts, was probably not surprised to learn recently that his FOIA request had been rejected on a number of different grounds, including the unashamed acknowledgement that making the legal data public would hurt West's private market. Harming West's market is clearly not something the Department of Justice is prepared to do. Debrovir's FOIA is on appeal.

All the legal back and forth between West, William Debrovir, James Love, and the Department of Justice has left a few people hoping that Juris, in one form or another, will be revived. But even if the data is saved, the page numbers will still belong to West. Unless West is moved by a fit of altruism to give up its lucrative copyright, the well-guarded barrier at the entrance to the law will remain in place.

West's Role

A fit of altruism may not be entirely out of the question. West's copyright of the page numbers of federal case law has brought small sudden squall of hostile publicity upon the company, which is not used to being cast in the role of corporate evildoer. Last year, Congress undertook hearings on the page-number issue, and during the latter part of 1993, legal librarians, computer researchers, and small publishers jumped at the chance to attack West's monopoly.

Rebecca Finch points out that a whole generation of computer-assisted legal research has been stymied by a lack of available data. Under Finch's guidance, the Linguistic Data Consortium helps computer scientists gain access to large databases in order to develop advanced electronic search techniques. "We're getting multilingual text, news wire text, medical text; but the problem with legal data is that it is copyrighted," she says.

One of the seminal researchers in the area of computerized database tools, Carole Hafner, was forced to give up her work on case law because she could not get any of the raw material. Hafner, whose highly technical 1981 book, *An Information Retrieval System Based on a Computer Model of Legal Knowledge,* helped define the field, now studies biological and medical data. "All this research has been stalled all over the world because nobody can get any legal text," Hafner complains. "The research effort, the fundamental research on case law and databases has been brought to a standstill because of the fact that these companies will not share their data with researchers. They will not sell their data. They will not sell a tape. You can forget it."

Hafner's characterization is not entirely correct; there is highly advanced database research going on in at least one location: West Publishing. One of West's in-house computer scientists, James Olson, has designed a natural language search tool called West Is Natural (WIN), which even Hafner admires. "WIN is great, everything about it is great," she says, "but the problem is there's no competition." Hafner points out that there is tremendous debate today over the best way to access a database; semantic nets, formal logic, and neural net approaches all have their advocates. "All these people should have a chance to work on legal

text," Hafner argues. "Legal text may have some unique characteristics, but nobody knows because we've never been able to
study it."

Despite the vociferous criticism from West's rivals and competitors, Congress declined to pass a law disallowing the copyright
on page numbers. While West's formidable political influence
may have played a role in the decision, a more important factor
was the ambivalence of other data vendors on the page-
numbering issue. Competing publishers would enjoy being able
to undermine the West monopoly, but at the same time the largest
players in the information industry realize that all sorts of copyrighted compilations of public data could be at risk if Congress
passes a law stating that page numbers cannot be protected.

After all, when you choose a particular portion of the public
record and put it into electronic format, what keeps the next guy
from coming along and ripping it off? West argues that it selects
and edits the cases it publishes, and points to its page numbers as
the unique signposts of the way it has decided to arrange the data.
Get rid of the signposts, says West, and the information landscape
becomes the site of a bloody free-for-all.

Interestingly, West's copyright of the page numbers of federal
case law has never received a full airing in court. In 1985, Mead
Data Central, West's main electronic competitor attempted to use
the West page numbers in its own legal database, Lexis. In a
preliminary injunction, the 8th US Circuit Court of Appeals up
held West's copyright, and West and Mead eventually signed a
secret agreement that granted Mead a limited license to use the
numbers. Widespread speculation holds that this agreement forbids Lexis to include the page numbers in CD-ROMs and other
electronic formats. Meanwhile, West's provisional victory has kept
other electronic publishers at bay.

The apparent disinclination in Congress to outlaw copyrighted page numbers has led West critics to mount a slightly
different attack. Many US courts offer electronic copies of their
decisions via local bulletin board systems; the decisions are not
organized into a database, but they are inexpensive and available
to everyone. Why not just stick official, publicly owned page numbers on them? If there were a consistent page-numbering system
acceptable in all jurisdictions, any publishing company could pull
the decisions into a database and compete with West on the bases
of who provided the easiest and cheapest way to access the law.
Various proposals for a page-numbering system have been wan-

dering around the Administrative Offices of the US Court of
Appeals for more than a year, but for one reason or another none
of them have "stuck."

To the anti-Westites, the court system's failure to promulgate
a simple, standard, public-domain citation system for US case law
indicates a condition of advanced backbone-enfeeblement. "The
courts have lost their moral compass," says Alan Sugarman,
whose company, Hyperlaw, produces CD-ROMs of legal data.
Sugarman points out that the US Courts have only two jobs: They
resolve individual disputes and they publish their decisions as
guidance for everybody else to follow. The fact that these decisions lack citable page numbers puts Sugarman into a state of
voluble outrage. "We are talking about the law, here!" he says.
"We're not talking about a by-product. Publishing cases for
people to cite is one of their primary jobs. So, why don't they take
some of their budget and spend it to get their materials into an
authoritative form?"

As for West, it holds that the page-number issue is a tempest
in a teapot. Gerry Sikorski, West's spokesperson on the Juris and
page-numbering issues, says that West would not oppose the idea
of a standard, nonproprietary electronic-numbering system. "We
have never asked a court to embrace our citation system," he
insists.

Still, Sikorski is quick to point out what he perceives as the
inevitable problems with public-domain page numbers. "The
question you have to ask is, what's broken?" he suggests. If the
government were to try to put standard page numbers on court
decisions, Sikorski believes that "there would be a lot of expense,
a lot of disruption, and it won't lead to anything more than a lot
of taxpayers, citizens, and legal writers and readers going
through a lot of gymnastics." Still, West's spokesperson shrugs,
"If somebody proposes something good, then what the heck?"

West's problem—and, of course, it's palladium—is that the
privately held company is intimately entangled with the federal
judiciary. Bad publicity could be deadly for a firm that depends
on the goodwill of courts and judges to maintain its position as
the bearer of the standard text of the law. West goes to great
lengths to enhance this relationship. The company sponsors year-
ly cash gifts of $15,000 to federal judges (an independent judicial
panel, not West, decides who shall receive the prizes), and West
has been known to work closely with judges in order to insure
accuracy in published decisions. The judges are reluctant to lose

the help of a good friend, and West's role is explicitly acknowledged in a number of jurisdictions.

At the same time, West needs to aggressively resist the implication that it has any special or unfair relationship with the judiciary. When West's president defended his company before Congress last year, he went through various jurisdictions one by one, arguing out that "there is no problem with access." Other publishers, he said, "are as free as we are to publish their own compilations" of legal material.

In its attempt to publicly downplay its position, West resembles a company that wants to have its cake and eat it too. West insists that it is the best and most popular legal publisher, and it is constantly assuring its customers that it can provide them with the standard text. On the other hand, it is also being forced to argue that it doesn't do anything any other publisher couldn't do. West's motto is "Forever Associated with the Practice of Law." This seems true; there is no other publisher whose copyrighted arrangements are as essential to attorneys as are West's. But maintaining this role for eternity—or even for another decade—has begun, paradoxically, to require certain efforts to protect and even to conceal it.

West's involvement in government does not begin and end with giving cash prizes to judges. Vance Opperman, West's president, is a leading Democratic party fund-raiser who has what a Minnesota newspaper called "hard-wired connections" to Vice President Al Gore. He is also finance chairman for the 1994 re-election bid of California Senator Dianne Feinstein. West may be standing on an ever-narrowing border between private enterprise and public service, but this border coincides with the territory occupied by the current administration. A politically progressive baby boomer, Opperman once told an interviewer that he listens to Bob Dylan's "Blowin' In the Wind" nearly every day.

Gerry Sikorski, West's spokesperson, is a retired Democratic member of Congress from Minnesota. Sikorski insists that West's role in the US judicial system is a benevolent and democratizing one. "West provided legal documents that weren't provided elsewhere, that weren't preserved or collected or put together," Sikorski says. "These documents are an important part of our democratic legal structure."

Again, though, West finds itself on ever narrowing ground. The company believes access to these documents is important, but it doesn't believe it is important enough for the government to put them online with public-domain page numbers. "Nobody is standing in the way of that," says Sikorski, "but are you willing to pay the money that will cost? Is it a better use than keeping criminals off the street or having more judges?"

In defending West's decision to sabotage Juris, Sikorski points to the growing need to "clarify" the conflict between public data in its raw form and public data that has been transformed by editing into private property. As the online resources grow more common, this conflict will intensify. Even James Love agrees that Juris was a bad mix: the case law was in the public domain, but the page numbers and headnotes belonged to West. "We feel very strongly that in this day of information superhighways, the concept of intellectual property is critical to success," says Sikorski. "This mixture of data complicates things." By turning off the main publicly owned database of case law, West found an effective way to eliminate the source of confusion. As for the Department of Justice employees, they are now free to purchase their case law from what Sikorski calls a "better, more useful, more advanced system." In other words, they can access Westlaw.

Sikorski asserts that the chorus of complaints aimed at West by Juris advocates is simply the carping of jealous rivals. After all, he says, it was West who more than a hundred years ago won the important legal battles that earned private companies the right to reprint court decisions, thus opening up the world of legal publishing to private enterprise. Today, he says, West's preeminent position is based almost entirely on its high-quality editing and its detailed headnotes that summarize and catalog the decisions. James Love and Alan Sugarman and other public access advocates "want West to do the work and then strip off the book covers and the spines and republish it."

In conversations with attorneys with no ties either to West or to the Taxpayers Assets Project, however, few agreed that West's great virtue was its editing or its notes. Most said that West's value lay in its completeness and its citability. Mike Rushford, president of the Criminal Justice Foundation, a conservative group that regularly files briefs with the Supreme Court, had one of the more explicit responses.

"That's bullshit," he said. "It is not editing or the headnotes, it is the page numbering." As head of a public interest law firm, Rushford is constantly looking for ways to save money. He regularly asks his attorneys if they could substitute legal data on CD-ROM for West's high-priced database and law books. "My legal staff says we can't cite to them," Rushford reports, "so we are going to have to buy the West books too. It is just a matter of practical concern. We have to make a judgement about what the courts will want." When you are filing a brief before the Supreme Court, Rushford points out, the last thing you want to worry about is whether your citation is acceptable.

In a sense, the West monopoly represents a classic economic logjam: Old property relations interfere with new technologies. Just as feudal relationships in the early modern era restrained, for better or worse, the development of a capitalist economy, so the outdated notion of copyrightable data monopolies obstructs new forms of commerce built upon widespread electronic access to basic information. If the text of the law were free, or nearly free, companies would be dueling with each other to see who could add the most value to the data. The competition would then genuinely be over search tools, interfaces, and commentary rather than over page numbers and citability.

All West's opponents have a slightly different vision of what this future will look like. James Love looks forward to a day when any citizen can access a legal database for free at a local library. Alan Sugarman hopes to be one of the publishers selling inexpensive and highly-focused CD-ROMs to specialty law firms. And Carole Hafner believes that if the legal text was available to computer scientists, in ten or fifteen years the need for headnotes and indexes might be eliminated altogether: lawyers and non-lawyers could query the law in a vast number of user-friendly and technologically distinct ways.

Still, it's impossible not to sympathize at least a little with West's uncomfortable situation. The company's importance is indisputable: its history is impressive. "West has performed a democratic role since the 19th century," says Sikorski, truthfully. Ironically, like the old AT&T/Bell Telephone system, West may simply have been too successful at making itself indispensable.

IV. POLITICAL AND POLICYMAKING ASPECTS

EDITOR'S INTRODUCTION

Although the Internet will probably not be a major campaign issue in upcoming elections, politicians will certainly discuss its applications to government functioning and efficiency. In the first article, Law Professor Fred H. Cate writing in the *Stanford Law and Policy Review* discusses the role of government in information policymaking.

The second article, "The Underpinnings of Privacy Protection," reprinted from the *Communications of the ACM*, reviews judicial and policymaking concerns for privacy, especially in the field of electronic technology. Next, the innovative ways politicians are using information technology is discussed in an article from *Campaigns & Elections*. Finally, "Democracy On-Line" from *The Futurist* speculates on the "electronic town meeting"—a possibility in the near future.

THE NATIONAL INFORMATION INFRASTRUCTURE: POLICYMAKING AND POLICYMAKERS[1]

Introduction

Communications policymaking in the United States is complex and unfocused. It is described by its acolytes as "an often paralyzing task," "an endless policy loop," a "tangled web," and a "regulatory round robin."

[1]Article by Fred H. Cate, associate professor of law at the Indiana University School of Law, Bloomington, from *Stanford Law & Policy Review* 6:43–54 '94. Copyright © 1994 by the Board of Trustees of the Leland Stanford Junior University. Reprinted with permission.

Yet the extension from communications to *information* policymaking poses even greater challenges. The creation, manipulation, storage, transmission, and use of information constitute both a vital component of the U.S. economy and an essential underpinning of other critical sectors. These activities pose a wide range of serious issues that may only be exceeded in number and diversity by the policymakers responsible for dealing with them.

This article examines three intertwined features of information policymaking—the vital role played by information in modern society, the diversity of issues that information products and services present, and the proliferation of information-related policymakers—and the extent to which the Administration has responded by narrowing and centralizing its policymaking inquiry. The article concludes by recommending a broader, more comprehensive approach to information policymaking, one that takes its direction less from the White House and more from the issues and experts involved in the policymaking process. As Henry Geller, a former General Counsel of the Federal Communications Commission (FCC) and the first Administrator of the National Telecommunications and Information Administration (NTIA), has written: "The Information Age, with its global competition, demands that we put our policy house in order."

The Role of Information

The "information superhighway" is all the rage today. According to the Clinton Administration's *Agenda for Action,* the potential benefits of the National Information Infrastructure (NII) are "immense":

The NII will enable U.S. firms to compete and win in the global economy, generating good jobs for the American people and economic growth for the nation. As importantly, the NII promises to transform the lives of the American people. It can ameliorate the constraints of geography and economic status, and give all Americans a fair opportunity to go as far as their talents and ambitions will take them.

Vice President Al Gore and Secretary of Commerce Ron Brown have canvassed the country claiming the NII will "bring an era of unprecedented prosperity to America." "In the future," according to one White House briefing paper, "the NII will enable all Americans to get the information they need, when they need it and where they need it, for an affordable price."

Whether an advanced information infrastructure is the key to the Promised Land remains to be seen. But information is nevertheless a key component of the U.S. (as well as the global) economy. Although figures vary, information services and products are either the first or second largest sector of the U.S. economy, accounting for between 10% and 12% of Gross Domestic Product. Taken together, telephone companies, information service providers, communications equipment manufacturers, and computer hardware and software companies account for more than 4.5 million U.S. jobs. The Commerce Department predicted in November 1993 that information sector revenues that year would reach $610 billion, up 8% from 1992.

Even these figures do not represent the real importance of information and, therefore, the real significance of the information infrastructure in the United States. "Information," writes Anne Branscomb, legal scholar-in-residence at Harvard University's Program on Information Resources Policy, "is the lifeblood that sustains political, social, and business decisions." Noncommunications businesses rely as much on information services and products as do telephone companies and computer manufacturers. During the 1980s, U.S. business alone invested $1 trillion in information technology. Between one-half and two-thirds of the U.S. workforce is in information-based jobs.

Consider, for example, the growing market for financial services—banking, securities and commodities trading, letters of credit, currency conversions, and loan guarantees. Approximately 5% of U.S. services exports are financial services; as of mid-1992, the United States held 66.3% of the world market for financial services. What is a global financial system but a "network of information"? As a result, banks in the United States and elsewhere are investing heavily in information technologies.

Information is equally significant for the activities of government. According to the Clinton Administration's *National Performance Review,* the "[f]ederal government lacks appropriate access to most effective, cost-efficient, information technology products and services." These services, the report predicts, can overcome "the barriers of time and distance to perform the business of government and give people public information when and where they want [it]." The importance of information is not limited to telephone and computer companies; it is indeed the lifeblood of modern society.

Information Policymakers and Policy Making

POLICY OBJECTIVES

During the 1992 presidential campaign, Bill Clinton and Al Gore pledged to make deployment of a "national information network" a priority of their Administration. The impetus for this commitment apparently came from Gore, who, as a Member of the House of Representatives, proposed a "nationwide network of fiber optic 'data highways'" in 1979. As a Senator and Chair of the Senate Subcommittee on Science, Technology and Space, Gore introduced proposals for a National Research and Education Network as the "Department of Energy High-Performance Computing Act" (S. 1976) in 1989 and the "High-Performance Computing Act" (S. 272) in 1991. Gore found a like-minded "fellow traveller" in Bill Clinton. Together, they campaigned on a promise to create a network that would "link every home, business, lab, classroom and library by the year 2015."

Once in office, the President and Vice President moved quickly. On February 22, 1993, just 28 days after the inauguration, they unveiled a five-part strategy for building the "National Information Infrastructure," described in subsequent releases as consisting of:

(1) thousands of interconnected, interoperable telecommunications networks, (2) computer systems, televisions, fax machines, telephones, and other "information appliances", (3) software, information services, and information databases (e.g., "digital libraries"), and (4) trained people who can build, maintain, and operate these systems

The Clinton/Gore strategy, *Technology for America's Economic Growth: A New Direction to Build Economic Strength,* included the following goals:

• Implement the High-Performance Computing and Communications Program, to help develop the basic technology needed for the NII.

• Through the Information Infrastructure Technology and Applications program, work with industry, universities, and federal government labs to develop technologies needed to support NII applications.

• Provide matching grants through the National Telecommunications and Information Administration to assist states, local

governments, universities and school systems, hospitals and other
health care providers, and other non-profit entities in NII pilot
projects.
  • Promote dissemination of Federal information through
consistent Federal information policies designed to ensure that
Federal information is made available at a fair price to as many
users as possible while encouraging the growth of the information
industry.
  • Reform telecommunications policies to afford a consistent,
stable regulatory environment necessary to encouraging private
sector investment in the NII.
  The Administration has energetically pursued the first four
strategies, with little fanfare and with perhaps even less consultation with relevant government agencies. The Administration sought $1 billion for the High-Performance Computing
and Communications Program and an additional $96 million to
focus specifically on Information Infrastructure Technologies
and Applications. The Administration has requested $40 million
for research by the Department of Energy's National Labs on
the Information Infrastructure and $600 million for the Tech-
nology Reinvestment Project, which funds technological development of NII applications in health care, manufacturing,
electronic commerce, and education and training. NTIA has
announced $26 million in matching grants to support NII appli-
cation pilot projects by not-for-profit organizations; the Administration has pledged to seek $100 million for these grants next
year.
  The Office of Management and Budget issued a circular in
June 1993 to encourage agencies to increase citizen access to public information. The *National Performance Review* report, released
in September 1993, contains eleven recommendations for the
improved use of information technology, including the creation
of a Government Information Technology Services Group to develop a "strategic vision" for the federal government's use of information technologies. The Administration has launched a series of inquiries into electronic dissemination of government
information and the use of networks for intra- and inter-
government communications. While it awaits the final outcome of
those inquiries, the Administration is making widespread use of
electronic bulletin boards (available through Internet, commercial services, and direct telephone links) to disseminate speeches,

press briefings, executive orders, and key Administration documents. As of February 10, 1994, the Administration had published electronically more than 1600 documents and had processed more than 220,000 electronic requests for information since September 1, 1993. The Fiscal Year 1995 budget includes $18 million for a new system to electronically distribute government information.

The fifth strategy—reforming telecommunications policy—is taking longer to achieve and involves the Clinton Administration's most visible information-related activities. The Administration released its *Agenda for Action* on September 15, 1993. Although ostensibly the product of an Information Infrastructure Task Force, the *Agenda for Action* was a White House initiative, led by Vice President Gore and Secretary Brown. The *Agenda for Action* sets forth the Administration's vision for the NII. While stressing that the private sector will "predominate" in developing, deploying and paying for the nation's information infrastructure, the *Agenda for Action* notes that "the government has an essential role to play." The *Agenda for Action* identifies nine "principles and goals" to guide the government's NII policies:

(1) Promote private sector investment. . . .
(2) Extend the "universal service" concept to ensure that information resources are available to all at affordable prices. . . .
(3) Act as a catalyst to promote technological innovation and new applications . . . [through] important government research programs and grants. . . .
(4) Promote seamless, interactive, user-driven operation of the NII . . . [to] ensure that users can transfer information across networks easily and efficiently.
(5) Ensure information security and network reliability. . . .
(6) Improve management of the radio frequency spectrum. . . .
(7) Protect intellectual property rights. . . .
(8) Coordinate with other levels of government and with other nations . . . to avoid unnecessary obstacles and to prevent unfair policies that handicap U.S. industry.
(9) Provide access to government information and improve government procurement.

By the time of the Vice President's remarks at the National Press Club on December 21, 1993—the first public statement on the NII by the Vice President since announcement of the *Agenda for Action* in September—the Administration had narrowed these essential principles guiding NII policy to five:

First, encourage private investment. . . .

Second, promote and protect competition . . . [and] prevent unfair cross-subsidies and act to avoid information bottlenecks that would limit consumer choice, or limit the ability of new information providers to reach their customers.

Third, provide open access to the network. . . . We need to ensure the NII, just like the PC, is open and accessible to everyone with a good idea who has a product they want to sell. . . .

Fourth, we want to avoid creating a society of information "haves" and "have nots." . . . The less fortunate sectors of the population must have access to a minimum level of information services through subsidies or other forms of a public interest tithe.

Fifth and finally: we want to encourage flexibility. . . . Technology is advancing so rapidly, the structure of the industry is changing so quickly, that we must have policies broad enough to accommodate change.

As noted by Secretary Brown, three of the Vice President's five goals address one issue: managing competition. Thus, the *Agenda for Action*'s original list of nine objectives is now reduced to three over-arching goals for the Clinton Administration's Information policymaking: manage competition between and among competing information product and service providers; assure regulatory flexibility; and provide for universal service—however defined—for all Americans. Virtually all Administration speeches and testimony concerning the NII have repeated these goals.

Such consistency is noteworthy in itself. On the one hand, the broad variety of information policymakers singing in harmony reflects the Administration's success in imposing some order on the policymaking process. On the other hand, such diverse policymakers all singing with one voice, in unison with the Vice President, raises concerns about the likely effectiveness of that process in identifying and resolving critical and difficult information policy issues. In addition, the government's narrowed focus has eclipsed other important issues originally identified in the *Agenda for Action*, such as the application of intellectual property rights to information networks. Both the centralization of the policymaking process and the exclusion of relevant issues from the Administration's agenda are discussed in greater detail below.

Information Policymakers

EXECUTIVE BRANCH AND INDEPENDENT AGENCIES

Given the importance of information, it is not surprising that it falls within the purview of multiple government agencies. What is surprising is the sheer number of government entities with jurisdiction over some facet of information creation, storage, transmission, manipulation, and use. No single agency is vested with primary jurisdiction or responsibility for coordinating information policymaking. Kimberly Patch, writing in *PC Week* magazine, observed that the development of the NII is being guided by a "virtual alphabet soup of government agencies." Her reference to "more than a dozen government entities," however, underestimates the number of regulators involved. Admittedly, the prospect of the NII has rapidly organized the efforts of at least some of these entities, particularly the many executive branch and independent agencies involved. It has helped to coordinate their often disparate, even contradictory, policies, while at the same time bringing them more into line with the Administration's focus on managing competition in the information marketplace, assuring regulatory flexibility, and guaranteeing universal service.

Much of the leadership on NII-related issues comes from the Department of Commerce. Secretary Brown chairs the Information Infrastructure Task Force, created by the Clinton Administration on September 15, 1993, to guide development of the NII. Larry Irving, Assistant Secretary of Commerce for Communication and Information and NTIA Administrator, chairs the Task Force's Telecommunications Policy Committee and its Universal Service Working Group and Legislative Drafting Task Force. NTIA performs a number of important functions regarding communications and information. The agency serves as the President's principal advisor on telecommunications policies. It also coordinates telecommunications activities and policies within the Administration, conducts studies and makes recommendations on a wide range of telecommunications and information technology issues, and funds research into telecommunications applications. Further, it coordinates federal government use of the broadcast spectrum; participates in representing the Administration on communication issues before Congress, state regulators, and the FCC; and develops policies and programs regarding the regulation of domestic telecommunications industries, and the representation and promotion of U.S. telecommunications industries and interests in multinational conferences and negotiations. The bulk of NII-related executive actions falls within the purview of the NII.

Department of Commerce officials fill other key NII posts. Carol Darr, Deputy General Counsel of the Department of Commerce, chairs the International Telecommunications Policy Working Group. Arati Prabhakar, Director of the National Institute of Standards and Technology in the Department of Commerce, chairs the Applications and Technology Committee. Bruce Lehman, Assistant Secretary of Commerce for Patents and Trademarks, chairs the Intellectual Property Working Group. Jerry Gates, from the Department of Commerce Census Bureau, chairs the Privacy Working Group. The Department of Commerce also serves as Secretariat to the National Information Infrastructure Advisory Council, a 37-member group advising the Task Force. Also represented among the NII Task Force leadership are the Office of Management and Budget, Department of the Treasury, Advanced Research Projects Agency, and the Department of Health and Human Services.

Notably absent from the list of NII Task Force leaders is anyone from the FCC, the independent regulatory agency created by the Communications Act of 1934 and responsible for regulating all interstate and foreign communication by wire, radio, television, satellite, and cable. This omission may be due in part to the fact that, as an independent agency, the Commission is not part of the Executive Branch. When the NII Task Force was formed in September 1993, the Senate had not yet confirmed Commission Chairman Reed Hundt. It is nonetheless surprising that no other Commissioner or senior FCC staff member with primary communications policymaking responsibility was given a leadership role on the Task Force.

The FCC has extensive, although not always successful, experience promoting and regulating competition among telecommunications industries and assuring universal service in both telephone and over-the-air television service—the points of the Administration's current NII initiative. It is also the only federal agency with statutory jurisdiction over those responsibilities. Although Chairman Hundt has close ties to the Vice President and although they appear to share common ground on many information-related issues, the absence of the FCC from the NII Task Force leadership may prove especially troublesome when, and if, it comes time to implement Task Force recommendations.

The FCC, however, does participate in deliberations of the Task Force, along with many other federal agencies, including the Departments of Agriculture, Education, Energy, Housing and Urban Development, Interior, Justice, State, and Veterans Affairs, the Central Intelligence Agency, Environmental Protection Agency, Federal Trade Commission, General Services Administration, National Economic Council, National Science Foundation, White House Office of Science and Technology Policy, and the Vice President himself. The General Accounting Office also plays a significant role, in large part through its reports and studies of information technologies.

Other Executive Branch and independent agencies, while unrepresented on the NII Task Force, exercise substantial responsibility for information policy. The Antitrust Division of the Department of Justice advises the U.S. District Court overseeing the Modified Final Judgment—which broke up AT&T's telephone-service monopoly—regarding applications for waivers from the decree's restrictions on AT&T and local telephone-service providers. The Antitrust Division also develops competition policy, monitors compliance, and enforces antitrust laws. The Copyright Office in the Library of Congress and, as noted, the Assistant Secretary of Commerce for Patents and Trademarks, respond to the intellectual property challenges presented by digital information and enforce existing intellectual property laws.

The U.S. Trade Representative oversees international trade in information services and products and its impact on U.S. foreign relations. Information is inherently global and of such economic importance that it frequently is at the heart of international trade disputes. The United States has applied a variety of trade statutes—including the Omnibus Trade and Competition Act of 1988, the Telecommunications Trade Act of 1988, the Export Administration Act of 1979, and the International Security Assistance and Arms Export Control Act of 1976—to information services and products. U.S. Trade Representative Mickey Kantor has threatened action against the European Community and Japan for alleged unfair trading practices related to information products. Other officials involved in U.S. international information trade policy include the U.S. Coordinator for International

Communications and Information Policy in the Department of State, who is aided by an industry Advisory Committee on International Communications and Information Policy, and the International Trade Administration in the Department of Commerce.

OTHER FEDERAL AND STATE POLICYMAKERS

Congress affects information policymaking through a number of committees and advisory bodies. In addition to the traditional oversight exercised through appropriations and Senate confirmation proceedings, Congress has created a wide range of specialized committees and subcommittees dealing with telecommunications, intellectual property, constitutional (particularly First Amendment) issues, technical standards, government information, competition, and international trade in information products and services. The Congressional Budget Office evaluates the financial impact of proposed information policies and Congress' Office of Technology Assessment issues a wide variety of influential reports on the impact and regulation of information.

Although often overlooked, federal—and, to a lesser degree, state—courts play a substantial role in both developing and enforcing U.S. information policy. Not only may interested parties appeal adverse agency decisions, civil litigation between and among interested parties and the federal government has laid much of the de facto regulatory groundwork. For example, the U.S. Supreme Court's decisions in *Sony Corp. of Am. v. Universal City Studios, Inc.* and *Feist Publications, Inc. v. Rural Tel. Serv. Co.* did more to establish the parameters of "fair use" and the copyrightability of databases, respectively, than any administrative pronouncement. Also consider U.S. District Court Judge Harold Greene's role in the case brought by the Department of Justice against AT&T. Though Judge Greene rendered his decision approving the Modified Final Judgment in 1982, he has retained jurisdiction under the consent decree to control the operations of both AT&T and the Regional Holding Companies (RHCs). The court's control over U.S. telecommunications is so great that the RHCs have spent more than a decade litigating and lobbying to be freed from restrictions imposed by the decree. Most recently, the RHCs have applied to Judge Greene to remove the decree altogether. The breadth of that decree and the substantial discretion given judges to interpret antitrust laws, "probably makes him the single most powerful decisionmaker in U.S. communications policy today." It is little wonder Judge Greene is often referred to as the "telecom czar."

State and local governments also regulate telecommunications service providers, particularly local telephone and cable operators. Every state has a regulatory agency (i.e., Public Utility Commission or Public Service Commission) responsible for overseeing intrastate telecommunications. These state organizations not only exercise considerable power over telephone service within their respective states, they also act collectively through the National Association of Regulatory Utility Commissioners and with the FCC on Federal-State Joint Boards. In addition, many cities exercise some continuing control over cable television through local franchising authority. These cities may act collectively on issues of common concern through the National League of Cities.

In short, information policymaking in the United States involves every cabinet department, more than 100 Executive Branch and independent agencies, two dozen Congressional committees, subcommittees and expert advisory bodies, the federal courts, 51 state utilities commissions, and literally thousands of local regulators. These figures include none of the international policymaking institutions (e.g., International Telecommunications Union, World Intellectual Property Organization), domestic standard-setting bodies (e.g., American National Standards Institute, Institute of Electrical & Electronics Engineers), public interest groups (e.g., Action for Children's Television, Media Access Project), research centers (e.g., The Annenberg Washington Program in Communications Policy Studies, Columbia Institute for Tele-Information), or the many private industry associations (e.g., Information Industry Association, Telecommunications Industry Association), which all seek to influence the shape of the government's information policy.

The number and variety of information policymakers and organizations seeking to affect the policymaking process have always challenged the ability of government to identify and pursue rational, consistent, and effective information policies. President Johnson's Task Force on Communications Policy recognized 26 years ago the serious problems created by the absence of a single source of "coordinated and comprehensive policy advice"

in the more limited realm of communications policymaking. The
breadth of issues and players involved in information policymaking only makes the situation worse. To its credit, the Clinton
Administration has recognized the need for greater coordination
and, through its NII Task Force, has taken the first steps towards
achieving it. Those steps, however, have not come without costs.
The Administration's efforts have centralized and politicized the
policymaking process and excluded other important issues from
the Administration's agenda.

Expanding the Scope of Information Policymaking

The government has responded to the extraordinary breadth
of issues and entities involved in information policymaking by
narrowing the scope of inquiry. Senior Administration officials
promote only three of the original nine policy principles listed in
the *Agenda for Action:* encourage competition between and among
information product and service providers; assure regulatory
flexibility; and provide for universal service. The Administration
has deferred, dismissed, or relegated the remaining principles to
the bottom of its policymaking agenda. Given the central role the
NII initiative and the Task Force play in coordinating and orient-
ing the information policymaking efforts of many agencies, the
focus on three issues to the exclusion of others, such as privacy
and intellectual property, has a trickle-down effect in and outside
the government. As a result, key substantive issues go unresolved.
More importantly, the process of information policymaking—the
very means through which the substantive issues can be
addressed—is thwarted in two ways. First, the Administration's
top-down, focused approach unintentionally skews the debate
and overestimates the importance of its objectives. Second, this
approach obscures the significance of the principles either identified but not addressed publicly, or those omitted altogether.

The Focus on Universal Service

The ramifications of narrowing the policymaking inquiry are
nowhere clearer than in the focus on universal service, one of the
three objectives the Administration champions. The Administration has widely touted universal service as an essential principle

guiding its information policymaking efforts. Universal service is certainly an important goal, but the Administration's singular commitment raises a number of questions, both about universal service itself and its impact on the policymaking process.

Universal service has historically been a minimalist commitment to providing a single, basic service—what is sometimes called Plain Old Telephone Service (POTS). POTS means no advanced information services, no unlimited calling, not even a telephone itself—just a single line connecting each house to the telephone network. Universal service did not occur overnight. The telephone was developed in the late 1870s and was commercially available for more than 50 years before passage of the Communications Act of 1934, which required universal service. Had universal service been an obligation from the outset, it would likely have stymied early expansion of the telephone network. Robert W. Lucky, Vice President of Applied Research at Bellcore, asked at a recent NII conference: "Would Internet have ever gotten started if people had presumed from the start that you have to have universal access? It is a great simplification to talk about some of these things as absolutes and not talk about the costs and timetable for those things happening." Even after more than a century of experience with the telephone, the United States has still achieved only a 94% national penetration rate, leaving 5.7 million homes without telephone service. Approximately 12% of African American and Hispanic homes have no telephone service; 17%, or one in six families, lack telephone service in the rural south and urban centers of America's largest cities. More than 20% of African American, Asian American, and Hispanic homes in California have no telephones. Even in the nation's capital, 12% of homes have no telephone service and the number of unserved residents is increasing—more than 6% between 1984 and 1992—as it is in other parts of the country. The Administration should be cautious about trying to emulate this "success."

Universal service has always been linked to monopolies and extensive government regulation. Prior to its breakup, AT&T could be counted on to provide universal service as part of its monopoly over U.S. telephone service. In fact, it was Theodore Vail, President of AT&T, who first coined the phrase "universal service" in 1910. After the break-up of AT&T, the Regional Holding Companies, which provide local telephone service on a monopoly basis, continued universal service partly because they were and are heavily regulated near-monopolists. In television, the government's extensive regulation of the industry facilitated its commitment to over-the-air television without direct charge. That commitment has created an intricate system of expensive indirect charges, for example, in prices paid for products advertised on television.

It is far more difficult to define universal service in an environment with as many information services and providers as the NII. Does universal service mean free access or low-cost access to some basic tier of services or to all services? Such distinctions will matter far more in the NII than they do today in telephone service (e.g., whether telephone access comes with call-waiting or without). An NII universal service commitment that does not go beyond the information equivalent of POTS will greatly divide the information "haves" and "have-nots," despite the Administration's populist rhetoric. Yet a more sweeping definition of universal service will impose high costs and threatens to delay widespread deployment of the NII.

Unfortunately, the focus on universal service has thus far obscured, rather than clarified, these issues, and, as a result, the process and players seem to be taking their cues from above. Rather than drawing on their expertise, experience, and ability to collect information from within industries or markets, these policymakers often seem to be imposing on these resources an agenda that originated in the White House or elsewhere among senior officials. The phrase "universal service" has become a mantra. The Vice President says it; the Secretary of Commerce says it; the Assistant Secretary says it; soon, people both in government and out are chanting it, especially when looking for preferment or grants in the NII process.

In addition to distorting the debate about its definition, merits, and costs, the focus on universal service distracts senior Administration officials from other policy goals. Assistant Secretary of Commerce Larry Irving, sounding a familiar Administration theme, recently said: "If 1992 was the year of the woman, 1994 promises to be the year of universal service." As important as universal service may be, the Administration's intense focus on it clouds the full range of objectives necessary if the government's information policy is to effectively guide the rapid, cost-effective deployment of a technologically advanced, digital infrastructure offering a wide range of information, communication and entertainment services.

The Missing Principles

Among the objectives the Administration is overlooking are intellectual property and the First Amendment. Although the *Agenda for Action* stressed the importance of protecting intellectual property rights efficiently and effectively in a digital environment, subsequent Administration actions have largely ignored this goal. The First Amendment has been ignored from the beginning. Whether this is a result of the focus on universal service (and ensuring competition while providing for regulatory flexibility), or the understandable desire to avoid controversial issues, is unclear. What is clear is that the failure to address both intellectual property and free-expression issues not only threatens the success of the NII, but also reflects a failure of the policymaking process itself.

INTELLECTUAL PROPERTY

According to the *Agenda for Action:*

The broad public interest in promoting the dissemination of information to our citizens must be balanced with the need to ensure the integrity of intellectual property rights and copyrights in information and entertainment products. This protection is crucial if these products—whether in the form of text, images, computer programs, databases, video or sound recordings, or multimedia formats—are to move in commerce using the full capability of the NII.

Protecting the integrity of digital works is likely to require revision of U.S. intellectual property laws, designed for a world in which copying was difficult, economically impractical, and relatively easy to regulate by focusing on the physical manifestation of the work and the actual incident of copying (e.g., photocopying a book). As more information becomes available in digital format, and technologies for digital copying are increasingly widespread and affordable, U.S. intellectual property law will become more and more outmoded.

In addition, U.S. copyright law protects only original expression. The Supreme Court held in *Feist* that a compilation, such as a database, can be copyrighted only "if it features an original selection or arrangement of facts," and the copyright protection is "limited to the particular selection or arrangement." Computerized databases, which can be searched by text strings or key words, rarely feature "original" organization. Under *Feist,* no matter how many resources were invested in creating a complex database, it would not be protected by copyright law. As a result, database creators today protect their investment through contracts and high user fees—disfavored by NII proponents' emphasis on open access.

Inability to resolve these issues threatens the success of the NII. Protecting intellectual property and responding to the challenges of digital technology are more than just moral or legal imperatives. Copyright is, according to the United States Supreme Court, "the engine of free expression. By establishing a marketplace right to the use of one's expression, copyright supplies the economic incentive to create and disseminate ideas." Failure to protect copyrights, patents, and trademarks will undermine the incentive to create. The *Agenda for Action* stressed that the Task Force should "[e]xamine the adequacy of copyright laws" and "explore ways to identify and reimburse copyright owners" through either alternative market structures or new technologies. These are important inquiries that the Administration should not ignore or defer.

Yet intellectual property issues have apparently slipped from senior Administration officials' fields of view. These issues receive nowhere near the same attention from the Vice President and Task Force leaders as, for example, universal service does. A Task Force working group is examining these issues; perhaps its preliminary draft report, *Intellectual Property and the National Information Infrastructure,* will generate more interest from the Administration, Congress, and the public. Certainly the communities that create and disseminate programming are concerned. But the lack of overt attention from senior officials, and the vague, shadowy impression that the Administration might eventually take some action in this area, combine to dissipate the pressure for action and the incentive for attention. The identification of intellectual property issues in the *Agenda for Action,* followed by their subsequent disappearance from high-level discussion, has created a wait-and-see atmosphere. The Copyright Office and the Intellectual Property Working Group toil on, but the NII leadership's attention is focused elsewhere. As a result, their efforts go largely unnoticed, except by concerned outsiders who are persuaded to wait.

The First Amendment

None of the Administration's NII pronouncements mention the First Amendment. It does not appear in the *Agenda for Action* or in a single speech by Vice President Gore, Secretary Brown, Assistant Secretary Irving, or any other senior Administration official. Free expression is not the subject of any NII committee or working group.

The omission of the First Amendment from information policy is all the more significant in light of the substantial regulatory role that the Administration anticipates the government should play. In his December 21, 1993, address at the National Press Club, the Vice President analogized the current information marketplace to the environment that, in his view, permitted the sinking of the *Titanic:*

Why did the ship that couldn't be sunk steam full speed into an ice field? For in the last few hours before the *Titanic* collided, other ships were sending messages like this one from the *Mesaba:* "Lat 42N to 41.25 Long 49W to Long 50.30W. Saw much heavy pack ice and great number large icebergs also field ice." And why, when the *Titanic* operators sent distress signal after distress signal did so few ships respond? The answer is that—as the investigations proved—the wireless business then was just that, a business. Operators had no obligation to remain on duty. They were to do what was profitable. When the day's work was done—often the lucrative transmissions from wealthy passengers—operators shut off their sets and went to sleep. . . . Ironically, that tragedy resulted in the first efforts to regulate the airwaves. Why did government get involved? Because there are certain public needs that outweigh private interests.

The Vice President's vision of the proper role of the government's information policy, to judge from the *Titanic* example, is to regulate the information infrastructure, to restrain those "private interests" that are outweighed by unspecified "public needs." It is no wonder that the First Amendment is not mentioned, because it would pose a clear obstacle to such regulation. The provision of information products and services is a profitable business. To lament that fact both undermines the government's reliance on private investment to deploy the NII and raises important First Amendment issues.

The Supreme Court has found that the First Amendment's simple command—"Congress shall make no law . . . abridging freedom of speech or of the press"—erects a very high barrier to government intrusion into communications. Under the First Amendment, governmental regulations based on the content of expression are generally subject to "strict scrutiny" by courts. In the context of over-the-air broadcasting, however, the Court requires only that broadcasting regulation be "narrowly tailored" to achieve a "substantial government interest." That lower standard is premised upon the physical scarcity of the electromagnetic spectrum, which permits the operation of only a finite number of broadcast stations and therefore, according to the Court, permits greater regulation of broadcast programming.

The developing information infrastructure has little to do with over-the-air broadcasting. Instead of scarce electromagnetic spectrum, the infrastructure utilizes the abundant capacity of fiber optics. As a result, proposed regulations dealing with the content of information provided via the NII would likely be subject to "strict scrutiny" by courts. This conclusion is supported by the Supreme Court's recent decision in *Turner Broadcasting Sys., Inc. v. FCC*. In that case, eight Justices supported the proposition that "the rationale for applying a less rigorous standard of First Amendment scrutiny to broadcast regulation . . . does not apply in the context of cable regulation." The abundant capacity of the cables that deliver television to the home is multiplied many times in the networks that form today's Internet and tomorrow's NII. But even if treated under the less restrictive test reserved for over-the-air broadcasting, such regulations would still have to meet the "substantial government interest" test. And that less restrictive test is under fire as the proliferation of media technologies undermines the scarcity justification for permitting some content-based regulation of broadcast programming.

The First Amendment is vital to the NII because it reflects a constitutional commitment not only to free expression, but also to reaping the benefits of free expression without government interference. "[A] cardinal tenet of the First Amendment is that governmental intervention in the marketplace of ideas . . . is not acceptable and should not be tolerated." The First Amendment also serves as a positive barrier to impermissible restrictions on information. No matter how desirable such restrictions may be in the eyes of the Vice President, the Task Force, the Congress, or anybody else, the First Amendment forbids policies that abridge the freedom of speech.

Information policymaking that ignores the First Amendment wastes time and resources; it fundamentally disserves the public interest. The absence of the First Amendment from the policymaking debate calls into question the debate itself. How serious is the commitment to the NII and to assuring access for everyone, if the policymaking process ignores the principles and limits of the First Amendment? One is reminded of the politically popular but constitutionally deficient actions of a unanimous U.S. Senate in banning indecent telephone calls and flag-burning—the latter only three months after the Supreme Court had found that flag-burning was constitutionally protected—only to have both provisions struck down by the Supreme Court. Such actions undermine policymakers' commitment and their wisdom. Given Congress' renewed interest in regulating the content of broadcast television, cable television, and video games, the First Amendment fills a more crucial role than ever in information policymaking. Ithiel de Sola Pool wrote more than a decade ago about the ironic tendency of policymakers to seek to regulate new information technologies:

The easy access, low cost, and distributed intelligence of modern means of communication are a prime reason for hope. The democratic impulse to regulate evils, as Tocqueville warned, is ironically a reason for worry. Lack of technical grasp by policy makers and their propensity to solve problems of conflict, privacy, intellectual property, and monopoly by accustomed bureaucratic routines are the main reasons for concern. But as long as the First Amendment stands, backed by courts which take it seriously, the loss of liberty is not foreordained. The commitment of American culture to pluralism and individual rights is reason for optimism, as is the pliancy and profusion of electronic technology.

Conclusion

Information policymaking today is dominated by the number and diversity of issues and parties that it involves. These two features vastly complicate the task of information policymaking and also substantially increase the cost of delay or failure in achieving rational, effective information policies. The Clinton Administration deserves enormous credit for both recognizing the widespread importance of information and seeking to address explicitly the complexities of information policymaking. Yet the most tangible manifestations of the Administration's response in the policymaking arena reflect neither the ambition nor the comprehensiveness of the Administration's early moves to organize information policymaking.

Faced with a dazzling array of difficult issues and often conflicting principles, the Administration has chosen to concentrate its most visible energies on only three. This approach is skewing the policy debate about those areas of inquiry, while restricting discussion of other important issues. A more comprehensive and balanced approach, incorporating the broad array of issues identified in the September 1993 *Agenda for Action* and critical First Amendment concerns, is necessary. Such an agenda, addressed by the wide range of policymakers with expertise in, and responsibility for, information policy, should be driving the information policymaking process.

THE UNDERPINNINGS OF PRIVACY PROTECTION[2]

The concept of privacy as a separate right was first articulated over 100 years ago when then attorney Louis Brandeis and Samuel Warren wrote an article in the *Harvard Law Review* urging recognition of a right to privacy, or as they so eloquently phrased it, the "right to be let alone". Law review articles, however, are not the same as legislative acts. For several decades only a scattering of jurisdictions have recognized this right, permitting private tort actions and invasions of privacy. For example, the Court of Appeals for the District of Columbia cited the Brandeis and Warren article as the source of the District's common-law action for invasion of privacy in *Pearson vs. Dodd*, 410 F.2d 701, 703 (1968). Significantly, these early privacy cases do not deal with the question of governmental invasions of privacy, but with civil tort actions brought by one individual against another.

The government's involvement in privacy was the subject of an important Supreme Court decision in *Olmstead vs. United States*. Before discussing this constitutional milestone, it is important to elaborate on an axiom which underlies much of the privacy discussion to follow.

The U.S. Constitution is essentially a limitation on government power. It was written over 200 years ago in an effort to strike a balance between the need for greater governmental authority in the 13 newly independent colonies and the fears that government represented the greatest threat to individual liberty.

[2]Article by Frank M. Tuerkheimer, professor of law at the University of Wisconsin, from *Communications of the ACM* 36:69–73 Ag '93. Copyright © 1993 by *Communications of the ACM*. Reprinted with permission.

The founding fathers based their fears on several hundred years of British history during which the Crown fought intensively to retain its political and economic prerogatives.

Ultimately, the Constitution represented the compromise between the twin evils of anarchy and tyranny. The principle mechanism by which this compromise was reached was to separate powers at the federal level into three branches and then to specifically enumerate the totality of those powers, inferentially leaving the remaining powers to the states. This compromise was not enough to ensure adoption of the Constitution. Many were concerned that it did not contain sufficient specific restraints on government power. As a result, 10 amendments, which we call the Bill of Rights, were added to the Constitution.

There can be no doubt that the drafters of the Bill of Rights looked to the British experience and the abuses of the Crown to determine exactly what kind of governmental conduct should be prohibited. One of those abuses was the historical practice of the Crown of invading and searching persons' homes and then utilizing the information obtained in subsequent criminal prosecution. As a result, the Fourth Amendment to the Constitution provides that:

The right of the people to be secure in their persons, house, papers and effects against unreasonable searches and seizures shall not be violated; and no warrants shall issue but upon probable cause, supported by oath or affirmation and particularly describing the place to be searched and the persons or things to be seized.

To understand some of the major privacy issues currently on the national agenda in the U.S., the scope of the Bill of Rights must be examined. Persons generally labeled as "conservative" in legal parlance say judges should not be allowed to expand the protections of the Bill of Rights beyond its specifically enumerated provisions. The argument underlying this view is that judges with lifetime tenure will legislate their own particular views of constitutional scope if allowed to expand the document in that manner. Such judicial legislation is undemocratic and undesirable because federal judges are the government officials least responsible to the electorate.

The opposing view, which was at one time the prevailing Supreme Court view on the Constitution but may no longer be, is that the Constitution represents a broad statement against governmental excess. Thus, it cannot retain any vitality if it is interpreted to prohibit only those excesses engaged in by the British

Crown in the 500 years before the American revolution. According to this view, the intent of the writers of the Constitution in limiting government's powers is a guide to its interpretation, not a limitation on it. Some of the leading constitutional cases of the past half century have been predicated on this approach, including *Brown vs. Board of Education* (striking down school segregation), *Griswold vs. Connecticut* (striking down Connecticut's prohibitions on the sale of contraceptives), and *Roe vs. Wade* (striking down prohibitions against abortion). Certainly the latter two contain explicit privacy protection components.

The defendants in *Olmstead* were convicted of violating the National Prohibition Act. Evidence of the defendants' involvement in a large-scale liquor importation and distribution conspiracy originated with a wiretap placed on several of their telephones by federal agents without a court order. The defendants urged that this violated their Fourth Amendment rights. A majority of the Supreme Court held that protection of the sanctity of one's home, governed by the Fourth Amendment, did not apply to telephone communications. Justice Brandeis, the author of the famous *Law Review* article on privacy 30 years earlier, dissented.

Justice Brandeis's dissent was predicated on the notion that the words of the Constitution were designed to "approach immortality as nearly as human institutions can approach it" and that "in the application of a constitution, . . . our contemplation cannot be only of what has been but of what may be." He readily acknowledged that the Fourth Amendment was directed against invasions of the sanctity of the home, but added that "time works changes, brings into existence new conditions and purposes. Subtler and more far-reaching means of invading privacy have become available to the Government. . . . [A] principle to be vital must be capable of a wider application than the mischief which gave it birth. This is particularly true of constitutions."

Brandeis then shifted privacy concepts from the "right to be let alone" value of his earlier article to communications privacy. Relying on a case that applied constitutional protection to the mail, he noted there was no difference between a sealed letter and a private phone call. In fact, "the evil incident to invasion of the privacy of the telephone is far greater" because "the privacy of persons at both ends of the line is invaded. . . . [t]he tapping of a man's telephone line involves the tapping of every other person whom he may call or who may call him." His synthesis of the two privacy concepts under what he felt should be constitutional protection then followed:

The makers of our Constitution undertook to secure conditions favorable to the pursuit of happiness. They recognized the significance of man's spiritual nature, of his feelings, of his intellect. They knew that only a part of the pain, pleasure and satisfactions of life are to be found in material things. They sought to protect Americans in their beliefs, their thoughts, their emotions and their sensations. They conferred, as against the Government, the right to be let alone—the most comprehensive of rights and the right most valued by civilized men. To protect that right, every unjustifiable intrusion by the Government upon the privacy of the individual whatever the means employed, must be deemed a violation of the Fourth Amendment.

Brandeis's dissent in *Olmstead* became the law in the U.S. approximately 40 years later in *Katz vs. United States*. In overruling the *Olmstead* case, the Supreme Court in *Katz* held that "the Fourth Amendment protects people, not places. . . . [W]hat [a person] seeks to preserve as private, even in an area accessible to the public, may be constitutionally protected." Because there was a "reasonable expectation of privacy" in connection with a call placed in a public telephone booth, the Fourth Amendment was held to apply, requiring that a court order be obtained before a telephone tap was placed. Legislation specifying the need for a court order to permit a wiretap was then passed. It set forth standards for permitted wiretaps and also for conduct designed to minimize privacy invasions once taps were permitted. Use of information obtained from a tap was also restricted. Thus, under federal law today, for either the federal government or state government to obtain a domestic wiretap, an application must be made to a magistrate or a judge in which the government establishes reasonable grounds to believe such a wiretap will reveal evidence of a crime. (Such taps were obtained and used with great success in the recent conviction of organized crime boss John Gotti in New York City.)

While the wiretap legislation passed in the wake of the *Katz* decision contemplated assistance to law enforcement on a case-by-case basis, the legislation did not require that systems facilitate wire surveillance. The FBI has proposed that communications systems not be wiretap proof. If adopted, such subordination of technology to law enforcement techniques would be a major first.

From Katz *to the Present*

Since *Olmstead* and *Katz*, advances in electronics, computers, and other technologies have accentuated privacy concerns in two broad arenas—surveillance and personal data protection.

The surveillance category embraces, among other things, the government's increasing facility for undetectable electronic wire-tapping and monitoring of computer network traffic. The most profound expansion in surveillance monitoring, however, is not governmental but private. Today, businesses routinely monitor employee work habits and personal proclivities by recording key-strokes per minute at employee workstations, by scanning employees' e-mail messages, or by recording the destination, duration and time of outgoing personal phone calls by employees. In the interest of efficiency, airlines instruct their reservation clerks to take reservations in under two minutes "total average talk time (TATT)". Directory assistance operators are evaluated against a standard that imposes a 29-second average call length. There are even reports of journalists drafting stories at their computers being interrupted by networked supervisors objecting to the au-thor's choice of words.

The inclusion of personal information is a myriad of databases and the ease with which one's name, address and per-sonal information are transferred and used for purposes unre-lated to the one for which it was originally obtained is a source of great concern. Such lists are often effortlessly integrated with one another (often by reference to a common identifier such as the U.S. Social Security Number) to produce rather detailed portraits of individuals and their habits, purchases, histories. Often the individual is unable to avoid inclusion or to correct informational errors.

The legislatures in many countries recognize both the politi-cal and emotional value of privacy protection and have, in the last 20 years adopted a variety of strategies for achieving meaningful protection. At the heart of these efforts are a set of guiding principles concerning collection, use and dissemination of per-sonal information.

In the U.S., those principles were articulated in a 1973 report by the Department of Health, Education and Welfare, which pro-posed a Code of Fair Information Practices for automatic person-al data systems. These, however, apply only to the federal govern-ment. The following year, Congress passed the Privacy Act, which purported to incorporate the Code in restricting public sector uses of federal, but not state, local or private, records. Yet, in practice the Act has come to be recognized as a weak protector of personal privacy because an exception, which permitted "routine use" of data, has been so widely applied as to diminish the Act's force.

The U.S. Congress has passed laws attempting to deal in part with Privacy Act limitations, such as "routine use" and specific subjects not covered by the Privacy Act. These have addressed individual problems with separate pieces of legislation, each of which functions under the broad canopy of the 1974 Privacy Act. In the communications privacy sector, the leading legislation is the Electronic Communications Privacy Act of 1986. That Act requires the government to obtain a court order before intercepting most forms of electronic communications, broadly defined. Exceptions that permit electronic monitoring in the regular course of business and with an individual's prior consent many permit employer monitoring of e-mail systems, though this issue has yet to be settled by a court. Legislation since the enactment of the Privacy Act has not, however, created an effective oversight mechanism to give teeth to existing privacy protections.

In contrast to the U.S.'s approach of adopting specialized legislation to fix particular problems as they arise, other nations have adopted broad prospective data protection codes which may require data collectors to register with the government (UK, Sweden), or may impose a blanket prohibition on public and private data uses without the consent of the data subject (as in a proposed directive by the European Community).

The broad approach to data protection was expressed in a set of Guidelines issued in 1980 by the Organization of Economic Development. The Guidelines, which echo the principles behind the Code of Fair Information Practices, apply minimum standards to data collected, stored, processed or disseminated in either the public or private sector which identifies or could identify an individual. Many member nations and private organizations look to the Guidelines when drafting data privacy laws or policies.

Recently, the European Community has debated adopting a directive that would harmonize the data protection laws of its member states and, restrict transfer of personal data from a member state to another state that lacks "adequate" protection for personal data. Furthermore, a more recent proposal would protect personal data and privacy in the context of public digital telecommunications networks, in particular the integrated services digital network and public digital mobile networks. The new proposal would extend existing principles to the collection, storage and processing of personal data by a telecommunications organization.

It should be apparent from this brief overview of present

privacy protections that we are behind. Historically, it is clear that the law has adapted to technological changes, but not at a fast pace. The antecedents of electronic communications had been in place for almost a century by the time *Katz* was decided. The rate of technological change since *Katz* makes it unthinkable that a comparable period will lapse before legal constraints are developed that take into account the extraordinary changes in technology that computer electronics represent.

Certainly, we are not there today. In the U.S. a patch-work of laws deal with smaller problems, but none approaches the breadth of the problem, either at the governmental or the private level. While Guidelines and Codes represent broader efforts in the right direction, these are just guidelines and are not self-enforcing. They do not give anyone a legal claim that can be used across the board to deal with governmental or nongovernmental privacy invasions. We are, then, approaching a crossroads: either legislation with teeth will be enacted or the technological changes will simply swallow up privacy rights. As this task is approached, it must be remembered, however, that privacy is not the sole interest involved.

Countervailing Considerations

A world of total privacy is neither attainable nor desirable. Perhaps the most compelling policy against total privacy is the government's right to prosecute violations of the law. For example, if one's financial records were totally protected by a right to privacy, it would be difficult, if not impossible, for the government to prove tax evasion. Surely, it cannot be contended that the government's power to enforce its tax laws should be subordinated to a citizen's right to privacy so that tax evasion prosecutions would be a practical impossibility.

This illustration is, however, merely part of a larger perspective in law enforcement. If law enforcement is left to investigate only crimes in which neither communications nor data are essential proof, it is unlikely that prosecution of crimes such as murder, assault, rape, and robbery, would be significantly affected. What would be affected, however, is prosecution of business crime. The end result would be a contour to law enforcement that is decidedly class-focused.

Generally speaking, persons commit crimes in the most likely manner to get what they want—usually money or injury to another—in a way least likely to result in detection. Thus, crimes of violence tend to be committed by persons without the means of committing more subtle criminality. The robber of a bank or the mugger on the street does not have the means to steal more quietly. The president of a bank, or a Savings and Loan institution, however, has the luxury of stealing quietly, where not just the criminal, but the crime itself, must be uncovered, unlike the case of the robbery or mugging. If privacy rights precluded the government's ability to obtain information necessary to prosecute the crimes of those with means, the wealthy would essentially be immune from criminal prosecution and law enforcement's efforts would be directed almost totally at the poor.

While investigation and prosecution necessarily require the government to obtain information that might otherwise be private, the government's obtaining of information does not necessarily mean it will be made public. When the government subpoenas bank or other financial records as part of a criminal investigation, these records are subject to the same secrecy constraints that apply to any information obtained by a grand jury. It is only if criminal charges are brought that such data may become public. However, in such cases, the government's interest in enforcing its criminal laws seems paramount. While privacy protections may weaken in the case of criminal investigation, it should be remembered that such an investigation is an exceptional case and establishes no general rule. Moreover, even in the case of a criminal investigation, there are internal privacy constraints such as the need for a warrant and grand jury secrecy.

Not all litigation is criminal litigation. When a person sues for injuries relating to an automobile accident, the person sued has the right to obtain the plaintiff's medical records in an effort to show that either the injuries complained of are not as severe as alleged or that they are attributable to an injury antedating the accident. In such a case, the plaintiff has no valid privacy right to such records, and court process—a subpoena or a formal discovery request is the mechanism by which otherwise confidential information is provided to the defendant and perhaps, ultimately made a part of the public record. It makes no sense to say that the plaintiff, who has placed his or her medical condition in issue, should have a privacy right to keep that condition from being fully litigated. And because it is court process that permits access to otherwise confidential data, the court is available to curb excesses or needlessly broad discovery into the plaintiff's medical condition.

Conclusion

There is little doubt that in the future, many records presently stored in nonelectronic form will be retained in electronic
databases. This poses the risk that through networks such records
will be accessible to large numbers of persons to whom these
records would otherwise be inaccessible. It is axiomatic that whatever privacy protections apply to such records must not be lost
simply because the mechanism of retention has changed. Thus,
for example, medical or bank records which are afforded privacy
protection under existing law should not lose the privacy protection they have under present law simply because the way in which
they are stored leaves them vulnerable to electronic detection.
The required privacy must be maintained.

There is an inverse to this conclusion. Just as privacy should
not be lost when the storage mechanism becomes electronic, privacy rights should not be acquired when otherwise nonprivate
records are stored electronically. If business records, for example,
are transferred from cumbersome books and ledgers onto an
electronic data base, that transfer does not render them subject to
privacy constraints simply because they are stored electronically.
Otherwise, law enforcement of any kind of business crime would
be heavily burdened and for no valid reason.

With respect to communications privacy, the constitutional
prohibition against unlawful searches and seizures, held to create
a zone of protection within a reasonable expectation of privacy,
should and does extend to electronic communications. The 1986
Electronic Communications Protection Act prohibits government
interception of electronic communications without probable
cause. Similar constraints apply in other countries. Caller-ID
technology, which gives the recipient of a phone call access to the
source of the call raises additional privacy issues.

Although private wiretaps are also prohibited, restraints on
private interception of e-mail and network communications are
presently not promising in terms of individual privacy protections. Certainly if the "reasonable expectation" standard is the
legal basis for private privacy protection, an employer, by notice,
can effectively remove such expectation from an employee by
simply stating that all information placed on a company
computer is the property of the employer, a practice that has
been followed. It would follow almost inevitably that if an employ-

er does not so advise an employee, the expectation of privacy would be reasonable.

There is no doubt that we are now at a crossroad. Technology will have a major impact on our lives and values as we understand them, unless we act and act quickly. Those to whom Brandeis's description of privacy and its importance in a civilized society evokes assent do not have much time. The rate of technological change will render privacy obsolete. During the critical period in which we can prevent the destruction of privacy, we cannot proceed on the assumption that those with power share our views and can be counted on to preserve our values. Brandeis saw the pitfall in such hopes as well when he said that "the greatest dangers to liberty lurk in insidious encroachment by men of zeal, well-meaning but without understanding.

We must understand, and we must act.

ACKNOWLEDGMENT

Bennett Berson, a third-year law student at the University of Wisconsin, provided invaluable assistance in the preparation of this article.

WINNING VOTES ON THE INFORMATION SUPER-HIGHWAY[3]

· It's two days before the city council is scheduled to vote on your client's plan for downtown development. You've spent months making your case to local leaders, the business community and the citizenry at large. In fact, all of the council members have at one time or another indicated they'll support your client's project, including the financing.

A well-planned grassroots lobbying blitz by a national environmental group—including a flood of phone calls and letters from around the country—seems to be giving several of the coun-

[3]Article by Roger S. Conrad, editor of the *Utility Forecaster*, from *Campaigns & Elections* 15:22–27 Jl '94. Copyright © 1994 by *Campaigns & Elections*. Reprinted with permission.

cil members second thoughts. Worse, the local newspaper has added to the momentum to kill the deal by printing a number of articles questioning your client's financial dealings. It's critical that you do something now to turn the tide.

The solution: You organize a rally downtown to protest underdevelopment and to support your client's plan by communicating with your supporters over your campaign's on-line, computer bulletin board. You also contact citizen activists your campaign has identified using computer assisted or "predictive dialing" and urge them to attend as well. In addition, you ask them for permission to phone "patch" them in to offices of the council members to voice their support.

The result is an "earned" media event with a grass roots flavor that generates momentum for your plan's approval, as well as a barrage of favorable phone calls that at least partially balances out the negative effect of the environmental group's effort. As it turns out, it gives the wavering council members all the backbone they need to say yes.

Sound farfetched? What I've just described is something savvy campaigns around the country are doing every day with existing technology. In fact, many believe high-tech campaigning will ultimately revolutionize the business of politics, particularly once telephone and cable companies have completed their ambitious plans to wire America into a digitally-switched, fiber optics-based "interactive network."

It's important to remember, however, that any technology, no matter how exciting, is just a tool. It doesn't relieve you of responsibility for making the right decisions or crafting the right substantive messages. And if used poorly, it could cost you irreplaceable votes and money. Below, we look at how successful campaigns are avoiding these pitfalls, and how they're using information highway technology that's already available and tested to boost success rates.

Interactive Systems

Much of the focus on the information highway has been on interactive communications systems, such as that being built by the year-old alliance between "Baby Bell" U.S. West and cable giant Time Warner. Bell Atlantic, Pacific Telesis and other phone and cable companies have also committed billions of dollars to construct interactive systems by the turn of the century.

Interactive systems are to be based on two relatively new telecommunications technologies: Digital switching and the use of fiber optic cable. Used together, these dramatically increase the speed and volume of data that can be shipped from one place to another, making it possible for the same network to simultaneously provide everything from telephone and "500 channel" cable television entertainment service to home shopping and visual teleconferencing.

Many of the details of full service networks, however, are still very much in question. Most phone and cable company executives envision the television set becoming an interactive telecomputer. Andy Grove, CEO of computer chip maker Intel, believes the vastly more powerful personal computer will expand its role as the engine of future high-tech communications. Others see more of a mix, with homes owning a variety of appliances, each capable of sending and retrieving vast amounts of information. Finally, the Palo Alto Research Center—which correctly foresaw the rise of the personal computer—predicts that wireless or cellular networks will dominate.

Another question that's emerged is whether or not anyone will want to pay for these new services. In politics, the two-way contact that interactive communications offers holds great promise. But even the projects of the most firmly grounded people may ultimately prove to be pie-in-the-sky.

For example, Doug Bailey, publisher of the successful daily, on-line political briefing "Hotline," and three other equally well-situated consultants, are planning to launch the American Political Channel, a futuristic system using "movies on demand" technology. If all goes as planned, viewers will someday be able to watch regular programming, as well as access videos on candidates and issues on demand. As of yet, however, the group has yet to launch its first broadcast.

Campaign consultant Scott Walker, who has worked for such Beltway mainstays as Senator Howard Metzenbaum (D-OH), believes ultimately federal and state legislators could be able to debate and vote on issues over interactive, audio/visual, tele-cable systems, regardless of whether or not they're actually in the capital at the time. But even if technology permits this at some future date, few are likely to abandon Capitol Hill because of the networking and lobbying that goes on.

There are, however, three relatively new information superhighway technologies that are already being used by campaigns nationwide:

• Telephone technologies such as "Predictive Dialing," and related computer hardware and software. These now well-established techniques allow far faster voter contact than ever before by automating dialing to eliminate extra motion by callers and by rapid, careful selection of prospects to call.

• Audio-Visual technologies, such as satellite transmission and narrowcasting of commercials on niche cable channels. These are limited in range now. But these innovations can speed up media production and provide lower-cost alternatives to expensive broadcast advertising.

• On-Line computer technologies, including databases such as Lexis/Nexis and Time Net, and the interactive forum/database "Internet." These have two major uses. First, they enable campaigns to do very focused issue and opposition research, to transmit their own messages within networks and to keep up with the media cycle in several locations simultaneously. Second, they're now being used by larger campaigns, political parties and PACs, to communicate with supporters far more quickly and cheaply than is possible using the mail or the telephone.

One caveat: These technologies are only as effective as how well they're used in each specific campaign.

The key is focus and cost. Don't try to adapt what you do just for the sake of having a flashy new technology at your disposal.

Predictive Dialing

Whether you're running a local candidate's campaign or advocating approval of a statewide initiative, "predictive dialing" can dramatically improve your results at a reasonable cost.

In layman's terms, predictive dialing is a computerized time management system for telephone banks. It involves special dialing equipment and software together with a live caller (unlike completely automated calling systems that play a prerecorded tape). With it, telephone bank operators have a computer screen and keyboard in front of them with a headset. Lists of names and phone numbers to be called are loaded into the system on tape or disk. When a phone number is dialed, the predictive dialing software can recognize and distinguish a live "hello," a busy signal, an answering machine, or the phone company saying the number is no longer in service. When a live "hello" occurs, the call is sent instantly to the first available operator who hears the "hello" in the headset as the name of the person being called appears on the screen.

Written into predictive dialing software are complex algorithmic programs that regulate and monitor the speed of dialing and the number of phones being answered so that people being called aren't forgotten on the line without a ready operator to handle the call. In effect, it predicts when someone will answer their phone and when a phone operator will be available to take the call.

There are two major advantages of predictive dialing over conventional phone banking. First is speed. The computer is capable of dialing dozens of numbers every minute. All busy signals, answering machines, disconnected lines and endless ringing is filtered out. Telemarketers are consequently free to concentrate exclusively on the task at hand: Asking the right questions and/or delivering the right message. The result is a greatly increased number of calls per hour.

The second major advantage is targeting. Computers can instantly select only the numbers of the people who are members of a key demographic group or who answered yes to a specific question during an earlier phone call. The computer can also store dozens of pieces of information from questions asked to be used to select future calls.

Predictive dialing was first developed by large financial institutions for corporate proxy fights. But today, campaigns are using it in new ways. Mac Hansbrough of National Telecom Services, a telemarketing firm working for Democrats nationwide, identifies four major uses: Fundraising, polling, voter contact and mobilizing "grass roots" support for key legislative issues. "We can literally target any market we want, depending on the database," says Hansbrough, "and the potential savings in time and manpower are huge."

Predictive dialing's speed and targetability has induced more than a few state party organizations to use it for fund raising, including Republicans in Florida, Texas and most recently Wisconsin. R. J. Johnson, executive director of the Wisconsin Republican party, expects to use it to more than double his donor base from 1992.

Johnson has been able to cut the party's costs per communicator hour literally in half. That in turn has cut the average level of contributions needed to make telemarketing profitable to the $17 to $25 dollar range, dramatically increasing the party's ability to pursue donors, particularly when used in combination with direct mail.

According to Johnson, their productivity ratio will rise in coming years, as the percentage of calls shifts from simply cold calling partisans to renewing current donors, whose response rates will be much higher. Johnson is also using the information storage power of new software packages. This will help not only fundraising, but could be used down the road for voter identification and "get-out-the-vote" (GOTV) calls as the party's donor base becomes larger.

Wally Clinton, whose telemarketing business operates 300 telephones (many of which are equipped with predictive dialing), says that the new technology has "doubled our productivity." Clinton also points out that predictive dialing is most efficient when making a large volume of phone calls for political persuasion and mobilization but that a less expensive CATI (computer assisted telephone interviewing) system with "power dialers" is more economical and is better geared to doing fewer and longer calls that involve qualitative interviewing for public opinion surveys.

Many telemarketers use new phone technologies for voter identification. For example, suppose Candidate Smith is running for Senate and wants to focus his effort on undecided voters. First, the computer is fed a list of voters based on prior surveys and election data. As calls begin, interviewers ask voters who they supported in elections. Those who answer Smith's Republican opponent will be weeded out. They may be worth pursuing later, but not in this effort. Those who answer Smith, meanwhile, will be reminded to get out and vote. They may also be notated for a GOTV call or letter closer to the election.

Those who are undecided or who say no can then be wooed by a combination of direct mail and future phone calls.

Once the caller hangs up after any of the calls, a computer automatically enters the new information into the database. For those listed for a follow-up letter, names are sent via modem to the list vendor, who can then print a letter and envelope thanking the voter for listening and urging he or she to vote on election day for Smith. The letter, which is mailed that day, serves as a powerful reinforcer of the phone message.

Voter identification's power can be dramatically enhanced by combining it with "desktop mapping." According to Joe Pindell of Election Data Services, a voter's address or phone number allow attitudes to be automatically compared with demographic characteristics to aid in gauging the mood of particular groups.

Patch-Ins

John Davies of Santa Barbara-based Davies Communications, who manages campaigns for Republicans and business groups nationwide, says predictive dialing can be particularly effective in grassroots lobbying when combined with the commonly used phoning technique of "patch ins." Strongest supporters of an issue—those who have been identified, educated and motivated—are selected from the database and phoned using the speed of computer-aided dialing. But rather than simply asked to call or write their congressman or county commissioner, supporters are requested to be patched-in or immediately connected to the office of the public official. The result is a motivated caller who feels strongly about an issue, something most public officials find difficult to ignore.

For an issue in California, predictive dialing-located patch-ins helped Davies turn a 4-1 negative vote before a county commission into a 5-0 victory for the proposal. Such a powerful tool, however, is in Davies' words "like a power torch. You can either build a bridge or cut off your hands." The principal danger, he says, is the risk of a backlash from too many phone calls in. "You want constant calls to build into a crescendo as the vote nears," he warns, "Too many calls at once look like astroturf, not grassroots." In one instance, for example, a Davies-orchestrated patch-in campaign resulted in a local government being paralyzed with too many calls. The upshot was a backlash against the callers.

One negative in using this new technology is the upfront cost. Experts estimate that it can run upwards of $5,000 per phone for the necessary hardware and software to do predictive dialing. For a phone center with, for example, 50 work stations, that involves a capital investment of over $250,000. In addition, it also requires sophisticated, well-trained administrative and supervisory personnel, which is why many campaigns prefer to hire professional phone firms as opposed to developing in-house "boiler rooms."

Will this technology ever cut the costs of political telemarketing? Perhaps, some suggest, in the long run when hardware and software costs decline and more people are familiar with them. In line with this, pollster Bill Hamilton believes these new technologies "may eventually bring down the price of public opinion polls" which use telephones extensively to interview scientifically selected samples. That would be good news for candidates who find it necessary to budget more and more for survey research. But for now, the costs of new technology often offset added efficiency, limiting cost-savings. Speed—no small factor in politics—is the big advantage, not cost.

If you choose to purchase equipment or services, be sure to shop around. Also, figure out in advance what you want and be sure it's the most cost-effective way of achieving it. When shopping for equipment, be sure you're not paying for more power than you need before you plunk down dollar one.

Channels of Influence

By far the most hyped feature of the information super-highway is the so-called "500 channel" network to be built by telephone and cable companies. Rather than actually provide 500 individual stations, this system (if built) will supposedly have the huge transmission capacity necessary for two-way audio/visual communication.

With channel compression—squeezing four, six or eight channels into one—moving forward and the increased use of fiber optics, National Media, Inc. president Robin Roberts estimates that "within four years 40 percent of the country will have 500 channel capability. Roberts says he expects about 20 percent of channel capacity will be dedicated to pay-per-view and video-on-demand. The remaining 400 channels, he says, would be programmed specifically.

The extent to which new channels are used, and used effectively, is another matter that is affected by not only technology and economics but also audience habits. Media research has shown that in cities with cable systems ranging from 35 to 150 channels, only about 12 are regularly viewed. Apparently, added channels does not increase viewing. It only further fractures the audience by adding new, specialized options. Roberts foresees the day when political TV spots will be targeted not just to large market areas (as they are usually done now) and not just to smaller zip code zones, but to separate rooms in individual households.

"A micro-computer converter box will allow campaigns to send their messages to the family room and the parent's bedroom, while avoiding the children's room," says Roberts. "This technology will clearly have a greater impact on voters who receive targeted messages."

Another issue raised by increased channel options will be

measuring the effectiveness of advertising messages, a critical problem for political time buyers. Roberts, whose firm specializes in media placements and research for Republican candidates, believes the answer to the measurement problem will be "direct response" advertising. He advises: "Direct response allows advertisers to quickly track results by measuring reaction to commercials. Cost-per-inquiry can be calculated to determine which networks and dayparts are working for you and which are not."

In one example of creative usage of cable channel programming, former Tennessee Governor and U.S. Secretary of Education Lamar Alexander hosts his own weekly one-hour issues-and-answers program called "Republican Neighborhood Meeting." Launched in May 1993 and based out of Nashville, Tenn., the show is broadcast to cable television stations nationwide via satellite every Tuesday evening at 8 p.m. Eastern Time and is basically organized under a "town meeting" format, with Alexander interacting with small groups in addition to taking telephone calls. Each broadcast costs about $50,000 to $60,000 and is financed by Alexander backers.

A new television technology perhaps more practical for most campaigns involves delivering more targeted messages by tailoring specific advertisements to key demographic groups held in favor by the community. The campaign of Maine Democratic Senatorial candidate John Baldacci recently won praise from the state's mainstream press by broadcasting a closed caption commercial for the hearing impaired. According to media advisor David Heller of Politics Inc., this free press "enforced the candidate's message of inclusiveness," a major plus in progressive-minded Maine.

Info On-Line

On-line databases are perhaps the most important avenue of the information super-highway for political uses. In fact, with the growing popularity of the "Internet"—an electronic, telecommunications-based network linking computers all over the globe—many believe they will revolutionize politics.

Today, most large repositories of information, and many small ones too, have put their files on-line, making them accessible by computer usually for a fee. Political research is one area that's already benefitting from this mushrooming of on-line ser-

vices. Opposition researcher Dan Hazelwood of Targeted Creative Communications, for example, makes broad use of
Lexis/Nexis searches in his investigations.

In Hazelwood's view, such searches are particularly valuable
where higher offices are concerned, because there's so much
more on record.

Hazelwood's also keen on using on-line data services for keeping up with the media cycle and for anticipating moves of opposing campaigns. During the recent off-year congressional election
for the seat of the late Representative William Natcher (D-KY),
Republicans were able to anticipate and respond to the moves of
Democrat Joe Prather by monitoring the media on-line. One example was the Republicans' timely response to Prather's attempt
to focus on the crime issue.

Another on-line data source with blockbuster potential for
opposition research is the Federal Election Commission's on-line
files, which list information on federal campaign contributions.
These are currently "published" on Time Net for an access fee of
$20 an hour. According to Hazelwood, however, the access is well
worth the expense. By finding out who the contributors are, he
says, you can often expose hypocritical stands by candidates.

Most campaigns today are familiar with on-line computer-
based services such as Compuserve, Prodigy and America On-
Line. But as Matthew Polutta of the research firm Science Applications International Corp points out, Internet takes a quantum
leap beyond.

Get Net, It Pays

First, the Net offers access to over 130,000 computer networks
worldwide with 20 million users. That's double the number of
users a year ago and it's growing by 10 percent a month. Growth
could accelerate even more once MicroSoft launches its Windows
4.0 program, complete with an InterNet interface. Second, the
Net is also an interactive medium. Users can communicate with
thousands of other users electronically through a wide variety of
"bulletin boards" on specialized topics, as well as send electronic
or "E-mail" to other users worldwide, including subscribers of pay
on-line services like Compuserve, Prodigy and America On-Line.

With such a wealth of data available, beginning Internet users
often must spend hours learning where to find the information
they want. As vast as the Net is, that's actually like trying to find a

needle in a barn full of hay. Fortunately, when it comes to demographic information for political campaigns, that problem appears to have been solved by B3 Corp. According to spokesman Tim Brown, the company has developed a computer software program that will allow users to access demographic information on the Internet in an easy and organized way, and at no charge.

Compuserve and other on-line services offer access to the Net, but only to subscribers who must pay a fee. In contrast, B3 Corp is offering free Internet access at its Wisconsin-based access point. Information on the service is available through both an on-line, computer access number and a voice line. Services include establishing an electronic mail box for users and the only expense is the cost of long-distance calls, for those who live out of state. Brown expects the service to attract some 250,000 subscribers in its first year alone.

Communicating quickly with supporters is another burgeoning use of on-line services. Provided enough members are on-line, political organizations can potentially mobilize their members far more quickly than is possible through the mail. In addition, there are no printing or storage costs for the paper.

Despite the Net's rapid growth, there are limits to its practical uses, at least for the moment. For example, most consultants view its audience as still too limited and self-selected to do effective polling. However, by offering the ability to communicate directly with the candidate, campaigns can generate a lot of good will. Texas direct mail consultant David Gold points to the "800" phone number as a good example of how a candidate can show that he or she "cares" about voter feedback. Gold also believes that going on-line can be invaluable in creating an image for the candidate of being "friendly to high-tech," helping he or she appear ready to lead their constituents into the future.

Bill Clinton's White House has won kudos by maintaining an InterNet access, which allows users to send suggestions and questions on a wide variety of issues via E-mail. Now, some campaigns are using the Internet to offer information on candidates' positions as well as to send the message that the lines of communication are open. In Texas, for example, Democratic Senatorial candidate Richard Fisher is in the process of listing his campaign's position papers on the Net, a response says campaign spokesman Martin Johnson to Fisher supporters sending E-mail messages on his behalf during the primaries.

Johnson maintains that being on the Net is "an important new way to spread the word about Fisher." Being listed on the Net can also be invaluable in notifying supporters in advance of a candidate's short-notice appearances by sending E-mail, much as the NRA does to rally support for its issues.

High-Tech Do's and Don'ts

The major advantage of the technologies discussed above is speed. All make it quicker and easier to do what campaigns have always done, thereby freeing up worker hours and money to concentrate on the things that will make the difference between winning and losing.

For example, by eliminating some of the human effort in dialing, predictive dialing allows campaigns to use phone banking as a powerful tool to mobilize overwhelming support for a candidate or issue in a matter of hours. In addition, phones can now also be used to do lightening fast and finely tuned voter surveys and fund raising. Satellite-based television makes it possible for a candidate to use television to reach small groups of viewers cheaply. The InterNet and other on-line data services allow instant communication with supporters, as well as a way to monitor and react to media events, effectively search for "silver bullets" to "kill" opposing candidates and compile demographic information.

Before you use any of the new technologies to pull out into the information super-highway's fast lane, there are a few commonsense rules to keep in mind.

First, remember that new technologies and products— whether you're talking about predictive dialing or the Internet— do nothing to change the most important factor in the campaign equation: The message. They're simply tools to help you do your job better. Don't expect them to relieve you of responsibility for decision making. How effective they'll be will depend on your decisions.

Second, have a clear idea that what you're buying is the best possible solution to your problem, before you pay for it. That means doing the math to calculate costs and benefits, as well as searching out alternatives. For example, though predictive dialing can often be done much more cheaply in house than through a vendor, it may not be feasible for some campaigns to hire all the people they need to do it themselves. In fact, because predictive dialing services can be expensive, it might even make sense to stick with conventional phone banking in some cases.

Conversely, never buy new equipment or implement a new technology just because it represents the latest technological innovation. You'll not only be squandering resources that can better be used elsewhere, but you'll also wind up wasting time learning how to use it.

Third, be sure to comparison shop for equipment, software programs and other technology, just as you would for any other product or service. Each of the technologies discussed in this article are widespread. No one has a lock on what you need. You can almost always find something cheaper or more effective if you check out the competition, say by scanning a few of the myriad publications on the subject. And don't forget to test drive before you buy.

DEMOCRACY ON-LINE[4]

Over the last 200 years, new information technologies have significantly transformed the possibilities and practice of democracy. For example, the early-nineteenth-century invention of the penny press for printing newspapers made the acquisition of political information by the masses both convenient and affordable. This, in turn, greatly facilitated the extension of suffrage during that period. Later, the advent of television weakened the traditional political-party system and led to the growing influence of the media in elections.

Over the next 20 years, many experts believe that information technology may change more than it has over the last 200 years. If they are right, we can expect major changes in the democratic system of government.

Problems with Democracy

Today, it is hard to imagine that such a large democracy as the United States, with its 250 million citizens, could survive if information technologies such as books, magazines, newspapers, ra-

[4]Article by James H. Snider, university fellow of political science, Northwestern University, from *The Futurist* 28:15–19 S/O '94. Copyright © 1994 by *The Futurist*. Reprinted with permission.

dio, and television suddenly vanished. Indeed, until the last few hundred years the most-respected political thinkers uniformly agreed that only small-scale democracy was possible, in part because of communication limitations. Aristotle argued in the fourth century B.C. that democracy could not work in a country larger than a small city-state such as Athens. One reason was that in a democracy all citizens should be able to assemble at one place to hear a speaker. Thus, the range of the human voice limited a democracy's size. As late as the mid-eighteenth century, political thinkers of the stature of Montesquieu and Rousseau continued to echo this conventional wisdom and argue against the possibility of large-scale democracy.

After the birth of the United States—a huge democracy by historical standards—such arguments were discredited. But as evidence mounts that America's democratic system is moving farther away from the democratic ideal, it is easy to wonder if the pre-modern thinkers weren't on to something. According to a widely quoted study by the Kettering Foundation entitled *Citizens and Politics: A View from Main Street America,* "Americans are both frustrated and downright angry about the state of the current political system. [They] do not believe they are living in a democracy now. They don't believe that 'We the people' actually rule. What is more, people do not believe this system is able to solve the pressing problems they face."

Perhaps the early political thinkers simply got the maximum democratic size wrong. Instead of it being 5,000, or 20,000, or even 100,000, maybe it is 250 million. Convinced that large-scale democracy was impossible, the early political thinkers surely would have had little trouble identifying at least part of America's main governmental problem—its growing size and complexity.

Over the last 200 years, America's population has grown from 3 million to 250 million. At the same time, the size and complexity of government has grown exponentially. In 1831, there were only 11,491 federal employees; today there are millions. As government grows larger and more complex, it is harder to keep it accountable. And as the proportion of citizens to representatives increases (thus decreasing the odds of any individual citizen making a difference), citizens have even less incentive to try and keep it accountable.

The development of mass media such as newspapers and television has helped to alleviate these problems. The maximum range of a politician's message is no longer the hundreds or thousands within the physical range of the voice, but the tens of millions who can watch television. Similarly, the mass media usually offer better and more convenient political news than could word of mouth.

Unfortunately, the technology and institutions of democracy are no longer keeping up with its growth. America continues to have democratic ideals, but not an informed and engaged electorate able to act upon those ideals. The result is a government that neither knows nor implements the public's will. The savings-and-loan scandal is a notorious example: If the government had regulated banks in the public interest, taxpayers would have saved hundreds of billions of dollars.

There are, of course, non-technology-based approaches to solving our democratic woes; for example, we might instill a better sense of civic duty in schools, or overhaul campaign-finance laws in order to minimize the influence of special-interest groups. A more fundamental approach might be to use information technology to transcend the inherent historic limitations of democracy. In moving from today's Industrial Age democracy to tomorrow's Information Age democracy, both direct and mediated democracy can and should be enhanced.

Direct Democracy

Most of the literature on the democratic significance of new information technology has focused on its ability to enhance direct participation by citizens in the political process. For the many people who have lost confidence in the ability of both elected representatives and the media to act in their interest, direct democracy, such as the ballot referendum or the town meeting, offers an appealing alternative.

Clearly, the new technology facilitates new forms of voting and thus direct participation. For example, instead of physically going to the polls, people could vote from their homes. With more-convenient and less-expensive voting, people could be expected to vote more frequently and on more issues. Ballot referendums and polls could proliferate.

Another benefit of the new technology is improved access to the deliberations of public bodies. Already, cable television's C-SPAN channel gives us coverage of the U.S. House and Senate chambers and many congressional hearings. Similarly, the California Channel provides coverage of the California House and

Senate chambers and legislative hearings. At a local level, many public-access cable television channels cover city council and school board meetings. In the future, coverage of such meetings at local, state, and national levels is likely to expand dramatically, thus making government deliberations much more accessible to the average person.

New technology also facilitates previously impractical forms of democratic deliberation. With the electronic town meeting via television, computer, or some synthesis of both, citizens are offered direct contact with public officials, unmediated by journalists. The idea is to force politicians and the media to talk to the public about important issues that might otherwise escape the political agenda. Combined with televoting, the electronic town meeting offers a potentially significant improvement on the ballot referendum or traditional telephone poll, both of which are poor at fostering deliberation and thus lead to uninformed voting.

Government records could also be made more accessible. The cumbersome procedures necessary to gain access to information under the federal Freedom of Information Act or the local public records laws could be replaced by instantaneous computerized access. Information that is an expensive nightmare to get from government today would thus become available, inexpensively and conveniently, with a few keystrokes. Congress' recent passage of the Government Printing Office (GPO) Electronic Information Access Enhancement Act, which provides Internet access to GPO documents, is a major step in this direction.

Mediated Democracy

As the many critics of direct democracy have argued, the average person does not have the time, ability, or inclination to become an expert on issues and candidates. Direct democracy, which inevitably leads to information overload can, at best, only be a minor palliative to the political information problem. What people want are trustworthy information sources that will do the hard work of gathering and digesting political information for them. This is already a function of the media, but only in a primitive form. The greatest potential of new information technology to improve democracy lies in its ability to enhance mediated democracy.

The importance of today's passive mass media is likely to diminish greatly over the coming decades. Passive media may be replaced by a new type of interactive multimedia, characterized by highly specialized media outlets often described as "information agents." For example, a typical city today has one dominant newspaper. This newspaper achieves its dominance largely because of huge economies of scale associated with its distribution system. In the future, the reporters who work for such newspapers are likely to become independent information entrepreneurs, selling their information wares directly to the public over the telecommunications network.

Part person and part computer program, these information agents will gather and digest information, then disseminate it to their clients just as high-priced consultants do today. Accordingly, their customized advice will be short and clear and allow for as much background and explanatory information as desired.

A vast literature exists criticizing our current mass media. While there is no guarantee that the media of the future will cure all these ills (and avoid creating new ones), the potential for more competitive, diverse, and customized media in the future is good cause for hope.

The new media could lead to some important qualitative changes in politics. In the past, the growing influence of mass media in the political process has led candidates to rely increasingly on media-based self-promotion (as opposed to the political parties) to get themselves elected. The new media, while continuing to weaken the political parties, could nevertheless greatly diminish the utility of candidate self-promotion.

The reasoning is that voters in the future will increasingly get their political information from the impartial information agents, not from the candidates directly. If that turns out to be the case, then not only will traditional candidate self-promotion become obsolete, but so will the power of lobbyists and special interests who derive their power from the ability to fund candidates' media campaigns. A candidate could spend huge sums taking out television ads, but it would do no good if the voter has come to rely on agents for political information.

In many respects, this argument merely extends to the political realm what many have argued is likely to be an effect of interactive multimedia in the commercial realm—the making of advertising, especially unrequested advertising, much less effective, if not completely useless.

Citizens in Action

An important new form of mediated democracy facilitated by new information technology has average citizens, not specialized information agents, doing the mediation.

This approach entails bringing together a random sample of voters to deliberate on issues and candidates. They, in effect, do the hard work of democracy that the rest of us don't have the time or motivation to do. Curiously, this is a form of mediated democracy widely used in ancient Athens more than 2,000 years ago and has continued, in a vastly restricted fashion, in the American jury system. New information technology facilitates its expansion in historically new ways.

Many variations on this idea have been proposed. In one of the three 1992 presidential debates, the Gallup Poll randomly selected 200 Americans to serve as the audience. In the 1992 U.S. Senate race in Pennsylvania, a small, random group of citizens were convened as a citizen jury to interview and evaluate the candidates. A more rigorous form of citizen-mediated democracy has been proposed by political scientist Jim Fishkin in his book *Democracy and Deliberation.* In what Fishkin calls a "deliberative opinion poll," a scientifically representative microcosm of American citizens deliberates on issues and candidates with the purpose of finding out what the public would think if it had the motivation and resources for informed decision making.

If we accept the assumption of modern polling techniques that a group as small as 500 people can be an accurate barometer of the public sentiment, then such an approach preserves the essence of the democratic ideal while substantially solving the problem of the individual voter's low motivation and inadequate resources. Members of the sample would know that their voice has disproportionate weight (maybe by as much as 500,000 Americans) and that they are getting otherwise inconceivable access to special resources, such as one-on-one contact with candidates and leading experts.

Public Policy Recommendations

New public policies are necessary to facilitate the new forms of democracy made possible by emerging information technology. To make sure that we don't disintegrate into a nation of information haves and have-nots, it will be necessary to ensure universal access to the coming information highway.

More important are the less obvious political institutions made possible by new information technology. For example, the new technology will make possible new ways to publicly finance elections. Instead of money going to candidates, money could be given directly to the voters. Instead of tens of millions of dollars in communication vouchers being given to presidential candidates to spend on 30-second television ads, money could be given directly to citizens to spend on information about presidential candidates. Such voter-based vouchers are far more democratic than candidate-based vouchers but have never been practical before.

Similarly, new laws and policies need to be developed to maximize the social utility of information agents. A special class of information agent—the electoral agent—could be given special treatment much like nonprofit organizations, which receive privileges such as tax exemptions and reduced postal rates. As with nonprofits, electoral agents could provide a public good that would otherwise be underproduced. If mass-media advertising becomes obsolete and thus no longer able to subsidize "free TV" or cheap newspapers (the traditional media for election information), then the need for electoral agents could become even more acute than it is today.

The obligations for electoral agents could include: (1) No funding from candidates or candidate proxies (that is, no financial conflicts of interest), (2) a complete public record of all contact with candidates or their proxies (for example, a video if a personal contact and an electronic letter if a text-based contact), (3) agent computer systems that facilitate candidate rebuttals of any agent assertion (the candidate could ask for a "rebuttal button" to appear on the screen when the challenged assertion appears), and finally (4) information structured to help voters make decisions between candidates (for example, a news format would not qualify).

In return for meeting these obligations, electoral agents would be entitled to receive the voter information vouchers as well as significantly reduced liability for libel.

The First Amendment needs to be reinterpreted. Too often today it only protects the rights of information producers, not consumers. If the media become even more important in the political process, it is vital that the public have the right to know as much about the media as they do about politicians, lobbyists, and government agencies. The White House Correspondents Association already requires members to disclose their major financial interests, including investments, speaking fees, and perks. Similarly, new technology facilitates enhanced rights of rebuttal and rights to diverse information sources.

The traditional right-to-know laws that pertain to government information also need to be rewritten. In many states, the public-records laws and the open-meeting laws were conceived when the photocopier and audiotape recorder were the most-advanced forms of information technology. These laws need to be brought into the present and made to anticipate the future so that public access to government and candidate information can be improved. Even if the public doesn't avail itself of this information, it is absolutely necessary for the effective functioning of the emerging media.

Perhaps the party system could be abolished as well. Already the growth of television over the last few decades has seriously diminished the power of the parties. This trend toward weakened parties is likely to continue as a result of the emerging information infrastructure and the new agent-based media it engenders. A logical implication is to institutionalize the growing powers of the media over the nominating system. For example, an electoral agents' association could set dates and criteria for nominations—something the media currently do in a much less democratic way with so-called "hidden" nominations. The hidden nomination is the process, most pronounced in presidential primaries, whereby the media anoint a handful of candidates as serious contenders.

More generally, the practical realities limiting nominating systems can be rethought in light of new information technology. The current nominating systems in the United States are based on certain assumptions about communications and transportation requirements. As the information infrastructure changes, so do the possibilities for creating nominating systems that will attract and select the best candidates. Theoretically elegant but heretofore impractical voting systems could come into widespread use. Instead of starting with an initial pool of five to 10 candidates preselected by political parties or mass-media pundits, it might be practical with computer voting to start with hundreds or thousands of candidates and have the public do the selecting. With the advent of relatively inexpensive and convenient home voting, we could also have three or four nominating rounds instead of the two customary today. And the new media rather than the parties could be given control of the basic nominating system protocols.

Modern civilization requires a large and complex government because the private sector alone simply cannot provide many vital services such as defense and environmental protection. It is unfortunate that its immensity has made the government so unaccountable to its citizens and their general welfare. But new information technology, combined with forward-thinking public policies, can help bring the democratic ideal much closer to reality.

EDITOR'S INTRODUCTION

The Information Revolution has raised profound cultural and social questions. In the first article, reprinted from the *Wilson Quarterly,* Tom Maddox analyzes the "Cultural Consequences of the Information Superhighway." Next, in a piece reprinted from *National Review,* George Gilder favorably contrasts the intelligence of computers to the banality of television, and praises the information superhighway for revitalizing capitalism. Characteristic of American life, a gender gap exists in the business world of computers. In an article from *Working Woman,* Bronwyn Fryer hopes for a greater role for women in technical and management positions. In the final article, *Christianity Today* staff writer John Zipperer discusses a growing problem for parents: the growth of pornography on the Internet, and the methods to combat it.

THE CULTURAL CONSEQUENCES OF THE INFORMATION SUPERHIGHWAY[1]

The coming of the information superhighway, or, more modestly, the National Information Infrastructure (NII), has reanimated America's running debate about the vices and virtues of technology. It has also reshuffled the ideological deck in interesting ways. Latter-day counterculturalists who have joined the ranks of the technological optimists, such as Howard Rheingold of the *Whole Earth Review,* find themselves encamped alongside the likes of George Gilder, the onetime apostle of Reaganomics. Even as Theodore Roszak, one of the popular prophets of the

---

[1]Article by Tom Maddox, writing coordinator at Evergreen State College, from *Wilson Quarterly* 18:29–36 Summer '94. Copyright © 1994 by Tom Maddox. Reprinted with permission.

1960s, assails the emerging "cult of information," staid members of the academic establishment scramble to log on to the Internet. In truth, these new ideological divides are little more helpful than the old, for it is as right to be hopeful about the future unfolding before us as it is to fear it.

As technophobes are fond of pointing out, technology's effects are generally unpredictable, often negative, and almost always produced at the expense of traditional ways of life. From the technophobe's point of view, therefore, a moral, sensible response to the NII is to reject it in principle and fight against it with whatever means are at hand—to sabotage it intellectually and combat the policies that would bring it into being.

Persuasive as some of its concerns may be, such a neo-Luddite view of the NII seems beyond the pale of serious consideration. As a people we are wont to explore the paths along which our desire leads us, and it seems virtually foreordained that our desire will lead us to build and use the NII. Even after one sets aside the reflex reactions of the technophobe, however, there is much reason to feel uncertainty and anxiety over the NII. The history of electronic media, especially television, is a powerful reminder that new information technologies can easily be turned to malign ends. Through advertising and other means, they have been used not only to exploit our hearts' desires but to manufacture new ones. Along with the specter of greater government control over citizens' lives that becomes possible with the new information technologies, this "commodification of desire" must be considered one of the darker prospects of the NII. Add to it the inescapable unease one feels in contemplating a wired world, an almost subliminal fear of the accession of what historian Manuel de Landa, in *War in the Age of Intelligent Machines* (1991), calls the "machinic phylum"—the set of things that operate according to the machine's laws of rationality and order. To put these fears more succinctly, with the NII, it seems likely that the machines will grow stronger, as will marketers and governments.

It is possible that another, less defined group, at once the weakest and least organized and also the most numerous, subtle, and relentless, can wrest control of the NII. That is the group of each of us, insofar as we represent ourselves and not the need to consume, on the one hand, or to behave obediently, on the other—each of us as we represent what the philosopher Michel Foucault called "a certain decisive will not to be governed."

Certainly, in many situations this group has virtually no voice and no power. Against it, Foucault insisted in books such as *Madness and Civilization* (1961) and *Discipline and Punish* (1975), is the power of the modern state. And there is as well the vast array of businesses and organizations that exist primarily to sell us images of our wants and needs, to ply us with our own fantasies. Their most effective and characteristic medium is commercial television, where the advertising surrounds and overwhelms a content that, as MTV videos and elaborate "infomercials" illustrate, increasingly becomes indistinguishable from it.

The same groups can be seen working, along with others, to create the NII. Government spokespersons and telecommunications industry flacks ply the media promising manifold blessings, at least to citizens of the United States. "All Americans have a stake in the construction of an advanced National Information Infrastructure," according to a U.S. government "Agenda for Action." "Development of the NII can help unleash an information revolution that will change forever the way people live, work, and interact with each other." In *Business Week,* an MCI Telecommunications ad fantastically asserts: "The space-time continuum is being challenged. The notion of communication is changed forever. All the information in the universe will soon be accessible to everyone at every moment." All because of a dream known as the information superhighway and a vision known as network MCI. The pitchman's hyperbole and the government's bland assurances alike should tell us that we are being hustled, worked—like a crowd standing in front of the ring-toss stand at a traveling carnival.

Note the two passages' common theme of changing things forever: "communication," according to MCI; "the way people live, work, and interact," according to the government. Oddly, just here, where the hyperbole appears to be at its worst, both advertising agency and government are telling the simplest of truths: Should the NII come to pass, it will change things forever. Like the magician's showy gesture or the pitchman's barked promise, these declaiming voices serve to distract our attention from something else: in this case, the subtler, more disturbing truth that no one— neither the White House nor MCI nor anyone else—can predict the nature of the changes that will be brought about by the NII.

Consider some of the characteristic technologies of the last 100 years: the telephone, the automobile, the radio, the television, and the computer. At the time of their inception and for many years afterward, no one understood the implications of their invention and use. Sociologist Colin Cherry, writing about the history of telephone systems, says, "The new invention can first be seen by society only in terms of the liberties of action it currently possesses. We say society is 'not ready,' meaning that it is bound by its present customs and habits to think only in terms of its existing institutions. Realizations of new liberties, and creation of new institutions means social change, new thought, and new feelings. The invention alters the society, and eventually is used in ways that were at first quite unthinkable." That the automobile would become such a common killer of adolescents, for example, or the telephone a powerful instrument for the gratification of a distinctive brand of aural sexual pleasures that did not exist as such before its invention—who could have predicted these and a myriad other such things?

"Mechanical properties do not predestine the development and employment of an innovation," social historian Claude Fischer notes in his study of the social consequences of the telephone, *America Calling* (1992). "Instead, struggles and negotiations among interested parties shape that history. Inventors, investors, competitors, organized customers, agencies of government, the media, and others conflict over how an innovation will develop. The outcome is a particular definition and a structure for the new technology, perhaps even a 'reinvention' of the device."

One could write the history of the broadcast media in the United States in very similar terms. When radio stations began broadcasting in the 1920s, they sprang up almost at random and did pretty much what they wanted. "Radio" was still up for grabs; the nature of the medium was undefined. Advertisements, for example, were extremely controversial in the early days, many people (including Secretary of Commerce Herbert Hoover) holding that the airwaves should be employed for the public good, not for commercial purposes. In 1927, motivated in part by the need to keep stations on separate wavelengths, Congress created the Federal Radio Commission (FRC), directing it to regulate the radio waves according to "public interest, convenience, and necessity." This remains the standard for the regulation of broadcast media today by the FRC's successor, the Federal Communications Commission, the justification for de facto censorship of radio and television and other regulation of program content.

There were dissenters, of course. Radio preacher Aimee Semple McPherson, who in fact trampled all over other stations' wavelengths, telegraphed Washington: "Please order your minions of Satan to leave my station alone. Stop. You cannot expect the Almighty to abide by your wave-length nonsense. Stop. When I offer prayers to Him I must fit into His wave reception. Stop."

Despite her plea, the situation was becoming clear: If the Almighty wanted to go on radio, he would have to play by the U.S. government's rules. Anybody who has listened to much radio or watched much television can draw his or her own conclusions about how well those rules have served the public interest, the public convenience, or the public necessity. Whatever defects unregulated radio and television might possess theoretically, it is difficult to imagine that they would be more numerous and thoroughgoing than those of the existing regulated varieties.

The NII today is in a condition much like that of radio during the 1920s. The stakes, however, are much greater. Through the NII, it may become possible for businesses and arms of the government to acquire an intimate knowledge of every citizen—what we love and hate, what compels us and what we ignore—and with it perhaps the ability to manipulate our needs and our behavior. Every choice we make could be recorded, as could every moment of consumer bliss or image consumption. We could be profiled in terrifying detail, almost casually, as a kind of side-effect of the network software. Viewed this way, the NII becomes the Panopticon triumphant, to borrow Michel Foucault's notion of a machine for constraining our desire within socially acceptable limits, on the one hand, and commercially viable ones, on the other.

The experience of the Internet suggests how this can be prevented. It shows that the individual users of telecommunications and computer technology can sometimes achieve a kind of victory by wresting control of the technology. Originally created by the Pentagon to keep defense-related computers connected even in the aftermath of a nuclear war, the Internet has become one of the prime sites of many kinds of individual and collective activity. Almost from the beginning, the Internet has served the individual's purposes with enormous flexibility—as much as, if not more so, than it has served the institutions that brought it into being. As personal computers became nearly ubiquitous during the 1980s and Internet connections commonplace, they unlocked possibilities entirely unforeseen by the technicians or the managers who oversaw the system. Defense Department bureaus found their employees swapping recipes; staid and reputable organizations of all sorts found their members or employees engaging in unlicensed and uncontrolled debate, discussing the theory and practice of sado-masochism or chatting about whatever they wished with people from all over the world. In short, while the technology (of computers and networks) made such things possible, it neither anticipated nor encouraged them, nor could it stop them.

Perhaps we can expect more of the same from the NII. If, as seems likely, there emerges out of today's struggles and negotiations over the new medium considerable freedom for individuals in their use of the NII, people will exploit it in currently unimagined and unsanctioned ways. To many people, some of what occurs will seem wasteful, disgusting, obscene, sexist, racist, even criminal; to others, merely vulgar and depressing. Some already lament the waste of network resources—or "bandwidth"—resulting from the storage and transmission of binary files of explicit sexual images or from "anti-social" modes of behavior such as "flaming" (i.e. sending abusive E-mail to an individual one finds annoying). Such practices stand as honorable evidence of that "certain decisive will not to be governed," and so we must protect them above all, as we must protect the speech that most offends us and the religious beliefs we find most stupid and repulsive.

In fact, because the new information technology we are creating seems to lend itself more readily to improvisation and freedom than to rigid planning and control, it is not unreasonable to hope for triumph. Still, the possibility remains that the NII could turn into a largely one-way street, one where "consumers" receive information but will not have freedom to retransmit or alter it. This is the "500 channels of TV" model, the worst scenario for the future because it implies an audience composed of inert consumers and passive paracitizens, easily manipulated by any technically adept spin doctors with access to the profiles. Many of today's cable television providers are eager to offer just this sort of service.

The history of American broadcast media is not greatly encouraging. Network and local programming alike have proceeded according to unspoken canons of propriety that defy adult standards of free speech and journalistic practice. As a result, we have a national standard of infantilized media, which allow necessary human chaos only as it sneaks through in the form of eroticized violence and violent eroticism, both typically subtextual, subliminal, and dishonest. If we wish the NII to escape such a malign fate, we should work toward an opaque and open NII, one that, for instance, allows universal and near-anonymous access, guarantees the individual the right (which the government does not currently do) and means to encrypt information, and provides individual control over content, both outgoing and incoming. Taken together, these technical attributes would combine to create an NII that might actually serve us without entangling us even more in the embrace of commercial and governmental forces.

Telecommunications and computer technologies are themselves also forces to contend with. Building the NII, we create a vast and productive niche for the enlargement of de Landa's "machinic phylum," worlds in which machines can grow and evolve, and this eventually may have profound implications for human consciousness. Even in the relatively primitive forms it takes today, information technology seems to encourage a fixation on virtual rather than real experience—on technologically mediated perception, not direct apprehension. It can also saturate us in a hypnotic image-repertoire that works to render us passive and dream-struck no matter who, if anyone, controls it.

Marvin Minsky, the dark knight of the information age, generally considered, along with John McCarthy, one of the founding fathers of the field of artificial intelligence, said in a speech a few years ago that he preferred virtual sunsets to real ones because the virtual sunset could be constructed so as to be perfectly enjoyable. Provocative lunacy, I thought at the time, not realizing how many people agree with him.

The virtual can seduce us because it offers the promise of being completely shaped to our wishes, while the material world remains refractory—there we suffer and die and live out fates that cannot be edited or replayed to render them more beautiful, more charming, less disastrous. The virtual worlds we can master, the material world we cannot. Even the most open model of the NII—one that does not lock individuals into passive roles as consumers and citizens—forces us to contend with this dialectic of virtual and real, and especially with the ethical dimensions of an allegiance to the virtual.

As the electronic media make us more aware of conditions around the world—or, at least, of images of such conditions—we realize how much horror exists and how connected we are to it. Thus, despite our prosperity and plenty, we find ourselves intolerably affronted by images of disease and destruction. We do not wish to see starving children or piled-up bodies as we wait for our evening meal. However, through the virtual worlds we master the horrors, discovering ways to prevent them from deeply disturbing our composure. And virtuality has a wide domain. The Holocaust becomes a museum and a Spielberg movie, a spectacle, as the Situationists say, and we watch and weep yet are strangely exultant at the end of it all, and why not? We are alive and have our technology to instruct and amuse us. Today the corpses pile up in Bosnia (or was that Croatia?) and Rwanda, and the day's bald television images and puerile narrations haunt us, but tomorrow they will have become elements of an aesthetically rewarding film.

The NII will serve us efficiently in this regard. In Wim Wenders's film, *Until the End of the World* (1992), characters become addicted to image technology, lost in reliving memories of their infancy through a device that turns their thoughts into pictures. The NII would not grant us this power, but it would put rich, complex sets of images at our command—"All the information in the universe will soon be accessible to everyone at every moment"—and thus generate the potential for its own kinds of addictions: to beautiful images and to virtuality itself.

Ultimately, the NII finds us being ourselves in the late 20th century: caught in the web of our own fantasies, governed by forces that inscribe their orders into our being, fighting nonetheless, through a stubborn will, to manifest something like authentic individual desire. The sharp-edged technology of the NII can cut a number of ways: It can enlarge the domain of the commodifiers and controllers; it can serve the resistance to these forces; it can saturate us all, controlled and controllers alike, in a virtual alternative to the real world.

Meanwhile, most of humanity will live and die deprived of the wonders of the NII, or indeed of the joys of adequate nutrition, medical care, and housing. We would do well to regulate our enthusiasms accordingly—that is, to remember where love and mercy have their natural homes, in that same material world. Otherwise we will have built yet another pharaonic monument to wealth, avarice, and indifference. We will have proved the technophobes right. More to the point, we will have collaborated to neglect the suffering of the damned of the earth—our other selves—in order to entertain ourselves.

Yet as William Gibson says in *Neuromancer* (1984), the canonical work of cyberpunk science fiction, "The Street finds its own uses for things," the Street referring to the unauthorized, unsanctioned play of human desire. Thus, we can approach the NII in a properly skeptical or suspicious frame of mind and yet remain open to its possibilities. After all, the Internet has shown that even a technology designed to enable the military to fight on after a nuclear holocaust can be made to serve the unfettered human imagination. With this experience to guide us, it is possible, perhaps even likely, that the same can be accomplished with the NII.

BREAKING THE BOX[2]

When Bill Gates, chairman of Microsoft, declared on live TV this March that he did "not have to take any more of this," got up, and strode away from Connie Chung's cameras, he was symbolically crashing through the media mirror and stepping into a new historic era. A man without a television in his home, Gates in his defiance was offering an omen of an America free of TV within the next five years.

Yes, TV's reign can end that soon. Without giving up any current pleasure or service, all Americans can be emancipated like the Microsoft liberator to spurn the tyranny of the tube. The computer industry is already three times the size of the TV industry and growing ten times as fast. Current projections show that American companies will sell more than 50 million personal computers in 1994, about half of them in the U.S. and some 60 per cent for residences and home offices. Over the last five years the share of computers in the U.S. linked to networks rose from under 10 per cent to over 60 per cent. During the next five years, the capacity of those connections can rise at least a thousandfold, allowing PCs to summon digital films and files of news, art, and

[2]Article by George Gilder, fellow of the Discovery Institute in Seattle, from *National Review* 46:37–43 Ag 15 '94. Copyright © 1994 by National Review, Inc. Reprinted with permission.

multimedia from around the world. The television cable can become a computer connection. The personal computer can rule American culture as decisively as broadcast TV has ruled it for the last forty years.

The downfall of the liberal media, the rout of the rodent kings of the networks, the overthrow of Ken Auletta's "three blind mice" gnawing at the pillars of civilized life in America—what, one might wonder, could be sweeter news for conservatives?

Yet many conservatives are strangely ambivalent. They share the view of the existing broadcasters that the more power wielded by customers over what they can see the worse the programming will be. In this view, the boob tube will give way to what H. L. Mencken might have termed a new Boobissimus, as the liberated children rush away from the network nurse, chasing Pied Piper pederasts, snuff-film sadists, and other trolls of cyberspace.

Affirming these fears, NBC's prime panderer, Phil Donahue, asserts with relish: "The information highway will have a lot of sex." In late January he presented James Erlich of ICFX, the developer of Penthouse Interactive, showing off a future technology in which a viewer with a click of the remote could capture himself on screen jousting with the virtual software of a Penthouse "pet."

Is this the future of mass media—more brutal and banal and salacious TV? Or is it Bill Gates's vision of arts and letters and encyclopedias and empowered citizens visiting the wonders of the world without leaving their homes? The issue will be vital to the prospects for capitalism, for we live and work in our technologies, in our phones and TVs and computers, as much as we do in our homes and schools and neighborhoods.

On both the Left and the Right, television culture has long been the main exhibit for the case against capitalism. John Kenneth Galbraith, E. J. Mishan, Christopher Lasch, Barbara Ehrenreich, and Robert Bellah on the Left all land their most crushing blows merely by pointing to the obvious crudeness of mass advertising and entertainment. Pope John Paul II, Aleksandr Solzhenitsyn, and other titans of the age point to the crass pandering of broadcasters and the commercials that sustain them and the consumer culture that feeds them as the supreme evidence for the essential vanity of a Western "cult" of individual freedom. Indeed, even the most fervent supporter of enterprise may well blanch before the sort of entrepreneurial mind that capped this spring's Nielsen-ratings race with a contest of Can

You Top This? in which one network responded to the Menendez brothers on Court TV by offering up an interview with Charles Manson posing as a born-again Barabbas, and another countered with Jeffrey Dahmer, poignantly pondering his troubled childhood.

Supporters of capitalism must come to terms with the essential truth of the case against U.S. commercial TV—and even acknowledge the obvious superiority of public programming in both the U.S. and Europe. Under the sway of television, democratic capitalism enshrines a Gresham's law: bad culture drives out good, and ultimately porn and pruriency, violence and blasphemy, prevail everywhere from the dimwitted "news" shows to the lugubrious movies. As can be seen by anyone unblinded by libertarian dogma, no culture can long endure if its average citizen spends between four and seven hours a day gripped in passive contemplation of such stuff.

Boobissimus has already laid waste a generation of American youth, who have slipped to the very rear ranks of the industrial world in academic and intellectual achievement and leapt into the lead in violence and bastardy. Now, impelled by the still more far-reaching Kultursmog of direct broadcast satellite technology, Boobissimus is preparing to lay waste the rest of civilization as well.

Like Randall Jarrell, many a conservative thus finds himself with a "Sad Heart in the Supermarket." Soon after writing that lamentation, Jarrell stepped out on one of the superhighways financed by Albert Gore Sr.'s National Defense Highway Act and was run over by a truck. Many of us bear similarly sad hearts before the new information superhighway being rhetorically promoted by Al Gore Jr. We fear Boobissimus will rule the superhighway as it rules the mass media.

These fears, however, feed on a mistaken notion of the nature of mass man and mass culture. The information superhighway in fact is nearly a perfect antidote for Boobissimus. It promises to revitalize capitalism and culture in the U.S. and around the globe and to retrieve the hopes of a conservative era in politics.

TV is a boob tube not because the people are boobs but because it is a broadcast technology. Any broadcast medium, by definition, concentrates intelligence and control at the center. The nature of the technology dictates that the receivers be dumb terminals, or even idiot boxes, that make no demands on the user and that restrict him to a small selection of programs. As Nicholas Negroponte of MIT's Media Lab has pointed out, despite all the talk of interactivity and digital intelligence today's TV is still dumber than an airport urinal that can detect your presence at the stall.

The personal computer championed by Bill Gates is the opposite of this reductionist broadcast technology. Where television technology is essentially centralized—a tool of tyrants— computer technology amplifies both the intelligence of its owners and their power to choose and create.

Impelling the expansion of computer and networking technology are two exponential laws. Microchip technology is ruled by the law of the microcosm: Take any number n transistors and put them on a single sliver of silicon, and you get n^2 performance and value. Over the last thirty years, the number of transistors on a chip has doubled every eighteen months, yielding a millionfold rise in cost-effectiveness. Today's multimillion-dollar supercomputers inexorably become the pocket appliances of tomorrow.

This computer technology is now converging with communications technology. Networks feed on the law of the telecosm: Take any number n of computers and connect them in networks, and you get n^2 performance and value. The advance of networks is now even faster than the onrush of computing power.

Over the last five years, the network of networks known as the Internet has grown at a pace of 15 per cent a month; it now reaches some 20 million computers. The spearhead of the new era is electronic mail, on the verge of expanding to video or multimedia mail. When last estimated, there were 42 million active users of electronic mail around the globe, including nearly 30 million in the U.S., but the numbers were rising too fast to trust.

Within the next ten years, this explosive technological advance in both networks and processors virtually guarantees that the personal-computer model of distributed intelligence and control will unseat the emperors of the mass media and blow away the TV model of centralization. The teleputer—a revolutionary PC of the next decade—will give every household hacker the productive potential of a factory czar of the industrial era and the communications power of a broadcast tycoon of the television age. Broadcasting hierarchies will give way to computer heterarchies—peer networks in which the terminals are essentially equal in power and there is no center at all.

When the center cannot hold, one might wonder with Yeats, "what rough beast . . . shuffling its slow thighs . . . slouches toward Bethlehem to be born." It is centralization, however, that feeds the monsters of mobocracy and the mobcult of television.

Disguising this tendency for many years was the persistent influence of TV's sources in the more local and specialized culture of books and theater and the moral capital of an era before mass media. Nonetheless, any broadcast medium, appealing to miscellaneous crowds at a single time, ultimately must reduce its audience members to their lowest common denominator of tastes and responses.

What do we have in common? Well, we share a number of ideals and aspirations. But we share them in different idioms and accents. A richer and easier target by far beckons to the programming entrepreneur in our prurient interests, our morbid fears and anxieties, our ambivalent dread of violence and suppressed longings for it, our hunger for sexual images and fantasies, all the undertow of lusts and rages and derangements that it is the prime goal and glory of civilization to overcome.

This means commercial television is necessarily the enemy of civilization. If it tries to target special human interests and aspirations, TV must ultimately fail. In any particular crowd of viewers, there are not enough high-church Catholics, or ham-radio hobbyists, or quantum physicists, or rose gardeners, or libertarian intellectuals to sustain a program. To reach an adequate market, mass broadcasts almost necessarily must pander to prurient interests and morbid fears and anxieties.

Check into a hotel in America today. There on the bureau is the inevitable TV and the nearly inescapable Spectravision box. Some 37 channels of miscellaneous midden, 6 "blockbuster" movies, and 2 offerings of hard- or soft-core porn beckon the tired traveler. The Hollywood hits begin at inconvenient times and end deep into the night. The 37 channels are all in progress and none are just what you want. Zapping through the gauntlet, you tend to stop at the most arresting images—the smoking gun, the hurtling car, the nude breast, the crashing fist, the splash of blood. Even the eloquent Republican congressman on C-SPAN discussing the flaws in the financing scheme for Clinton's health-care plan may well not suffice to pull you away from the arms of Miss April on the beach in Aruba.

Any mass-media or broadcasting regime rides an inexorable gradient toward the gutter. But by changing radically the balance of power between the distributors of culture and the receivers of culture, the teleputer will forever break the broadcast bottleneck.

Potentially there will be as many "channels" as there are computers connected to the global network. In essence, this means one channel for each person, which he himself programs and controls and which always offers his very first choice. The creator of a program on a specialized subject—from Canaletto's art to chaos theory, from GM car transmission repair to cowboy poetry, from Szechuan restaurant finance to C++ computer codes—will be able to reach everyone in the industrialized world who shares the interest. Artists will be able to command a large audience without catering to lowest-common-denominator tastes.

People in a crowd, as Ortega y Gasset explained in his masterpiece, *The Revolt of the Masses*, are mostly boobs. But in their first choices—in their individual tastes, hobbies, career aspirations, educational goals—people show huge diversity and higher refinement. Of course, individual tastes and interests can also veer toward the depraved and self-destructive. There is no doubt that this fare will thrive on computer networks as it does in today's mass media; sin and perversion we will always have with us. But the key to the culture is not its perversions but its aspirations and opportunities for distinction. By refracting the mass media into myriad media, the teleputer will open the way to floods of new programming.

Those who think that there are too many channels already should imagine entering a bookstore with just 37 or 50 or even 500 books and magazines. In a bookstore, in contrast to a TV, you do not expect to settle for what is on the counter; you expect to get your first choice. Not only would the sparse bookstore normally fail to give you your first choice, it would offer an extremely misleading notion of American print culture.

To understand the future of computer culture, one need only contemplate one of the new super-bookstores such as Books-A-Million, Borders, or Barnes & Noble, which are rapidly gaining market share in the book trade. Or as Bill Gates has suggested, imagine "a Library of Congress" where all the publications are instantly and randomly reachable from your desk.

In variety, morality, and substance, the first-choice arena of text culture differs radically from reductionist broadcast culture. Some 55,000 new trade books are published every year, together with many thousands of magazines and other publications. About half the trade-book market is religious books, a $2.5-billion business. Over the last several years, for example, some 1.3 million copies of the Christian novels of the nineteenth-century Scots

novelist George Macdonald, who inspired C. S. Lewis, were sold
in America. Beyond religious and inspirational literature, science
tomes, technical manuals, career education, and a variety of
literature—from porn to piety—also sell heavily.

The best-seller list is not a good index of the real book culture
of America. Much of it is an offshoot of Boobissimus. Half the
nonfiction best-sellers are written by or for TV and movie stars
who gain monopoly rents because of the capital costs and distribution bottlenecks of old media technology. Moreover, the best-
seller lists entirely omit the religious books that account for half
the market.

The new multimedia culture will afford a huge new range of
variety. Teleputers will allow many of the fifty thousand screen-
writers who now queue up before the Hollywood bottleneck instead to reach substantial audiences around the world not by
pandering to mobs but by appealing to special interests and pas-
sions.

Providing a harbinger of the change is talk radio. The most
important development in politics since the retirement of Ronald
Reagan has been the rise of Rush Limbaugh, whose heroic energy
and forensic flair have transformed AM radio into a counterforce
to the monolithic liberal dominance of TV. In a primitive form,
talk radio has three of the features that the teleputer will soon
lend to multimedia and video: interactivity, low costs, and numerous local outlets.

The impact of information superhighways will be vastly more
powerful. Within the next five years the entire American economy is going to be reshaped around these new digital networks.
Telecommuting, teleconferencing, telemedicine, teleputing will
change from buzzwords into the basic fabric of business and life.

In politics, the teleputer will break the bondage of public
opinion. As Walter Lippmann showed some sixty years ago, public opinion is mostly a myth. People do not truly hold enduring
opinions on most of the subjects on which they are surveyed.
Unlike votes, opinions are not even remotely equal, as polls assume. Knowledgeable views are incomparably more significant
than the statistical figments of bogus majorities. On most issues,
the public en masse possesses not opinions but impressions.
Evoked by the media in league with politicians, these impressions
are echoed by the pollsters' questions, which therefore tend to
trigger the desired response. Ross Perot's instant-TV interactive-

town-hall concept was a virtual parody of existing mass politics, keeping the most crucial power—the definition and framing of the issues—in the hands of the czar of the net.

TV will soon expire and transpire into a new realm of real communities rather than reductionist masses and majorities. Using the on-line services that link to the increasingly global Internet, people no longer have to look for love, affinity, or political allies in all the wrong places. Perhaps as an omen, Limbaugh is said to have found his new wife on Compuserve. On the *NR*/Heritage Town Hall, conservatives can communicate with others across the country and around the world. They need restrict themselves no longer to the group at the pub or the park or the families at a local church.

The Internet has already made this era a golden age of letters. The future of media will see the further ascendancy of the word. As screens improve their resolution they will increasingly compete with paper as a high-contrast, flicker-free vessel for text. Great cities will hollow out, as the best and brightest in them retreat to rural redoubts and reach out to global markets and communities. The most deprived ghetto child in the most blighted project can escape the local demagogues who hold him down and can gain educational opportunities exceeding those of a suburban preppie today. Families will regroup around the evolving silicon hearths of a new cottage economy.

Contrary to reductionist polls and media, conservatives already dominate the real culture of the society. Conservatives account for some 80 per cent of the entrepreneurs who generate the overwhelming bulk of the nation's wealth and pay the huge majority of taxes. Conservatives account for perhaps two-thirds of the married men whose labors in the provider role are the productive heart of the national economy. Liberals dominate the parasite classes—the broken families, the litigious Left, the hedonist criminals and pushers, the educationist child abusers, the Planned Parenthood condom hawkers, the guilt-ridden heirs, the bureaucracy pimps, the foundation flakes, the mush peddlers of the academy and the welfare state, and the pied pipers of the mass media.

TV has substituted the values and visions of Washington and Hollywood for the real facts and faiths of America. Intellectuals have so forgotten how real cultures and communities work that they often confuse the passive experience of being in a mass audience with the active experience of participating in a real community. Thus, on the basis of evidence from the tyranny of television, they sink into pessimism about the future of democracy.

Ken Auletta declares that the networks are all we have as a "national church." In a sense he may be right. But it is a bogus church that reduces its worshippers to boobs. As Richard Vigilante answers, conservatives should "thank God" for the chance to disestablish this false church and restore the real life of Americans. Participation in a community is not a passive posture; it is an active commitment. The computer culture will blow away the façade of TV and allow the conservative Americans who sustain the economy once again to realize that their private lives make up the real culture of an America that can survive and prosper.

SEX & THE SUPERHIGHWAY[3]

It is a topic that has provoked almost as many headlines as health-care reform or Beavis and Butt-head: the inevitable information superhighway. Across America, virtually everyone from Al Gore to your favorite morning talk-show host has speculated for months about this informational interstate, although few agree on what direction it will take.

The superhighway—or hypeway, as one skeptic calls it—is supposed to knit our computers, televisions and telephones into networks that will allow us to work, shop and run errands in "virtual communities" without ever leaving our armchairs. All this activity is expected to generate a mind-boggling $3.5 trillion global-communications industry by the end of the century, according to no less an expert than John Sculley, the former CEO of Apple Computer. He might add that it could be rocky getting there: He himself left Apple for a job that didn't pan out. Meanwhile, high-tech companies like Silicon Graphics, Intel and Microsoft are jockeying for a place in the fast lane with such communications juggernauts as Bell Atlantic, US West, Time Warner and Paramount.

So what's wrong with this picture? In story after story, deal

[3]Article by Bronwyn Fryer, freelance writer, from *Working Woman* 19:51–60 Ap '94. Copyright © 1994 by Working Woman, Inc. Reprinted with permission.

after deal, the major players are the same white males who already run the leading cable, communications and computer companies. Just where are the *women* drivers on the information superhighway? Will women be shut out of this lucrative technological revolution, just as they have been shut out of real power and presence in the computer industry?

To answer this question, it helps to take a closer look at how women have fared in the computer industry itself, scene of the last seismic shift in technology. In fact, today's highway hype closely resembles that surrounding the birth of the PC in the late 1970s, when the press predicted that the new desktop machine would put "information at our fingertips" and offer huge economic opportunities to smart young entrepreneurs.

In theory, at least, this brand-new industry was also supposed to provide a level playing field for women—PC companies are less than 20 years old, and the average age of their employees is well below 40. But it hasn't turned out that way. Most of the Boy Wonders who started what became the biggest companies were just that—boys. These young entrepreneurs, like Apple Computer founder Steve Jobs, now 39, and Microsoft founder Bill Gates, now 38, had been playing with electronics for years. They invited other eager young guys into their start-up companies, which soon took on the forbidding, no-girls-allowed atmosphere of tree houses. Says leading industry analyst Esther Dyson, "You'd think the high-tech industry would be modern, but it really isn't. It's run by the old-boys network."

Not surprisingly, women didn't swarm to Silicon Valley and its counterparts. By 1992, reports the Bureau of Labor Statistics, women made up just 36% of the work force in computer and data-processing services and only 37% in hardware manufacturing. That compares to 59% in finance, insurance and real estate and over 50% in law, accounting and retail. On average, only such traditionally male-dominated areas as lumber production (where women account for 14% of the work force), automobile repair (10%) and construction (9%) employ fewer women.

Their numbers are even smaller near the top. None of the nation's publicly held hardware manufacturers have women at the helm, and only a handful of software firms do, most of them privately held and well under the $50 million mark. While 6% of directors of the Fortune 1000 are women, only 2.9% of the directors at 162 publicly owned companies in Silicon Valley (including some banks, but predominantly high-tech and biotech firms) are women, according to a report published last November in the *San Jose Mercury News*. As the *Mercury News* noted, "Women are 10 times more likely to be represented on the Supreme Court of the United States than on the average board of directors for a company in Silicon Valley."

The number of women who are corporate officers isn't much better. Overall in the Fortune 1000, women hold fewer than 5% of senior-management positions. In the computer industry, according to a January 1993 report in *Upside*, a high-tech magazine, the ranks of women vice presidents and above at hardware firms ranged from a high of 16% at Tandem Computers to zero at National Semiconductor. Even in the younger, faster-moving software industry, only one firm surveyed by *Upside* came close to equality in the executive suite, with three of the seven top positions belonging to women, and that was Autodesk of Sausalito, Calif., where the CEO is a woman, Carol Bartz.

Bartz, of course, has long been a leading role model for women in technology, and there are other bright spots in the industry. Women enjoy visibility and respect—not to mention impressive fees—as industry analysts, including Esther Dyson of EDventure Holdings and Patricia Seybold of the Patricia Seybold Group. There are venture-capital luminaries like Ann Winblad, a founding partner at Hummer Winblad Venture Partners, with $95 million under management, and pioneering entrepreneurs like Sandra Kurtzig, who founded the software company ASK Group. Some women are well-positioned to speed down the superhighway once it is built. Two new government appointees will be supervising its construction: Mary Lowe Good, undersecretary for technology at the Commerce Department, and Arati Prabhakar, head of the National Institute of Standards and Technology, which helps small and medium-size companies with technological development. And one of the hottest new vehicles is expected to be multimedia—software that combines digitized images and sound, usually packaged in disks to run on the CD-ROM drives of personal computers. Women like Brenda Laurel, a virtual-reality expert, have already established themselves in this sector, which is expected to grow to $25 billion by 1995.

Unfortunately, though, the majority of the women employed by computer companies tend to cluster, as they often do elsewhere, not in bottom-line positions but in less powerful staff jobs: human resources, sales administration and public relations. "The positions are what I call low-risk 'girl jobs,'" says Kathy Vieth, a former vice president of mobile computing at IBM, who last year took early retirement and now consults out of Vail, Colo. "There's nothing wrong with them, but unless you fill your dance card with a variety of experience—you don't stand a chance of getting into the corner office."

Why aren't more women plugged into the power elite? To some extent, it is a pipeline problem: The Engineering Workforce Commission reports that women earned only 16% of the bachelor's degrees in engineering awarded in 1993. The number's up from the 13% of 10 years earlier, but is still minuscule. Meanwhile, only 30% of the undergraduate degrees in computer science, the other main source of techies, went to women. The pipeline has been blocked by an educational turnoff that begins with young girls.

By the time they finish high school, many girls have already bought into the common perception that a "technical female" is an oxymoron. Helen Bradley, now vice president of systems-software engineering at Sunsoft, a Sun Microsystems subsidiary, remembers that as an engineering student at MIT in the 1970s, she had to make her way through a virtual minefield of discouragement. "My professors told me I was wasting my time and that I should go home and have babies," says Bradley. "I got pretty pissed off."

While Bradley turned her anger into an iron determination to succeed, many other women lose heart in the testosterone-tinged atmosphere. Go to just about any high-tech company, for instance, and you'll see many male programmers working through the night; at Microsoft, for instance, the programmers' offices look more like dormitory rooms, with futons rolled up under desks. For most women, especially those with families, hanging out at the all-night watercooler is simply out of the question. Sometimes the men don't even want them there; Deborah Willingham, general manager of product-support services at Microsoft, who previously ran an engineering team at IBM, has encountered men who refused to work with her because of her sex.

Some women compare the hostility they encounter to that faced by military women. That's not surprising, says Barbara Simons, a senior engineer at IBM. "The roots of technology development are military," she says, "and most developers tend to be competitive young men. Most women aren't comfortable in that kind of culture." Sometimes the culture can be positively oppressive: At last November's Comdex, the largest computer-industry trade show, among the biggest draws were the booths displaying pornographic software.

At work, women often find their technical competence challenged. Willingham is frequently asked by male colleagues to confirm that she holds a degree in industrial and systems engineering. "The men are never asked," she says. "It's just taken for granted that they are technical." Similarly, Erika Williams, a vice president at the computer company Amdahl, still makes a point of wearing her MIT class ring every day to underscore her credibility—after 15 years in the business.

Even Bartz, who runs a $400 million personal-computer software company that is the sixth-largest in the world, continually runs up against credibility checks. After joining the board of the California Chamber of Commerce, Bartz was surprised to find herself one of only 10 women among 85 men. But she wasn't surprised that some of the men in the room wanted to grill her about her background. "I obviously wouldn't be there if I weren't accomplished," she says, "but I still get asked about my credentials."

Then, too, some industry critics wonder whether technical expertise isn't an artificial barrier. Many of the senior managers of these companies come from sales, marketing or finance. And the lack of an engineering degree, the critics note, certainly didn't hamper men like Sculley, who came from Pepsico, or Lou Gerstner, the new IBM CEO, whose background is in consulting and marketing—both got their tech training on the job.

Even when they have the training, women seldom feel they get encouragement. In a 1989 survey by Cooper Union, 47% of female engineers said that they were not being used to their fullest potential, and one-third felt that they were not being steered into advanced positions. Female mentors are few and far between, and male mentors can be just as hard to find. "A friend of mine who's a CEO told me confidentially that he doesn't mentor women, and that none of his CEO friends do, either," says Judy Bitterli, senior vice president of sales and marketing at Softbank, a CD-ROM distributor in Monterey, Calif. "He's afraid that a close relationship to a woman might be perceived as more than a professional relationship, and he's terrified of a sexual-harassment suit."

Given this inhospitable climate, self-doubt runs rampant among high-tech women. That's particularly damaging in this arena, where aggressiveness and decisiveness are rewarded. "If a man and a woman are vying for the same job or assignment, the man will say, 'I'm the person for the job,' while the woman will say, 'OK, I think I might be able to do that,'" says Bartz. "Faced with that kind of hesitation, who is the boss more likely to choose?"

Considering their odds inside corporations, more and more women in technology are turning entrepreneurial, just like their sisters in other fields. While a promising route for those who have the know-how, it's obviously risky—and especially tough for those seeking funding from the financial or venture-capital community; most venture capitalists in high tech are the same set of suits that sit on the corporate boards. Heidi Roizen, founder and CEO of the $10 million Mountain View, Calif.-based software firm T/Maker, managed to raise two rounds of venture capital for her company while visibly pregnant during the second round. "Legally, people can't ask you about your pregnancy when you're applying for a job," she notes, "but when you're raising money, all bets are off. One venture capitalist kept calling me 'babe.'" Eventually, she managed to get $2 million—half of it from Ann Winblad's firm.

Representative Pat Schroeder (D-Colo.) wishes more women would take advantage of the Clinton administration's efforts to convert defense technology to civilian applications. The government is committed to paying half the cost of bringing products based on defense research to the general market, but few women have applied, and most have offered only services like marketing and teaching. "Women scientists and entrepreneurs should be leaping at the chance to, say, convert imaging technology used in the Navy into a product that takes better mammograms," says Schroeder, who chairs the House Subcommittee on Defense Technology Conversion. "But almost no women have come up with hard-core applications. That worries me, because this is such a great opportunity, and women are taxpayers, too."

Indeed, there have never been better opportunities for women in high tech, industry experts say. In spite of a difficult past, things are slowly changing for the better as corporations adapt to the times, women continue to gain experience and the ever-evolving technology itself aids the process. To begin with, current management trends seem to favor female advancement; as organizations continue to trim down due to the intensely competitive nature of the business, fewer levels will separate women from the top. "Successful companies are now being built on teams instead of hierarchies," says Lotus CEO Jim Manzi. "The old, male-dominated system is blowing up."

Organizations like Lotus are beginning to place women in advanced positions; senior vice president June Rokoff, for example, shares responsibility for technical direction and product development. Many companies are also actively seeking women for their boards. Manzi told *Working Woman* that he was "frankly embarrassed" by the lack of women on Lotus's board and vowed to have the situation corrected around the time this article appeared. Bill Gates told the magazine that he intends to name at least one woman to the Microsoft board by the end of 1995.

Technology is also bringing about change, says Microsoft's Kimberly Ellwanger, a lawyer who is the company's director of corporate affairs. "Electronic mail, which most large companies now use, has a way of flattening the organization," she notes. "You don't see the person you're dealing with, and you can send a message directly to the CEO." Likewise, the Internet, a giant worldwide electronic network that links many networks in a huge communications web—and that is perceived by many as the forerunner of the information superhighway—is a democratizing agent, although comparatively few women are on-line. Says Anita Borg, a researcher at Digital Equipment and founder of the Systers network, an electronic community of more than 1,500 technical women, "When we as a society are connected through this technology, we will see more women sharing experience and helping each other break through barriers."

And e-mail is making it easier to balance work and family within the computer industry. Take Carla Lewis, director of treasury operations at Microsoft, whose doctor ordered complete bed rest during the last trimester of her pregnancy. Lewis was able to continue her work by using a home computer and a modem; she even received a raise and an additional department to manage during her subsequent maternity leave.

Even more encouraging is the multitude of new openings on the superhighway. In the promising area of multimedia, says Richard Landry, publisher of *NewMedia,* a leading multimedia publication, about a third of the managers he meets are female. And Sueann Ambron of the Paramount Technology Group in Palo Alto, Calif., says, "We are on the perimeter of a whole new economy. There will be huge opportunities for creative, innovative new people, products and services."

Many of these new positions may not require traditional technological backgrounds. Artists, writers, musicians and other creative types who can conceive characters, stories and situations for multimedia games and educational software will be in demand. "It's kind of like TV or book plot development," says virtual-reality expert Diana Hawkins. "Today, most multimedia titles are targeted toward young boys. It's just a matter of time before we see more women involved and the offerings change."

Jacqueline Woods, president and CEO of Ameritech Ohio (formerly Ohio Bell), whose company is investigating joint ventures with other telecommunications firms in an effort to merge onto the superhighway, sees all kinds of opportunities for nontechnical types. Woods, herself a nontechnician with a background in marketing, sales and public relations, notes, "Women are very good at solving problems, educating, communicating and building consensus, and there will be a big need for that."

Industry analyst Denise Caruso believes that as the groundwork for the highway is laid, the high-tech industry will eventually begin to look more like the less male-dominated cable-programming, newspaper and magazine industries, where women hold some powerful positions. "Women can take a quantum leap forward now because no one knows what's going on," declares Caruso, who edited a closely followed newsletter on multimedia and is now editorial director of Friday Holdings, a high-profile partnership that invests in media deals. "Women always do well at the beginning of a new market, when it's wide open." But Caruso cautions that new technology and starry-eyed optimism too often go hand in hand. "Start-ups are generally bought out by bigger companies, and we all know who runs those," she says. "My only hope is that consciousness will be raised along the way."

Consciousness, as always, is key. It was only when the auto industry became aware that nearly half of its consumers were female that it began more actively recruiting and promoting the women who could speak to them. A similar recognition of the potential buying power of women might change the minds and hearts of the computer industry. And masses of new female customers are being developed right now in homes and classrooms around the country. "Young girls today are beginning to understand that the computer is a tool, and even a creative one," says Ameritech Ohio's Woods. "They won't be nearly as threatened as we were."

Is there a chance that one will grow up to be, well, a Girl Wonder version of Bill Gates or Steve Jobs? "Absolutely," says

Marilyn Bohl, the ASK Group's chief technology officer and a 30-year veteran of the high-tech wars. "But it won't be in an established field. It will be in some new area, like interactive TV."

Clearly, women will not be in a position to demand an equal share of high-tech success overnight, and they may have to spend some time in the slow lane, with maybe a detour or two. But more women are likely to be drawn to the field as it becomes more and more of a growth industry. Managers like Sunsoft's Helen Bradley had better enjoy their isolated visibility while they can. "When I'm the only red dress in a room full of blue suits at a conference, I really get attention," says Bradley. Sooner rather than later, a lot more women are going to be brightening up those rooms.

THE NAKED CITY[4]

This summer's trial of Robert and Carleen Thomas was more than a routine bust of a dirty-books distributor.

The Thomases, both 38, of Milpitas, California, were convicted on July 28 of transmitting obscenity through interstate phone lines via their computer bulletin board system on the Internet. The case, which is being appealed, served to open the eyes of both the computer network industry and Christians to the growing availability and acceptance of sexually explicit images over the emerging information superhighway and the eroding control of parents over the information their children take in.

"Now, with the advance of technology, [porn] can come right into the privacy of your own home," says Donna Rice Hughes, spokesperson for the Fairfax, Virginia–based Enough is Enough, an antipornography women's organization. "A lot of parents are still trying to figure out how to set the clock on their VCR while their kids are in their bedrooms accessing cyberporn," says Hughes.

There may be other milestone convictions in the near future, as the ever-resourceful pornography industry exploits computer and communications technology. In recent months, other instances have surfaced:

[4]Article by John Zipperer, staff writer, from *Christianity Today* 38:42–49 S 12 '94. Copyright © 1994 by *Christianity Today*. Reprinted with permission.

• Officials at the Lawrence Livermore nuclear weapons laboratory near San Francisco announced in July that the lab's advanced computers were being used by computer hackers to store and distribute more than 1,000 hard-core pornographic images.

• Pedophiles have used computer bulletin boards to contact children, learn their names and addresses, and set up meetings with them. "We've already had rapes of children occur through that type of setup," says antipornography activist Len Munsil.

• Phone-sex operators, stymied by legal and business barriers from drawing consumers with costly 900 numbers, have begun using 800 numbers—normally toll-free, but used by phone-sex corporations to charge enough to make 800-number phone sex an annual $100 million business. (Ameritech will no longer bill customers for charges resulting from 800-number calls beginning this month.)

• Some phone-sex firms have relocated to other countries out of the reach of the Federal Communications Commission. Then, from Moldova, the Dominican Republic, or African islands, the companies receive calls rerouted from 800 or 900 numbers in the United States. Businesses are often unaware that they are paying thousands of dollars in phone sex bills, because the overseas porn provider is not identified on the phone bills.

• Sexually explicit discussion groups on the Internet, a "network of computer networks," are regularly logging the greatest number of messages by Internet's 25 million estimated users.

The difference between the red-light district of the past and the home cyberporn connection of today is the tolerance that has grown with the relaxation of public attitudes and prosecutorial zeal. After a decade of high-profile convictions of people such as major pornography distributor Reuben Sturman, and highly visible Christian involvement in fighting pornography, including Focus on the Family president James Dobson's work on the 1986 Attorney General's Commission on Pornography, broad-based Christian activism appears to be waning.

Jerry Kirk, a longtime antiporn activist and Presbyterian pastor, believes churches are often reluctant to remain involved in the fight over the long haul. "Christians don't like conflict. They don't like risk," he says.

"One of the difficulties we struggle with again and again with churches," says Deen Kaplan, vice president of public policy for the National Coalition Against Pornography (NCAP), "is that the problem of pornography and sexual exploitation in general is an extremely unpleasant problem. You're forced to confront things that you and I probably would wish didn't exist."

Some religiously based organizations have joined the fight, including the American Family Association Law Center, the National Family Legal Foundation, and the Religious Alliance Against Pornography. Other groups find themselves trying to defend traditional values on such a wide range of issues that they inevitably have to pick and choose.

Politics and Porn

Evangelicals and liberal First Amendment advocates are drawing different lines in the sand over the Thomas trial and its implications for pornography.

To *Village Voice* columnist Nat Hentoff, former Attorney General Edwin Meese's Justice Department set the stage for the Thomas prosecution by shopping around obscenity cases until it found a community likely to convict. Hentoff notes that the California-based Thomases were convicted in Memphis.

"Hard core is legal in some jurisdictions," Hentoff told *Christianity Today*. "I think it should be in all, as disgusting as it is." He urges a free standard for computer networks. "If this so-called electronic superhighway is to be of use for free speech, it should be considered a common carrier," like telephone companies.

People making their living off the information superhighway fear being held responsible for what users of their systems do, actions that may be beyond the reach of system administrators. Karl Denninger, administrator for MCSNET, a Chicago computer uplink to Internet, says the Thomases should have been forewarned that they should not sell accounts in conservative Memphis or be prepared to face the consequences of possible prosecution.

"If there is no way for me as an operator of this kind of system to ascertain ahead of time whether or not it is legal to deliver that information . . . what option do I have?" asks Denninger. "The only one that's immediately obvious is to pull access to all that material. The problem with that is it's impossible."

MCSNET does not carry Internet groups consisting of hard-core pictures because of their content and concern over copyright infringement. Furthermore, individuals using MCSNET must specifically request available adult services or their accounts will not be enabled to receive them. Though there is a small amount of policing that network administrators can do on their systems—such as canceling accounts of people who place inappropriate messages in general computer news groups—not all administrators avoid the material like Denninger does.

Despite his precautions, Denninger worries that local administrators such as himself could still be held liable, whereas phone companies and large computer networks that may be just as involved get off scot-free because of their size. If the Thomases' convictions stand, he predicts, the large online vendors will have to patrol their systems to keep out any potentially explicit material.

The U.S. Justice Department is not offering any consolation to nervous network administrators, though. "We've gone after computer bulletin board pornographers before and have been successful, and we'll still go after them" in the future, Justice Department spokesperson John Russell told *CT*.

"I don't know if we're sending a message," says Russell. "It's a matter that violated the obscenity laws that we have. Whether it's a deterrent . . . that's not for me to say."

The ongoing connection of home personal computers onto worldwide computer networks increases the ability of children to access obscene materials. NCAP's Deen Kaplan gives credit to the Justice Department for its recent cyberporn victory, but he qualifies the compliment. "When one takes a look at the sort of images involved—torture and mutilation of women, defecation on women, bestiality, and there are 6,000-plus child images on that bulletin board—it doesn't take a great leap of faith for any law-enforcement authority to make the decision to prosecute that sort of material."

Shifting Community Standards

Pornography that was once low-quality material sold in seedy, out-of-the-way stores is now mainstreamed in attractive packaging for sale in neighborhoods. In addition, the mass-market cable movie channel Showtime devotes air time to soft-core films or nudity-laden series, such as *Red Shoe Diaries*. In a similar vein, HBO's *Real Sex* series has had explicit segments on masturbation techniques and bondage. There also has been a crossover to public broadcasting. In January, some PBS stations aired *Tales of the City*, a three-part series about "bathhouse life" in San Francisco, including scenes with frontal nudity and foul language.

"I think we're seeing a shift," says Len Munsil, executive director of Phoenix-based National Family Legal Foundation. "The obscenity test is based on community standards, and as our culture continues to decline and standards of morality continue to decline, and as hard-core pornography becomes much more accessible, more and more people see it [and] it's harder to get prosecutions undertaken."

Munsil does not believe it is more difficult to obtain convictions. However, he says it is tougher to get prosecutors "to do anything about the problem or for people even to recognize that it is a problem."

He complains that prosecutors adhere to an "absolutist" view of the First Amendment and without public pressure are unlikely to declare war against smut. "Lawyers who end up as prosecutors . . . begin to think [porn] is really not much of a problem—these laws are just an anachronism, and we'll just prosecute these other things," Munsil says. They don't "recognize that where prosecutors have been successful in impacting the availability of pornography through obscenity laws, the rape rate drops."

Pornography and criminal behavior have been linked in recent research, including a University of New Hampshire study that demonstrated higher rape rates in states with broader availability of pornographic material. There is some evidence that the danger can be mitigated by enforcement of obscenity laws, as one Oklahoma county discovered when it closed 147 of its 150 pornographic businesses and experienced a 25 percent rape rate drop.

Antipornography advocates hope to stimulate greater public awareness and more prosecution of obscenity delivered by computer modem. "Computers will be the means of transmission for pornography in the next quarter-century," says NCAP's Kaplan. "Most people don't realize that their child can take the home computer and dial up electronic bulletin boards that functionally have the equivalent of an entire adult bookstore online."

Kaplan suggests new standards for what is permitted on computer networks, just as cable and broadcast television have different standards. "We need to look at [computer networks] more in terms of a broadcast medium and some of the careful restrictions that go into that to protect children."

The emergence of Enough is Enough—with its high-profile across the political spectrum—highlights the often-reluctant participation of men. Janet LaRue, senior counsel for the National Center for Children and Families in Santa Ana, California, admits that men are more difficult to get involved because "so many men are users of the product."

Friend or Foe?

During the Reagan-Bush years, significant strides were made in educating Americans about the effects of pornography on women, children, and men.

The Clinton administration has been sending a mixed message, however, Reno's Justice Department has found itself at the center of a firestorm over accusations that the department tried to dilute child pornography prosecution.

In 1991, during the Bush administration, Stephen Knox was prosecuted by the Justice Department over three videotapes showing partially clad prepubescent girls in sexually suggestive poses. Knox, who was convicted and sentenced to a five-year prison term, appealed his case, arguing that the videos did not constitute child pornography because the girls were not nude and genitalia were not visible.

Under Reno, the Justice Department switched sides and helped Knox win a round in court last year. That action prompted the U.S. Senate to pass an amendment disagreeing with the Justice Department's position in a 100-to-0 vote. In June, a federal appeals court upheld Knox's original conviction, ruling that nudity was not necessary for depictions to qualify as "lascivious."

"We all assumed that the battle over child pornography was won during the 1980s," Munsil says. "Then, all of a sudden, you have a few ideologues in the Justice Department getting into power, and now we're having to refight that battle."

Activists fear that the Knox case could result in the further spread of child pornography, despite the upheld conviction. "It really was incredibly naïve, because there's a tremendous amount of interest in child pornography out there that is fed by that kind of position," says Bruce Green, an attorney with the American Family Association Law Center. "It creates a climate of tolerance."

Many people worry that a signal from Washington that obscenity convictions are a low priority could be disastrous. "It leads to a greater tolerance of things that might very well in a different time be viewed as intolerable," says Green, "and that is the harm that comes from unregulated pornography and obscenity of any kind."

The federal government can bring the full force of federal law enforcement power against national distributors, Munsil says. Without that pressure, "it just means there is a faster flow of hard-core material into all of the communities."

Two-Pronged Strategy

In combating pornography's growing acceptance and avail- ability, pastors, lawyers, and other activists envision a two-track approach. One avenue is to insist on the resumption of aggressive federal prosecution on distributors of obscene material. The oth- er is to teach parents how to defend their children and their homes.

"There doesn't seem to be an initiative with an adequate num- ber of new cases being brought," says Alan Sears, a federal pros- ecutor in the Reagan and Bush administrations and executive director of the Attorney General's Commission on Pornography.

In some states that do not have grand juries, for example, there is no way to subpoena corporate records except for a trial, Sears says. "Without extreme difficulty, you can't conduct searches out of your own state." Federal prosecutors are able to get around those difficulties and can engage in multi-district prosecutions.

Enough Is Enough has assembled a board of technology ex- perts to help it develop strategies to defeat porn in its new tech- nologies. Donna Rice Hughes, who gained notoriety because of her relationship with politician Gary Hart, says many of these new technologies grew out of defense research. So her group took its experts from the defense industry as well.

"The main thing we need to do is protect our children by making parents aware that [cyberporn] is out there," Munsil says. "You can no more leave your children alone to travel the informa- tion superhighway than you can leave them alone in Times Square in New York. . . . You've got to supervise your children when they're on a computer system and not let them have hours and hours to fiddle around on a bulletin board system."

Christians also need to recognize that laws usually allow for prosecution of such transmissions, Munsil says. "The laws are there; it's a matter of enforcement."

Janet LaRue is working to toughen California laws against child pornography. LaRue, who was victimized as a child, says pornography is "nothing but molestation" and urges churches to raise the level of their involvement. "Most churches are unaware of the problem and the fact that there are men in churches who are not only viewers of pornography but are addicted to it."

Kirk says, "We haven't believed God wanted us to go after the scientific world, the media world, the education world. We need to begin to believe God and not believe our limited abilities."

In some ways, the fight against pornography is a war of attrition, a grueling test to see which side will outlast the other. Kaplan says pornographers are in the business for one reason: to make money. According to the *New York Times,* one West Coast firm, Evil Angel Productions, reported gross revenues are "skyrocketing" from $34,000 in 1990 to more than $1 million this year. *Adult Video News,* a trade journal, says rentals and retail sales of adult videos have grown to $2 billion annually. And the industry is quickly moving into new technologies, such as interactive compact disks. In Rhode Island, South Pointe Enterprises Inc., a publicly traded adult entertainment firm, is digitizing some films for playback on personal computers.

Kaplan, commenting on the profit motive of the industry, says, "They don't care about speech rights, the rights of women, religious freedom—any of these loftier goals that are put out there in the public forum as reasons to protect what they're doing.

"So even when they are breaking the law, they will continue breaking the law until citizens gather and fight."

BIBLIOGRAPHY

An asterisk (*) preceding a reference indicates that the material or part of it has been reprinted in this book.

BOOKS AND PAMPHLETS

Barry, John A. Technobabble. MIT. '91.

Cunningham, Ann Marie & Wicks, Wendy, eds. Three views of the Internet. National Federation of Abstracting and Information Services. '93.

Dery, Mark, ed. Flame wars: the discourse of cyberculture. Duke University Press. '94.

Ermann, M. David; Williams, Mary B.; & Gutierrez, Claudio, eds. Computers, ethics, and society. Oxford University Press. '90.

Johnson, Deborah G. & Nissenbaum, Helen, eds. Computers, ethics & social values. Prentice Hall. '95.

Koelsch, Frank. The infomedia revolution: how it is changing our world and your life. McGraw-Hill Ryerson. '95.

Luff, Paul; Gilbert, Nigel; & Frohlich, David, eds. Computers and conversation. Academic. '90.

Lyon, David. The electronic eye: the rise of surveillance society. University of Minneapolis Press. '94.

McClure, Charles R. Public libraries and the Internet: study results, policy issues, and recommendations. U.S. National Commission on Libraries and Information Science. '94.

McClure, Charles R.; Moen, William E.; & Ryan, Joe. Libraries and the Internet/NREN: perspectives, issues, and challenges. Meckler. '94.

Negroponte, Nicholas. Being digital. Knopf. '95.

Rheingold, Howard. The virtual community: homesteading on the electronic frontier. Addison-Wesley. '93.

Roszak, Theodore. The cult of information: the folklore of computers and the true art of thinking. Pantheon. '86.

Rowe, Christopher. People and chips: the human implications of information technology. Blackwell Scientific. '90.

Shea, Virginia. Netiquette. Albion. '94.

Stoll, Clifford. Silicon snake oil. Doubleday. '95.

United States/Congress/House/Committee on Science, Space, and Technology. National Information Infrastructure Act of 1993. 103rd Congress, 1st Session. U.S. Government Printing Office. '93.

United States/Congress/House/Subcommittee on Science. High performance computing and network program. 103rd Congress, 1st session. U.S. Government Printing Office. '93.

————. Internet access. 103rd Congress, 2nd Session. U.S. Government Printing Office. '94.

————. Internet security. 103rd Congress, 2nd Session. U.S. Government Printing Office. '94.

United States/Congress/House/Subcommittee on Technology, Environment, and Aviation. Communications and computer surveillance, privacy and security. 103rd Congress, 2nd Session. U.S. Government Printing Office. '94.

U.S. Department of Commerce, Technology Administration. Putting the information infrastructure to work. U.S. Government Printing Office. '94.

Weinberg, Nathan. Computers in the information society. Westview. '90.

Williams, Frederick. The people's right to know: media, democracy, and the information highway. Erlbaum. '93.

Wriston, Walter B. The twilight of sovereignty: how the information revolution is transforming our world. Scribner. '92.

ADDITIONAL PERIODICAL ARTICLES WITH ABSTRACTS

For those who wish to read more widely on the subject of the Information Revolution, this section contains abstracts of additional articles that bear on the topic. Readers who require a comprehensive list of materials are advised to consult the *Reader's Guide to Periodical Literature* and other Wilson indexes.

A SLOW sign on the information highway. Lyle Denniston. *American Journalism Review* 16:54 Mr '94

Two recent events illustrate the legal conflict that might arise from the federal government's campaign to build the "National Information Infrastructure." In a recent speech to the Television Academy, Vice President Al Gore made it clear that the government proposes to mandate open access to the information highway. In other words, owners or operators of data or video channels could not refuse to carry messages that might not make it onto the highway on their own. Such a view, which treats the information industry as a public utility, ignores the First Amendment rights of a private communications manager to choose which messages to convey. The day after Gore's speech, the Supreme Court addressed this very issue in a case on the constitutionality of Congress's 1992 decision to force cable television stations to carry all local television stations for free. The justices suggested that the government may have to leave more discretion to private firms than planners now envision.

Invasion of the data shrinkers. Peter Coy. *Business Week* 115–16 F 14 '94

Digital compression is gaining popularity among electronics and communications innovators. Its appeal lies in its capacity to overcome one of the biggest obstacles to the multimedia and communications revolution: the large amount of digital information that is required to transmit analog sound and video. A rapidly developing branch of mathematics, compression can dramatically reduce the broadcast signals needed to transmit information, allowing major improvements in such developments as videoconferencing, compact-disc encyclopedias, video games, and audio recordings. Compression could also permit the information superhighway to be extended into people's homes through already existing copper wires instead of new optical fibers, thus reducing the cost of storage and transmission. Compression might even make data analysis in scientific research far more efficient. Several compression projects are discussed, and a sidebar explains the technique.

The ideal interchange for the data superhighway. Neil Gross and Peter Coy. *Business Week* 115–17 O 11 '93

A digital switching technology known as asynchronous transfer mode (ATM) has sparked intense interest throughout the communications world. ATM can switch streams of multimedia data traffic at incredibly high speeds along a single line, allowing rapid routing of everything from high-definition TV to computer programs, information, and ordinary phone calls. Faced with such great potential, the Clinton Administration wants to use ATM in its information superhighway scheme; the cable and telephone industries are seizing on ATM as a new weapon in their battle for control of the superhighway; and communications experts are concluding that ATM is the best way to send images, sound, and text over optical fiber into offices and homes. ATM may be too fast for existing infrastructures, however. Discussed are obstacles to the use of ATM and the competition among Fujitsu, NEC, AT&T, IBM, Northern Telecom, and others for control of ATM technology.

The information revolution. *Business Week Special Issue* 10–14+ My 18 '94

A special issue examines the Information Revolution. Over the last 50 years, the acquisition, use, and transmission of information in digital form has become a critical function in America's economy. Soon, it could become a critical part of civilization, as the power and reach of computers begins to touch and transform every aspect of life. Articles discuss the development of information economies in the United States, Japan, Europe, and the Third World; the technological foundation of the information superhighway; and the effects of technology on the workplace and society. A guide to buying computer hardware and software for business and personal use and an interview with Intel CEO Andrew S. Grove are presented. Computer images from the fields of technology, science, business, entertainment, and the arts are reproduced.

Tackling technophobia. Catherine Arnst. *Business Week Special Issue* 144–50 My 18 '94

Part of a special issue on the Information Revolution. Computers are entering the lives of even the most technophobic. Nearly 70 percent of U.S. homes remain computerless, but 70 percent of households with incomes of more than $100,000 currently own computers. Many of these upper-middle class families own computers because they are convinced of the educational benefits for their children. In addition, a home computer makes it possible to take work home from the office, gain a better understanding of one's finances, improve one's correspondence, or link up to the Information Superhighway. The home computer industry's fastest growing segment is the small office/home office market, populated by individuals starting their own businesses. Advice is provided on buying a computer, and several types of personal computers and on-line services are discussed. Sidebars describe how several individuals use their PCs.

The new face of business. *Business Week Special Issue* 98–102+ My 18 '94

Part of a special issue on the Information Revolution. Business is changing the way it views and uses information. After years of putting money into technology to automate tasks like ordering or billing, companies are now scrutinizing the information that their automated systems collect to find easier and more efficient ways to do business. Such corporate giants as IBM and AT&T are reengineering their businesses by rethinking work flows and encouraging information sharing among formerly autonomous purchasing, manufacturing, and marketing departments. Smaller companies and the self-employed are finding that recent price cuts and performance advances in PCs, wireless communications, and business software allow them to compete against their deep-pocketed rivals. Related articles discuss the new advantages enjoyed by smaller companies, technology's role in reshaping corporate hierarchies, and how Washington is faring in the digital age.

Churches and the new information technology. *The Christian Century* 110:1233–4 D 8 '93

Eli Noam, director of Columbia Business School's Institute for Tele-Information, believes that America's developing information superhighway has enormous potential but significant pitfalls as well. In an address at a meeting of religious communications specialists, Noam asserted that some people will be barred from this information network and thus will not have the means to access the data that lead to contacts, jobs, power, and, presumably, a better life. Noam also predicted the emergence of "tele-cults, or electronic communes," composed of highly specialized, fragmented audiences. Noam's advice on minimizing the negative impact of the information superhighway is provided.

Data is cheap. Jeffrey Young. *Forbes* v153:126 Ap 11 '94

Dialog Information Services, one of the first in the business of selling electronic data, is now facing the issue of how to survive in the age of desktop computers. In recent years sales and profits have flattened at the Knight-Ridder subsidiary. Among the reasons: Dialog remains a creature of the fast-disappearing mainframe era, the information superhighway has become too cluttered with data, alternative sources for data are surfacing, and Dialog does not create or own much of the data it sells. In an effort to boost Dialog's profits, president Patrick J. Tierney is trying to rewrite Dialog's information system from a remote mainframe environment to the more responsive and flexible one of client/server. To remedy Dialog's lack of experience in desktop applications, Tierney has also made minority investments in Personal Library Software and Individual Inc., two companies that have the necessary experience.

Futures lost—or postponed. Peter Nulty. *Fortune* 128:90 N 15 '93

The information superhighway may seem inevitable, but modern industrial history is replete with examples of technological innovations that failed to develop viable markets. The article recounts the failure of robots, the atomic age, ultrasonics, and the personal aircraft.

The new computer revolution. *Fortune* 127:56–63+ Je 14 '93

A cover story examines how information technology has forever altered the way business operates. PCs are helping companies get lean, smart, and close to their customers. The bottom line in the computer revolution is that those who seize opportunities are capturing important competitive advantages, while those who lag behind are forced to either play a game of catch-up or die. Although computing is not yet the largest industry in the world—at $360 billion a year, it is far behind autos and oil—it has become the most important because of its power to transform the way people work. Fifty-five companies (42 of which are American), each with over $1 billion in sales, dominate this industry. The article examines each of the industry's main segments and draws lessons from imagining infinite, inexpensive increases in hardware and software performance—increases that have occurred, are taking place, or will happen soon.

Who will wire America? William Fulton and Morris Newman. *Governing* 7:26–31 O '93

Across the country, state governments are trying to decide upon the best way to usher in the telecommunications revolution while guaranteeing that the interests of both the market and the public are served by the new technology. The creation of an integrated telecommunications industry is already under way, with telephones, television, computers, and data banks all converging through links between major providers of these services. However, states are taking very different approaches to defining the government's relationship with the telephone companies, cable systems, and information networks that will be part of the emerging markets. Some are using government funds and regulations to build networks, while others are encouraging private companies to take the initiative.

Speech may be free, but it sure isn't cheap. Steven Hill. *The Humanist* 54:6–8 My/Je '94

The U.S. Supreme Court's interpretation of the First Amendment will influence cases pertaining to the telecommunications industry and the information superhighway. Over the last 25 years, the Court has consistently interpreted the First Amendment in a rigid, literal manner, with little regard to the distinction between large and small media companies. It has established a precedent in matters of speech that could enable the new telecommunications technologies to exacerbate anti-democratic and authoritarian tendencies. With the Court's approval, large electronic media companies that can afford to buy speech will seek to monopolize it and make it homogeneous. The Court should seek to ensure that the public has access to the information superhighway, even if such access requires that expensive regulations be placed on the telecommunications industry.

Computer insecurity. Peter Neumann. *Issues in Science and Technology* 11:50–4 Fall '94

As more and more people and companies connect their computer systems to the information superhighway, the potential for unauthorized access and sabotage increases. Improvements in security systems have lagged behind the need, partly because of the assumption that most computer break-ins are relatively harmless. That assumption was true of the first generation of prankster hackers, but those of the future are more likely to be working for profit and other malign motives. System developers, citing weak market demand, have not anticipated the need for better and more easily administered computer security systems. Instead of funding research on improved computer security, the government has impeded progress by restricting the export of encryption technology. Relaxed export controls, updated laws on computer crime, more rigorous law enforcement, user education, and constant improvement of security technology are needed to prevent potentially harmful break-ins.

Public way or private road? Herbert I. Schiller. *The Nation* 257:64–6 Jl 12 '93

The interactive electronic environment taking shape in the U.S. promises to unleash an epic social transformation in which corporate concerns will take precedence over the public interest. With the enthusiastic support of the Clinton administration—which wants to link every business, home, school, and college in a National Information Infrastructure that will resemble today's Internet—the electronics, film, television, cable, information, and retail industries are rapidly moving to develop, control, and reap enormous profits from a single, all-encompassing interactive industry that will merge television, telecommunications, computers, consumer electronics, publishing, information services, and shopping. Unfortunately, transmissions on such a system seem destined to be determined by commercial criteria. The possibility that the networks might be used as a free social information facility seems remote.

Traffic jam. William Letwin. *National Review* 46:43–5 Ag 15 '94

Part of a special section on information and communications technologies. Vice President Gore's plan for an Information Superhighway, to be built with aid from the Federal Government, has attracted much less criticism than it deserves. The plan raises the questions of whether the existing information superhighway, built of optical fiber by private companies, should be upgraded and whether this upgrade should be funded by taxpayers. A faster and wider optical fiber network would require the copper wires that connect most homes and workplaces to this network to be replaced at great cost by optical fiber. Information services will likely make the necessary investment in such a project, however, if they believe that users will pay the cost. The government does not need to subsidize the effort with large sums of taxpayer money.

Populism + telecommunications = global democracy. Neal B. Freeman. *National Review* 45:50–1 N 15 '93

Part of a cover story on the worldwide surge in populism. The revolution in digital communications technology will transform the global political economy. The data superhighway is being built so quickly that the Clinton Administration will not have time to fund it or the opportunity to manage it. As a result, vastly more people will have much greater access to much more information than before. The digital era is likely to result in increased power for special interests who form their own networks, the retreat of telecommunications regulation, the loss of America's cultural hegemony, the rise of multinational organizations, the emergence of digital press lords, and the revitalization of democratic movements around the world. The people and groups that prosper in the information economy will be those with talent, energy, and, above all, speed.

Low fiber. Robert Wright. *The New Republic* 210:4 Je 27 '94

A recent study concluded that the data superhighway is bypassing the urban underclass, but it is questionable whether "electronic redlining" warrants a liberal crusade. The study, sponsored by a coalition of liberal groups, examined neighborhoods where the Baby Bells are testing fiber-optic "video dial tone" service and found that the beneficiaries tended to be affluent and white. The sponsors want "anti-redlining" rules to be included in the vast telecommunications legislation taking shape in Congress. This would amount to a subsidy to lay fiber in economically unattractive areas, financed by an implicit tax on fiber in upscale areas. However, people's living rooms are not where the inner city most needs the money. A fiber tax that would help fund inner-city public schools is a goal worthy of the civil rights movement; subsidizing teenagers who watch TV is not.

Under the wire. Ken Auletta. *The New Yorker* 69:49–53 Ja 17 '94

In the shaping of the information superhighway, the most frequently overlooked role may be that of the newly assertive federal government. Most of the current debate has centered on deals, technologies, and the shifting allegiances of players: cable, telephone, computer, studios, broadcasting, publishing, and consumer electronics. There is growing support, both within government and without, for government to set up rules for the electronic superhighway. Vice-President Al Gore, the Administration's acknowledged leader in telecommunications, believes that only government can prevent a multimedia electronic traffic jam and open new economic and social vistas. Battle lines are forming along ideological fronts, with liberals arguing for a more intrusive government and many conservatives asserting that decisions should be left to the marketplace.

Bound to the printed word. Marc Levinson. *Newsweek* 123:52–3 Je 20 '94

The newspaper industry is having a hard time moving beyond ink and paper. Anticipated tie-ins between the printed page and video, computers, and multimedia have been slow in coming. A misunderstanding of the technology and the markets has plagued newspaper spinoffs. For example, two chains—Dow Jones & Co. and Knight-Ridder—pushed into the rapidly growing field of selling computerized information to businesses, but both companies were blind to the very different nature of business information; the newspapers were slow to grasp that subscribers didn't just want to receive data but to chart it. Dozens of new news chain ventures are under way despite the bleak returns from earlier efforts.

Sex on the info highway. Barbara Kantrowitz. *Newsweek* 123:62–3 Mr 14 '94

X-rated computer networks and software comprise one of the most popular lanes on the emerging information highway. Adult-oriented bulletin boards offer personal ads, picture files, special groups, interactive games, and on-line orgies, while erotic movies are available on CD-ROM. Much of this material is poor in quality, and some computer-industry observers fear that it could overshadow more important uses of new technology, such as education. Some worry about the possibility of censorship, but computer bulletin boards are difficult to police. Jerry Berman of the Electronic Freedom Foundation admits that there is a need for software that would allow users to screen out objectionable material.

The complete survival guide to the information superhighway. Michael Antonoff, Arthur Fisher, and Robert N. Langreth. *Popular Science* 244:97–105+ My '94

An overview of the information superhighway. Envisioned as a nationwide and eventually worldwide electronic communications network, the information superhighway will connect everyone to everyone else via computer, interactive TV, telephone, or some future device that combines the features of all three. Some people see the information superhighway as an embellishment of the Internet, an existing network of computers devoted to the exchange of information. Others predict that it will be a more robust interactive TV network providing video entertainment services. The article discusses benefits of the information superhighway; specific functions, including video-on-demand, home shopping, interactive games, electronic banking and bill-paying, e-mail, and television channels; the definitions of "Internet" and "cyberspace"; the processes of building, paying for, regulating, and using the superhighway; and its effects on society and business.

Hearings on copyright and info highway. Howard Fields. *Publishers Weekly* 240:13+ N 29 '93

At a hearing by a National Information Infrastructure (NII) task force working group on intellectual property, publishers and other intellectual property owners said that they see no need to change the Copyright Act, including its fair-use provisions, to accommodate the Clinton administration's vision of the NII. The NII plan would provide a seamless connection of computer networks, television and radio transmissions, telephone service, and other forms of communication to make all those services available through a single wire or machine in the home or office. Witnesses at the hearing said that technical solutions would be needed to assure that the existing copyright law is applied and enforced, given the potential for unauthorized copying and retransmission of copyrighted works in electronic form on the NII.

Information please. Martin Morse Wooster. *Reason* 25:56–8 Mr '94

Americans' fear of the impending information superhighway is unfounded. Conventional wisdom holds that the superhighway will cause people to be enslaved by computers and subjected to "information overload." Several nonprofit groups and liberal lobbyists worry about equal access to information by schools and the poor. A more beneficial scenario, however, is indicated by articles in recent issues of several magazines. According to these articles, the information network—provided it is free from government restrictions—will make Americans freer, happier, and more self-reliant. The writer discusses articles on the information superhighway that have appeared in recent issues of Time, Wired, Regulation, Publisher's Weekly, and National Journal.

Beyond databases and E-mail. Robert Pool. *Science* 261:841+ Ag 13 '93

Part of a cover story on computing in science. Within the next 10 to 20 years, "electronic communities" will link scientists much more closely than ever before with information, instruments, and distant colleagues. The instantaneous give-and-take envisioned for future computer networks is not yet possible, but the foundation for the transformation is already in place. Cultural inertia is the only thing likely to slow down the revolution. Scientists' use of Internet and the development of software that facilitates searches of the databases accessible through Internet are discussed.

Domesticating cyberspace. Gary Stix. *Scientific American* 269: 100–7+ Ag '93

The source of next-generation electronic products is the computer network, which stands to revolutionize communications in the United States. The Internet, which incorporates thousands of computer networks, comprising 1.7 million computers in more than 125 countries, is undergoing an explosion of activity. Many legislators in Washington want to extend some version of electronic networking to every home, school, library, and hospital in the U.S. under the rubric of a National Information Infrastructure. The technical accoutrements are nearly in place to extend computer technology into homes via television sets. The writer describes activities of computer, communications, and entertainment giants that may lead to an "information superhighway," as envisioned by Vice President Al Gore. Sidebars present feedback from users of Internet and discuss today's cable and telephone networks and the evolution of local communications.

Seven thinkers in search of an information highway. *Technology Review* 97:42–52 Ag/S '94

A panel discussion on the potential and proper function of the proposed information highway presents the views of Amy Bruckman, a doctoral student in the MIT Media Laboratory and founder of an on-line community for media researchers; Michael Dertouzos, director of the MIT Laboratory for Computer Science; Robert Domnitz, a telecommunications industry specialist in the Massachusetts Executive Office of Economic Affairs; Nathan Felde, executive director of video information service development at the NYNEX Science and Technology Center; Mitchell Kapor, chairman of the Electronic Frontier Foundation; Martyn Roetter, vice-president and market researcher at Decision Resources of Waltham, Mass.; and Michael Schrage, a Los Angeles Times columnist and research associate at MIT's Sloan School of Management.

First nation in cyberspace. Philip Elmer-Dewitt. *Time* 142:62–4 D 6 '93

The Internet computer network has spread uncontrollably and now circles the globe. With as many as 20 million users, the anarchistic Internet is at once the shining archetype and the nightmare vision of the information highway that the Clinton Administration has been touting. With 5,000 discussion groups, 2,500 electronic newsletters, and many shared files, the Internet already provides for free much of what telephone and cable-TV companies are planning to sell—interactivity, 2-way communications, and multimedia information on demand. The Internet is owned by no single organization, and its operating costs are shared by its primary users: universities, national labs, high tech corporations, and foreign governments. Various uses of the Internet are described.

When the revolution comes what will happen to . . . Richard Zoglin. *Time* 141:56–8 Ap 12 '93

Television could soon experience a technological revolution thanks to the information highway, which will combine the switching and routing capabilities of phones with the video and information offerings of the most advanced cable systems and data banks. Not only will consumers have more channels from which to choose and the opportunity to interact with programs, but the transformation could bring about changes so radical that television may scarcely be recognizable. The amount of available channels will number somewhere around 500 to start. The eventual goal, however, is unlimited choice—virtually everything ever produced for television, plus a wealth of other information and entertainment options, will be stored in computer banks and available at the touch of a button. The article examines the potential effects that the new technology will have on channels, networks, commercials, video stores, and cable bills.

Take a trip into the future on the electronic superhighway. Philip Elmer-Dewitt. *Time* 141:50–5 Ap 12 '93

The information highway, a medium that combines the switching and routing capabilities of phones with the video and information offerings of the most advanced cable systems and data banks, will soon be a reality. Behind this technological merger are some rather simple technological advances: The ability to translate all audio and video communications into digital information; new methods of storing digitized data and compressing them so they can travel through existing phone and cable lines; fiber-optic wiring that provides a virtually limitless transmission pipeline; and new switching techniques and other breakthroughs that make it possible to put the technology in place without necessarily rewiring every home. The article discusses the development of the technology, its potential applications, and the role the government will play in its implementation.

How AT&T plans to reach out and touch everyone. Thomas McCarroll. *Time* 142:44–6 Jl 5 '93

AT&T has achieved one of the most remarkable makeovers in U.S. corporate history. In 1984, a federal court ordered the company to spin off its regional Bell operating companies, which own most of the local telephone lines in the United States. Through acquisitions and home-grown start-ups, however, AT&T has become one of the most powerful players in information technology. It is the nation's leading producer of electronic cash registers, the world's largest manufacturer of automated teller machines for banks, and the third biggest issuer of credit cards. It has also expanded into the field of multimedia. Ultimately, AT&T would like to become an all-purpose superplayer on the electronic superhighway that will provide America's homes with interactive services, information, shopping, and entertainment. The article discusses CEO Robert Allen's role in resurrecting AT&T and the company's efforts to create an electronic superhighway.

Hatemongering on the data highway. Richard Z. Chesnoff. *U.S. News & World Report* 117:52 Ag 8 '94

The Simon Wiesenthal Center, a Los Angeles-based center that exposes neo-Nazis and other bigots, recently submitted a report on cyberspace hatemongering to the chairman of the FCC, which has turned the information over to the Justice Department. The report, which is based on a three-year investigation by researcher Rick Eaton, was triggered by tips from Internet users who discovered violent, antiblack, antigay, antisemitic hate messages online. In response, some are calling for policing of the Internet, but others question the practicality and legality of such oversight. While some commercial networks have attempted to ban the use of their systems by hatemongers, some Internet enthusiasts say that countering the bigotry with well-documented responses is the best way to deal with the problem.

Fast lane to the future. William J. Cook, Jim Impoco, and Warren Cohen. *U.S. News & World Report* 116:56–8 Ja 17 '94

President Clinton and his technology guru, Vice President Al Gore, want to remove many of the legal and regulatory roadblocks that stand in the way of the emerging information highway while also ensuring universal access. Telecommunications policies are now a mixture of competition for long-distance telephone service, monopolies for local phone service, and exclusive cable franchises. Clinton and Gore want to promote and protect competition, encourage private investment, provide open access to the information network, and offer subsidies to make services broadly available. They face many hurdles in reaching these goals in the face of fast-moving and competing interests, as evidenced by the cases of MCI, which wants to compete with the Baby Bells for regional phone service; the bidding war for Paramount Communications; and direct broadcast satellite TV's challenge to cable television.

Policing the digital world. Vic S. Sussman. *U.S. News & World Report* 115:68+ D 6 '93

Part of a cover story on the information revolution. The rightful definition of free speech, the proper protection of intellectual property, and the limits of personal privacy are likely to be the most contentious social and legal issues raised by the unprecedented power of electronic technology. Currently, information can be disseminated by printed material, radio and television, and such "common carriers" as telephone companies, with each form subject to different rules on permissible content. It is unclear which, if any, of the sets of regulations applicable to these would be applied to electronic communications. With regard to personal privacy, credit companies now have the ability to compile large databases of customers to be organized, packaged, and eventually sold. The use and abuse of such information, as well as the issue of copyright protection of electronic information and the controversy over the use of encryption to protect electronic messages, are discussed.

Pioneering the electronic frontier. *U.S. News & World Report* 115:56–60+ D 6 '93

A cover story examines the effects of the information revolution. The changes in information technology promise a transformation with effects, like that of Gutenberg's printing press, as yet unforeseen. Although it was initially built 2 decades ago as a means of shuttling information between defense laboratories, the Internet soon spawned electronic mail, and people began using it to communicate on scientific and scholarly projects.

Recently, the Clinton Administration proposed sweeping legislation to fund basic research and promote regulations to help private industry create the "information superhighway." Changes in educational and political processes, as well as in the way people socialize with one another, can be expected. Internet pioneers Carl Malamud, Cynthia Denton, Wolfgang Staehle, Wam Kat, and Robert Weller are briefly profiled, and a sidebar presents a conversation with Al Gore. Related articles discuss interactive video, electronic privacy, and online services.

The information lockout. Laurie Ouellette. *Utne Reader* 24+ S/O '93

Some analysts are optimistic about America's approaching information revolution, but others fear that this development may increase the gulf between the haves and have-nots. An optimistic view is provided by media critic Jon Katz in the April 15, 1993, Rolling Stone; according to Katz, the trend heralds a new era of electronic democracy. In contrast, an article in the Feb. 12, 1993, Boston Phoenix argues that the new technology will disenfranchise the urban poor. An article in the Feb. 1992 MediaCulture Review contends that the poor cannot afford computer equipment or online fees, an article in the March 1993 MediaCulture Review warns that mergers between the media and telephone companies could result in a monopoly on information technologies, an article in the June 1993 Artspace warns of electronic colonialism, and an article in the May 8, 1993, New Scientist discusses access to the new technology on the global level.

Alice in Cyberland. Andrew Ferguson. *Washingtonian* 29:70–3+ Ag '94

The writer describes his experience using the online services Compuserve and America Online and notes that life on the Information Superhighway is dreadfully boring.

From the Center. Charles Blitzer. *The Wilson Quarterly* 18:152 Spr '94

The prospect of the information superhighway is an overwhelming and disturbing one. Using computers to read books, hear concerts, or enjoy operas is unappealing; not being able to browse at random in a bookshop or a library is frightening; and the notion of millions of people spending their lives in isolation while imagining that they are in touch with the whole world is appalling.

The rise of the knowledge society. Peter Ferdinand Drucker. *The Wilson Quarterly* 17:52–65+ Spr '93

An article adapted from Post-Capitalist Society. Radical changes in the meaning of knowledge have transformed society 3 times. In Europe around the year 1700, knowledge, which had always been seen as applying to being rather than doing, suddenly came to be applied to tools, processes, and products. This shift paved the way for the industrial revolution and the rise of capitalism. In the late 19th century and the first half of the 20th century, knowledge came to be applied to work, which ushered in the productivity revolution and averted a mass proletarian revolt. Today, knowledge is being applied to knowledge itself, a change that may be called the management revolution. While land, labor, and capital are still important as constraints on production, it is knowledge that is the single most important factor of production. For this reason, today's society must be described as postcapitalist.